HOME GROWN was
Designed, edited and published by
Spectator Publications Limited
91 St Martin's Lane, London WC2H 0DN
for Stanley Garden Tools Limited
Woodhouse Mill, Sheffield S13 9WJ
© Spectator Publications Limited 1977

Illustrated by Caroline Sharpe
              Robert Micklewright
              Anne Knight

Filmsetting by Citype Limited
Leicester LE1 5YP, Leicestershire

Printed by Colorgraphic Limited
Leicester LE8 2FL, Leicestershire

ISBN 90086931 3

HOME GROWN

FOREWORD

Gardening is the third most popular leisure activity in Britain, after watching television and reading. Unlike many other pastimes it has a wide appeal to all ages and both sexes. Now, at a time of national economic difficulty, its popularity seems to be increasing. The reasons for this have been generally explained by rising costs which have made vegetable gardening economically very attractive. No doubt this is correct but we at Stanley Garden Tools feel it neglects the pleasure and very real sense of achievement which gardening can bring. In Britain there are nearly two million keen gardeners who derive this pleasure and sense of achievement; there are about four times that number who approach their gardens with varying degrees of reluctance. In whichever category you find yourself, we hope and believe that this book will help you to get more from your garden in every way.

L.D. Gloyn-Cox
Managing Director, Stanley Garden Tools Limited

Two questions, really. Is it worth growing fruit and vegetables at all? Is it worth growing them in *my* garden?

There is no doubt about the answer to the general question; you can grow more cheaply than you can buy. There are, of course, other considerations than those of pounds and pence, and we shall consider them in a moment, but look at the cash side first.

It is difficult to quantify, because so much depends on soil, weather, skill, luck and other factors, but even the novice home grower comes out on the right side.

In 1975 the Royal Horticultural Society laid out a small demonstration vegetable plot in their Wisley gardens. It measured 48 ft by 17 ft/14.7 m by 5.4 m), no more than many a suburban lawn. It was sown with a variety of crops, and of course they were tended by experts. But otherwise they had no special privileges, everything was grown in the open from start to finish, no crop being started under glass.

It was a bad and difficult season. Everything harvested was recorded and valued at current retail prices, and the result was striking. For a total expenditure of about £20 the plot produced fresh vegetables worth £123. Prices at the greengrocers were high then, they are even higher as this is being written.

The cash advantages of home-grown fruit are less easy to demonstrate. Trees and bushes involve a long-term investment and spring frosts and similar disasters mean that in some years there is no dividend. Despite this, the planting of top fruit and soft fruit is very much worth while. A fruit tree is a source of pleasure and profit for half a lifetime, and although the soft fruits must be replanted every few years you can propagate your own replacements.

One good reason for growing your own soft fruits is that in the fresh state they become steadily more impossible to buy. Commercial growers sell in bulk to the canners and freezers and the opulent piles of berries and spreads of punnets that once meant the coming of summer have dwindled almost to nothing. If you prefer fresh to frozen you must grow your own soft fruits.

The value of freshness is, of course something that the home grower soon comes to appreciate. An early potato cooked within an hour of digging is more than a common spud. A lettuce heavy with overnight dew would seem no kin to the one trapped in a polythene bag for forty-eight hours.

The personal factor

The reader who has done little or no kitchen gardening up to now will wonder about other things.

Does it, even in a small garden, take up a lot of time? No more than the same area of ornamental garden. True, there is some winter digging and pruning to be done, and to the spare-time gardener this means a few hours at weekends when the evenings are dark, but it is spread over many months and is rarely a difficulty. Nor is the routine work of spring and summer, provided it gets a little regular attention in the evenings. After all, mowing the lawn presents problems if you neglect it for three weeks.

The growing of edible crops is an absorbing hobby, a fascinating aspect of gardening with greater opportunities for developing real skills than the decorative side. The latter has become too easy.

Anyone with a fat wallet can shuttle back and forth to the garden centre, grabbing every container-grown beauty in sight and have a magnificent display with no more expertise than that involved in the digging of holes. Give the same guy a patch of soil and a packet of seed and he might be at a loss to produce a decent bunch of radishes.

How big a garden is needed?

There is no minimum size. In the smallest garden you can grow food crops. You can grow them on the patio or in the courtyard. You can grow them in the house. And they will be worth growing.

Think of a square of soil measuring 4 ft by 4 ft/ 1.2 m by 1.2 m. Along each of its four sides plant tall bamboo canes a foot apart, slanting them together at the top and tying them. At the foot of each cane, plant three runner bean seeds in May, and supply the plants with water and liquid fertiliser. From this small square you will be unlucky not to pick 30 lbs of beans and the only substantial cost will be that of the bamboos, which will last for years.

On a strip 2 ft/60 cm wide you can plant cordon apple trees 2½ ft/75 cm apart and when mature each will give you a dozen pounds of apples in an average season.

You can edge the beds with alpine strawberries and dot the flower border with red seakale beet, variegated kale and clumps of sweet corn.

On the south wall of the house there may be room for a fan-trained peach. On the west a cordon pear or two. On the north or east, that sadly neglected sub-acid cherry, the Morello. And these things are as lovely in spring as any other flowering tree.

You can now buy a lean-to greenhouse only 2½ ft/ 75 cm wide, to cover your trained peach tree or row of indoor tomatoes.

Tomatoes in pots, too, on the balcony or in the courtyard. Especially the miniature Gardener's Delight with its sweet oval fruit and long trusses that transform it into a decorative pot plant. Or you might grow fruit trees in pots in the sheltered courtyard, a Victorian art which is beginning to flourish again. Or strawberries planted in holes in the side of a barrel or one of the specially-made tower pots. Even if you haven't a foot of bare soil the possibilities in these days of containers and prepared composts are endless.

Forced to garden indoors you can grow mustard and cress, many herbs in pots, mung bean sprouts if you go for Chinese cookery, and various other sprouts if you follow the current American fashion.

All these possibilities are explained in the book, but naturally we write for those who actually have a garden, small, medium or large. For them the home growing of food can make a very real contribution towards balancing the household budget, and our hope is that this book will give them a slight nudge towards starting and a little help along an interesting and rewarding road.

Why are some gardeners more successful than others? They may have the luck to garden on a very fertile soil or in an unusually congenial climate, but often their results are achieved with no special advantages. And we wonder why.

So came the notion of 'green-fingers', a special touch to which plants respond. Not just knowledge, for we can all learn how and when and what to sow and plant and what to do and what not to do, but something that goes a little further. It is the understanding of what sort of living creature a plant is, how it reacts to its environment, that the successful gardener has always at the back of his mind. It is significant that among professional gardeners the top-ranking expert is sometimes referred to as a 'plantsman'.

The green leaf

Any leaf will do - say, a cabbage leaf about to be consigned to the dustbin. If it did not exist, neither would you. Nor other animals, nor their food, nor timber, nor the energy of fossil fuels.

The green leaf takes water from the soil and carbon dioxide from the air and turns them into carbohydrates and other complex organic compounds. The starch in the potato, the sugar in the strawberry, the wood of the tree trunk, all are made by the plant from the simple chemical elements taken from air and soil.

The green leaf needs energy to work its miracle. It gets it from sunlight, not from heat but from pure light. The energy of light is tenuous beyond our imagining, but the green plant has been trapping it for a thousand million years and with it has built up the world we know.

So the plant needs light as much as air and water. Crowd it with its fellows or smother it with weeds and it will straggle upwards, weak and spindly, searching for the light on which its life depends.

The seed

The cabbage from which the leaf came started as a pin-head of living matter which contained the charateristics of its ancestors and the means of starting a new individual.

Take a runner bean - it's larger than a cabbage seed - and cut it open lengthwise along the convex edge. It will open into two halves, hinged at the scar where it was attached to the pod.

Inside you will find two tiny folded leaves, the seed leaves and a little stump of root. All round is food material to give the minute plantlet a start in life.

This is the miracle of the seed. However small, it contains an embryo plant and rations for its potential journey. To start that journey it must have a certain degree of warmth, water and oxygen. All these things are essential if cells are to divide and multiply.

So for the seed to germinate we must sow it when the soil has reached a growing temperature, if the soil is too cold it will rot. If it is sown too deeply or in water-logged soil it will die from lack of air. It will also die if allowed to dry out when germination has started, for its cells cannot then live without water. These needs the good gardener takes for granted. They do not mean that the seed is a feeble thing, it asks only a fair chance to survive and grow.

One other thing affects its chances of survival. As the root and the shoot emerge from the shell of the seed they grow in opposite directions, reacting in different ways to the force of gravity. The root extends downwards, seeking moisture and the soil chemicals it contains. The shoot pushes up towards the light where its seed leaves can expand and gather food from the air. At this point the tiny plant lives on the food reserves of the seed, and it must be self-supporting before they are exhausted.

If the soil is too lumpy, or the surface has set in a hard crust, the effort may be too great and the seedling will fail to emerge. So the soil of the seed bed must be fine and friable and adapted to the capabilities of the seed. The stout shoot of a broad bean can shove its way through a soil that would defeat the fragile seed leaf of an onion.

The root

As the stem and leaves of the plant grow, the root system must keep pace with them. It must keep them supplied with water and the chemical elements absorbed from the soil, and the greater the leaf area above the harder it must work.

From the pores in its green surfaces the plant gives off - 'transpires' - moisture, faster as the weather gets hotter. Look at

making and moving of complex organic compounds is done by the circulation of fluids from cell to cell. So is the swift passage of the hormones, which take the place of an animals nervous system, controlling the plant's growth and reproduction.

We tend to ignore the roots because we cannot see them. If we dig up a root system and shake off the soil its appearance will vary with the species of plant and the most important parts we shall probably not notice at all. These are the fine feeding roots and root hairs, barely-visible threads of cells which insert themselves between the soil particles and by dividing and increasing spread the whole network further and further, taking in the precious water and dissolved chemicals as they do so.

If the soil structure is good, made open by cultivation, the spaces between particles filled with the spongy organic matter called humus, the patiently exploring root fibres will take advantage of it, widening into a system to sustain the food-gathering leaves above.

Reproduction

Plants reproduce themselves in two ways, from a fertilised ovum like members of the animal kingdom, and vegetatively, when part of a plant become a separate and complete individual.

The formation of seed by the plant is of interest to all gardeners, not merely to the seed-grower. Some seeds we eat, like peas, beans and sweet corn, not to mention the cereals. Fruits containing seeds developed as a means of spreading them when the fruits were eaten by birds and animals. The fertilisation of the seeds has meant the evolution of many devices to transfer the fertilising pollen, and the gardener soon learns that pollen must be carried from male to female marrow flowers and from the male 'tassel' to the female 'silk' of sweet corn if the marrows are to grow and the cobs be full of kernals. He learns, too, that some varieties of fruit are strangely fussy and can only be fertilised by pollen from a different variety.

One oddity associated with the formation of flowers and seed is the way in which it sometimes

happens prematurely when the plant 'bolts'. A lettuce runs to seed instead of hearting, or a beetroot instead of making a proper root. Sometimes this happens with no apparent cause, but often it is caused by poor conditions - poor, dry soil, exposure to cold through sowing too early, and so on. Expressed in a very unscientific way, it seems that the plant has reacted to an apparently hostile environment. It has begun to doubt its own survival, and is making an attempt to perpetuate its species before it is too late.

The clone

One more preculiarity of plant life worth thinking about is the effect of vegetative reproduction - propagation from suckers, runners, tubers, cuttings, layering or grafting. Some of these processes are natural, some need the assistance of Man.

Biologically, all the individuals produced in this way are one. This is the clone, a word you will sometimes see in the nurseryman's catalogue. The plants have not come from the fusion of two germ cells, they are identical in make-up with all of their sort everywhere. There may be ten million Cox's apple trees, but biologically there is only one - it just happens to be growing in that many different parts.

One practical implication of this is worth remembering. If a clone is infected with a virus disease - and this has happened to strawberries, raspberries, loganberries and other soft fruits - it turns up in all the plants as faithfully as other characteristics. Then the only remedy is usually to breed new, virus-free varieties, growing them from seed and rooting out every trace of infection before it spreads.

So when buying soft fruit canes and bushes order certified virus-free stock.

We have looked at a few of the ways in which plants are affected by their environment. Good gardening is simply bringing that environment as near to the plant's ideal as possible.

Plants are adaptable, they survive maltreatment. But give them the care that comes with understanding and they will indeed repay you a hundredfold.

plants in the heat of a sunny day and you will see leaves flagging, even though the ground is moist. The roots cannot replace fast enough the water being transpired.

The plant most needs water when it has its greater leaf area and the crop reaches maturity. Then, unless its roots can cope, the crop may be disappointing.

Nor is this a simple sucking-up and giving-off of moisture. All the

The soil is your garden's principal raw material. Don't be discouraged when you read that such-and-such a crop 'prefers' a deep, fertile loam' and your soil is clearly nothing of the sort. Most crops can be induced to grow on most soils, though it is a good idea to concentrate more on those that perform well in your area than to waste time and money on coddling the persistently reluctant ones.

The character of a soil cannot be basically altered, but by regular cultivation and manuring, its fertility can be built up and its deficiencies reduced. In the long run you get back from a soil what you put into it, plus a bonus. What you put into it should not be limited to digging and manuring but should include observation - noticing if water stands on it after rain, what happens to the surface if you walk on it when wet, and so on. In fact, just getting to know it.

The making of soils

Soils begin as pulverised rock. Where it has been worn down into coarse particles the soil is sandy; where the particles are very fine they form a paste which we call clay. To this material is added, over great periods of time, the remains of dead animals and plants, and

Heavy or clay soils

Brown or yellowish in colour. Sticky when wet, dries to intractable clods if dug in the spring, or to something like cracked concrete if the wet surface is walked on. Subsoil is the same but more so, sometimes streaked with grey-blue, sometimes mixed with chalk.

Despite their faults, the clays are often inherently fertile. Crops fail in them through poor drainage or because the roots have such hard work exploring in search of food.

Dig as early in winter as possible, leaving the surface rough so that frost can penetrate the clods and crumble them to a tilth for sowing. Apply bulky organic manures, compost or peat during the winter digging, and every third year follow the digging with a dressing of garden lime, which improves the soil structure. But the greatest improver of the clays is organic matter, which opens up ways for the roots to travel.

Happy on clay soils. Runner and broad beans, peas, the cabbage family, maincrop potatoes, short-rooted carrots and parsnips, globe beetroot, most summer salads not sown too early. Apples, plums, maincrop strawberries, most soft fruit grown on bushes and canes.

Less happy on clay soil. Dwarf beans, long carrots, parsnips and beetroot, salads and vegetables sown in autumn and very early spring. Choice dessert pears, peaches, nectarines, early strawberries.

Light or sandy soils

Variable in colour, but always free-draining, quick-drying and easily worked. They warm up quickly in spring and are good for early crops in the open and under cloches. Plants grown in them make very large root systems. They are often poor because nutrient chemicals are soon washed away, crops respond to top dressing or fertilisers and the use of liquid fertilisers. These soils benefit as much as clay from organic materials such as manure and peat because they act as a sponge to retain moisture.

Happy on sandy soils. Winter or early spring salad and vegetable crops, perpetual (winter) spinach, New Zealand (summer) spinach, long-rooted carrots, parsnips and beetroot. Peaches, nectarines, figs, pears, bush and cane fruits if watered and mulched, early strawberries.

Less happy on sandy soils. Summer lettuce, round-seeded spinach, summer cabbage, autumn cauliflowers, late crops of broad beans and peas. Top fruits are often unhappy in dry summers, though small trees on dwarfing stocks are greatly helped by thorough watering and a thick peat mulch.

the infertile rock mixture becomes a fertile soil.

If you dig a hole about 2ft. deep you will see that the soil is in two layers. The lower one, the subsoil, consists of the basic material, clay, sand, chalk or whatever, and is solid and harsh in texture. The upper layer, the topsoil, consists of the same basic material with the addition of the organic matter that has accumulated. The top layer is more or less fertile, practically nothing will grow in subsoil. Where there is not much topsoil the soil is described as 'thin' or 'shallow', a condition often found in chalk soils.

Remember that Nature created soil fertility by accumulating organic material. When the gardener starts cultivating, he uses up that reserve. If he wants to stay in business he must put something back.

Types of soil
One should know approximately what kind of soil one is dealing with, since different soils need slightly different treatment. If you are new to gardening, or starting up in a new district, gardening neighbours will oblige with information.

The most common soil types are as follows.

Loams
Loam is a medium soil, not too much clay, not too much sand. The word covers a variety of soils, varying with the proportions of different ingredients in the mixture, heavy loams being a little lighter than the clays, light ones a little heavier than the sands. The important thing is texture. Squeeze a handful of moist clay soil and you get something like a lump of plasticine. Do the same with a sandy soil and the lump falls apart when your grip relaxes. Squeeze a handful of loam and it binds together but breaks up at a touch.

Loams are often fertile and contain plenty of organic matter. The soil of old pasture is an example, growing fine crops without much manuring. But stored fertility doesn't last for long and what you take out you must eventually put back.

All vegetables and fruits are happy in the medium soils except for a few eccentrics like blueberries, which only grow in acid peats.

Chalk or alkaline soils
The underlying subsoil is of chalk or limestone and the topsoil is sometimes thin. The soil dries quickly, though sometimes sticky immediately after rain, and it is often greyish in colour.

Chalk soils don't need lime. They are 'hungry' and benefit from all the manure or compost you can give them. Peat, dug in or applied as a mulch, retains moisture and helps crops like potatoes which do better on less alkaline soils. Fertilisers are necessary where there is poor growth and pale coloured foliage.

Happy on chalk soils. Peas, beans, brassica crops, chicory, many root crops if adequately watered in dry weather. All stone fruit, plums, gages, damsons, also peaches and nectarines if situation and climate are right.

Less happy on chalk soils. Potatoes, swedes and other late-sown root crops, successional sowings generally if made in June or July. Strawberries, raspberries, loganberries.

We now have to consider in more detail how to feed the soil and the crops growing in it.

We have seen that plants are largely nourished by water and by carbon dioxide taken from the air, and that to build up their tissues from these sources they must also gather a range of chemical substances from the soil.

A fertile soil is one containing an abundance of these nutrients and having a physical structure which makes it easy for roots to spread out and find them.

We can supply nutrients in 2 ways. First, by adding to the soils those materials we call organic manures, which are gradually broken down by micro-organisms to release the chemical foods. And, second, by supplying the chemicals in the concentrated form called fertilisers or inorganic manures, which can be taken up by the plants as soon as they dissolve in the soil water.

These 2 methods of feeding plants have been labelled 'organic' and 'inorganic' and their respective merits are a cause of controversy. The experienced gardener usually decides that the first is essential and the second is desirable.

The organic manures

We call them soil foods because their first function is to feed the countless billions of bacteria which flourish in a fertile soil, breaking down animal and plant remains into the brown mould called humus and releasing chemical nutrients in forms which roots can absorb.

The process of feeding the soil is slower than feeding plants directly with chemical fertilisers. It is also more lasting, the nutrients being available over a long period and increasing over the years in a well-fed soil. In the same way, it continually improves the soil structure, whatever the type of soil.

The main chemical plant foods are:

Nitrogen It promotes vigorous growth of leaf and stem and is most essential for brassicas, spinach, lettuce and all leafy crops.

Phosphates Affect germination, the growth of roots, maturity and the production of seeds. Important for all seedlings and crops such as peas, beans and sweet corn.

Potash Necessary for general health and disease resistance. Also for plants which store starch or sugar in tubers, roots or fruits - potatoes, carrots, beetroot, all fruits, especially soft fruits.

In addition to these elements plants must have minute quantities of others, such as manganese, known as trace elements. All are supplied by bulky organic manures used in sufficient quantity.

Victorian gardens had unlimited stable manure and were very fertile. Nowadays, we must find what organics we can and supplement them with fertilisers.

Buying bulky organics

Join a local Horticultural Society and find out if it has a joint purchase scheme. Transport is a major cost and manures are sometimes only available in large loads. Some societies buy and share out among members. Left to your own devices, try the following.

Farmyard manure There are usually farms within easy distance of suburban and some urban districts. Consult the Yellow Pages. The best time is late spring and summer, when covered yards are being cleared out.

Stable manure Usually over-priced, but worth enquiring for at nearby riding or training stables. Manure consisting of long straw and fresh droppings must be stacked and left to rot down for a few months before use.

Spent mushroom compost A good bet. Look for 'Mushroom Farms' in the Yellow Pages. Some sell the used compost in bulk, others by the bagful. The material

consists of straw, horse or poultry manure, peat and ground lime-stone. It is pleasant to handle, has a high nutrient value, and is a great soil improver.

Spent hops A wonderful source of humus, and small breweries sometimes sell or even give away the stuff to gardeners. Large breweries sell in bulk to makers of hop manure. Look for local breweries in the Yellow Pages or ask at the pub.

Wool shoddy Waste material from wool textile manufacture, and a long-lasting source of nitrogen. Probably still available in parts of the North of England, but a subject for bulk purchase and sharing.

Seaweed Once a primary source of fertility in many coastal districts, now neglected because no one has the energy to collect it. Make it into a heap and leave it for three or four months before digging in.

Green manure This is an old trick for increasing the humus content of soil. In late summer lightly fork over or rake any vacant ground to get a tilth. Rake in 1 oz per sq yd/ 33 g per sq m of sulphate of ammonia. Then rake in, also at 1 oz per sq yd, seed of mustard, rape or Italian ryegrass. When the crop is a foot/30 cm high, dig it in, inverting the spit so that the greenstuff is completely buried.

Peat Although without immediate nutritive value peat improves the structure of most soils. To get

maximum value, use it freely as a mulch during summer and then dig it in.

Making compost
Home-made garden compost is the cheapest manure. There is no mystique about compost-making, it is simply a matter of returning vegetable waste to the soil in a convenient form, broken down and with its plant foods available for use.

Compost is easily made in heaps, though containers may be used for the sake of appearance. Allow a space of about 6 ft by 4 ft/2 m by 1.2 m for a heap, and a total space large enough for 2 heaps. Dig the ground and remove perennial weeds. Never make compost on a concrete or other solid base, it impedes drainage and prevents the entry of earthworms.

Materials to use Annual weeds, tops but not roots of perennial weeds, crop remains such as pea, bean and potato haulm, if not diseased, soft, but not woody hedge clippings, lawn mowings, discarded bedding plants and flower garden trimmings, and household waste such as fruit and vegetable peelings, leaves and tops, but not edible scraps such as bread, which attracts vermin.

Building the heap Accumulate a layer of material 12 in/30 cm deep, sprinkle it with 1 oz/33 g of sulphate of ammonia and water thoroughly from a rosed can. Instead of sulphate of ammonia

you can use a proprietary activator or 2 in/5 cm layer of animal manure. This is a good way of using small quantities of manure from small livestock such as poultry. Cover the material with a 1 in/2.5 cm layer of soil.

Accumulate a second layer of waste, and this time sprinkle it with a double handful of garden lime. Water, and cover with soil.

Treat the third layer like the first, and continue with the sequence until the heap is about 4 ft/1.2 m high. It will sink continuously while being built.

Leave it alone for a month or so, then turn it over on to the plot alongside, placing any dry material from the outside in the centre of the new heap. Cover it with a layer of soil and with a sheet of polythene in very wet weather. Start a new heap on the vacated site.

The compost is ready for use when it reaches a uniform crumbly consistency, is brown in colour and smells pleasantly of leaf mould.

The simplest form of container is the two-compartment wooden bin, easily made of rough timber but tidier in operation than heaps. The sides should be about 3 ft/1 m high and the area sufficient for two batches of compost, with a partition in the centre. The fronts of the 2 bays should be removable so that the matured compost can be easily shovelled into a barrow.

Fertilisers supply plant foods in forms which can be assimilated very quickly, producing increases in growth and yields in the crops to which they are applied. For the most part they do not remain active in the soil for more than 1 season, nor do they improve its structure or create humus.

The fertilisers in general use are chemical compounds produced from mineral ores or by the fixation of atmospheric nitrogen. Their chief function is to provide in soluble form the 3 elements already referred to, nitrogen, phosphorus or phosphates, and potassium or potash, widely known by their chemical symbols, N, P and K.

When the chemical supplies only 1 of the food elements it is known as a 'straight' fertiliser. Those supplying all 3, perhaps with the addition of some trace elements, are known as 'compound', 'general' or 'balanced' fertilisers.

Straight fertilisers
For nitrogen Sulphate of ammonia, nitrate of soda, nitro chalk. Used on poor soils and as a top dressing to boost growth when a crop seems to be 'standing still'. Normal dose, $\frac{1}{2}$ - 1 oz per sq yd/ 17 - 33 g per sq m.
For phosphates Superphosphate of lime. Used as a pre-sowing dressing for all vegetable crops and especially good for peas, beans, sweet corn and Brussels sprouts. Normal dose, $1\frac{1}{2}$ - 2 oz per sq yd/50 - 66 g per sq m.
For potash Sulphate of potash, muriate of potash. Fruit trees on light land sometimes need an annual dressing of potash and if you find your trees and soft fruits are growing and cropping badly a soil analysis may reveal potash deficiency. Normal dose, 1 oz per sq yd/33 g per sq m.

The straight fertilisers may be bought at any garden shop or centre in small quantities and many gardeners keep a small quantity of sulphate of ammonia or nitrate of soda for use on the compost heap or as a stimulant top dressing. For general use however, compound fertilisers are preferable.

Compound fertilisers
In anyone wants to mix their own - and it may be slightly cheaper than buying a proprietary mix - the formula is 4 lb/1.8 kg sulphate of ammonia, 5 lb/2.2 kg super-phosphate, 2 lb/0.9 kg sulphate of potash. Mix all very thoroughly together before using.

A proprietary general fertiliser should carry an analysis showing its composition as regards the main nutrients. The analysis does not identify the chemical compounds used, but declares the actual percentages of the 3 elements present in a form which plants can assimilate. The analysis of a compound fertiliser like National Growmore, which is a good all-purpose one, would be about 7% N, 7% P and 6% K.

Buying and using fertilisers
They come in 3 forms, solid, liquid and as foliar feeds. The first is the most commonly used.
In solid form Straight fertilisers may be sold as powder or fine crystals. Compounds are prepared as small granules, clean and easy to handle.

Buy only the quantity you are likely to use in a season. Fertilisers absorb moisture from the air and may become a sticky mess during the winter. Put them into tightly tied polythene bags or airtight tins and close the containers after use.

When using compound fertiliser before sowing or planting, scatter it evenly over the area 1 - 2 weeks before you intend to sow, lightly forking or raking it into the top few inches. Fertiliser is not applied when digging because if deeply buried it would be dissolved and lost before the crop could reach it.

The usual rate of application for this type of dressing is 1 oz per sq yd/33 g per sq m. A simple way of

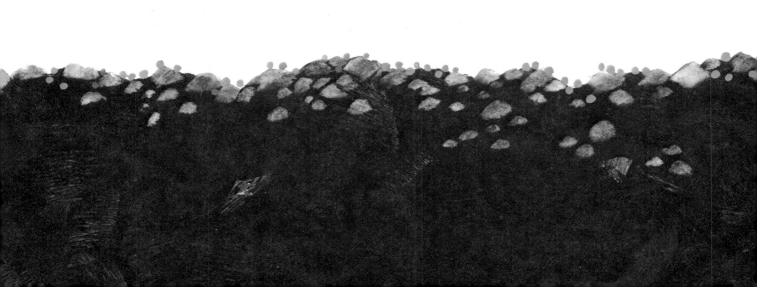

measuring the quantity is to weigh a number of handfuls of fertiliser on the household scales - say, 10 and work out the weight per handful.

When using solid fertiliser as a top dressing, scatter it close to the row at a rate of 1/2 - 1 oz per sq yd of row. Keep if off the leaves or it will scorch them. Work it into the surface with hoe or hand fork and water it in if the weather is dry.

Remember, fertiliser in dry soil feeds no plants. And, doses much heavier than those advised damage the delicate feeding roots and do more harm than good.

Liquid fertilisers Used for the feeding of growing crops and speedy in action. They are general fertilisers, though obtainable in different grades for special purposes. For instance, tomato fertiliser may contain added potash to assist ripening of the fruit.

Keep strictly to the makers' instructions on rates of dilution. Don't feed more heavily by making the solution stronger but if necessary increase the frequency of application, feeding, say weekly instead of once a fortnight.

Liquid fertilisers do not harm foliage if used at the proper strength, but avoid pouring them over the foliage of seedlings and soft-leaved plants in hot sun.

Foliar feeds These are liquid fertiliers formulated for application to foliage instead of to the soil. The nutrients are absorbed into the plants' tissues in a matter of hours rather than the normal days or weeks. Foliar feeds are now generally obtainable, but the technique is a new one and the sensible course is to use it on a portion of a crop and compare the result with that of the untreated part.

Lime
Plants must have calcium in the soil and this is applied as hydrated lime or ground chalk or limestone. All except chalk soils are likely to need an occasional dressing of this garden lime, best applied after winter digging at a rate of 6 oz per sq yd/200 g per sq m.

Soil testing Liming should not be overdone and if you are in doubt whether your soil needs it a simple testing kit, costing about £1, will tell you whether it is acid or alkaline - whether it needs lime or has plenty.

The acid/alkaline balance is expressed in a chemical statement called a pH factor. Soils with a reading pH7 are neutral, those with a higher reading are alkaline, those with a lower reading are acid. Most vegetables and fruit are happy with pH6.5, very slightly on the acid side, which is why lime should not be applied too generously.

Processed organic fertilisers
A number of organic substances are available in convenient forms and may be used as substitutes for organic fertilisers. They are safe in use, with little fear of overdosing, but are more expensive than the inorganics.

General purpose Hop manure, composted municipal waste (enquire of your local authority), dried poultry manure.

For nitrogen Dried blood, hoof and horn meal, fish meal. Some grades of fish meal also have a high potash content.

Phosphates Bone meal, steamed bone flour. The first releases soluble phosphates over a long period and is used when planting fruit trees and bushes. The second is a substitute for superphosphate.

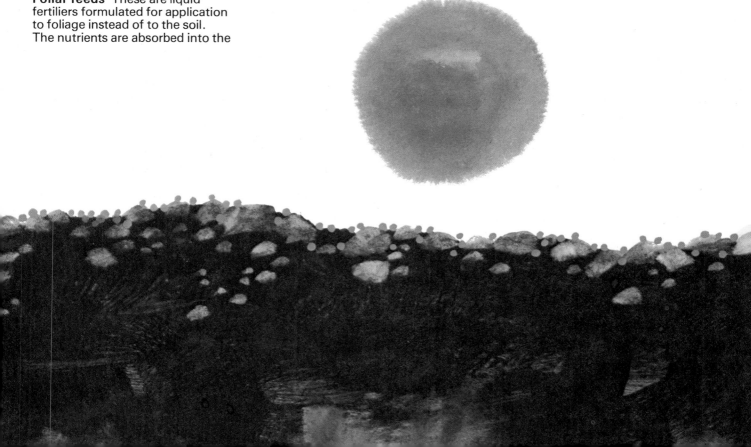

The garden tools you require may be dictated by either the state of your garden or the time of year. For those who are about to embark on gardening for the first time, the basic tools are a spade, fork, rake, Dutch hoe, weed fork and hand trowel. Spades and forks are manufactured in 3 sizes, digging size, small digging size and border size. The working heads are usually made either from stainless steel or from carbon steel and the handles from wood, aluminium, steel, polypropylene or a combination of two or more of these materials. Since your tools should last you a lifetime, it is advisable to purchase the best you can afford. Properly heat-treated stainless steel equipment is expensive but it will repay you many times over by its quality, ease of use and ease of cleaning after use. Make sure you choose sizes to suit you - it does not follow that the largest size will enable you to complete your digging work in the shortest time. A great deal of thought goes into the production of these tools and they vary from manufacturer to manufacturer in respect of weight, balance, lift and crank, so choose the one that feels right in your hands.

Stanley Garden Tools Limited manufacturer a range of stainless steel and carbon steel spades and forks which are fitted with unique aluminium alloy cored polypropylene handles. These are lighter than wooden handles, are stronger, quite impervious to the effects of the weather and they carry a lifetime guarantee against breakage in normal use. A further range of carbon steel spades and forks is also available. These are fitted with selected ash handles and either 'T' shape grips or the now popular moulded polypropylene 'D' grips.

Remember, however, that a lot of your digging will be done in the autumn when the ground is wet and heavy. At such times, a stainless steel spade or fork will prove its worth when other types become virtually unuseable due to the adhesion of wet soil to their surfaces. After use, you simply rinse a stainless steel tool and put it away until it is needed again.

Once your garden has been cultivated, you will find that border size spades and forks become invaluable for continuing maintenance and their light weight makes them very popular with lady gardeners who on some reckoning now outnumber the men.

Having completed the initial cultivation with spade or fork, you will need a rake with which you level the plot and produce a fine tilth ready for sowing. The same choice as with spades and forks is open to you. There are rakes which are inexpensive initially and quality products which will give many years' good service. The construction of rakes has improved dramatically over recent years and the traditional wooden handle which was subject to shrinkage and warping has been replaced with an aluminium alloy handle covered with P V C sleeving. These handles will not warp, are not subject to weathering and the heads are permanently fixed with modern epoxy resins.

As vegetable seed germinates, so does the unwanted seed of the weeds. You will find that a hoe is the ideal tool with which to keep them under control. You may prefer a traditional Dutch hoe or the push-pull type which, as its name implies, operates on a pushing and pulling motion.

Like rakes, hoes come in a variety of qualities and prices, and again, it will repay you to purchase a quality tool and preferably one manufactured from stainless steel. You will find that most of the better quality hoes are fitted with the same aluminium and P V C handles as the rake. Do not be misled by the weight of these tools. Modern materials and technological advances have enabled progressive manufacturers to produce ultra lightweight tools which have the same strength as their old-fashioned heavy predecessors. When selecting your hoe, you may be confronted by an alternative type called a draw hoe, but this is not a suitable substitute for neither the Dutch hoe nor the push-pull type. You will, however, find that a draw hoe is ideal in your vegetable plot for earthing up etc. As its name suggests, it enables you to manoeuvre the soil in a confined space. The most useful type of draw hoe is 'swan-necked' to enable you to work amongst your plants with maximum clearance.

A hand trowel and weed fork are vital garden tools for planting and transplanting and the choice available is perhaps wider than with any other. Cheap imported products are available but generally you will find that they are not as satisfactory as those produced at home. Whilst stainless steel tools are undoubtedly superior, beware of those which have not been properly heat-treated - the prongs of a weed fork must be spring-tempered. You can test this by deflecting one with your thumbs - if the prong springs back to its original position, purchase with

confidence; if it remains distorted, the fork is useless. Apart from their heat-treated stainless steel range, Stanley have recently introduced a new range of high quality carbon steel weed forks and trowels with heat-treated blades and ergonomically designed moulded polypropylene handles. These moderately priced tools will give you many years of satisfactory service. Long handled versions of both the stainless steel and the carbon steel weed fork are also available to enable you to reach the less accessible areas of your plot easily.

Systematic pruning of your fruit trees will reward you with heavier cropping. Established trees which have been neglected may require heavier pruning with either a saw or heavy duty lopping shear. Bow saws are manufactured in a variety of sizes, 24 in/ 60 cm and 30 in/75 cm being the most popular. Pruning saws have the advantage of being double edged - one edge for heavy and the other edge for finer cutting. Lopping shears are easier for branches up to approximately $1\frac{1}{2}$ in/3.75 cm thick and Stanley have recently introduced a new compound action lopping shear which gives substantial mechanical advantage in use. The coated cutting blade ensures a clean cut which helps to inhibit the formation of diseased wood.

Light pruning only will be necessary on those trees which have been regularly maintained and this can be best done with secateurs. The choice is almost limitless both in quality and price, but your first option must be to decide which of the two basic types you prefer.

Until recently, most secateurs consisted of two blades working together in a scissor-like fashion. Recently a new type has been introduced consisting of a single blade which cuts against an anvil. This type has certain advantages which tend to give it superior performance. When two moving blades are involved, there is a tendancy for them to spring apart and produce a rugged cut. To off-set this, the blades are made more robust but the additional thickness tends to reduce their cutting ability. Because the blade of the anvil secateur operates squarely against a fixed surface, a fine blade can be fitted which improves the cutting performance and requires less effort. This type of construction also allows the cutting blade to be coated with a patented anti-friction compound reducing even more the manual effort required to operate the secateur.

Stanley's latest introduction is an anvil secateur comprising 7 components only, all of which are available as spare parts. Whilst this secateur is lightweight in its construction, it out performs tools costing three or four times its price.

To cater for individual preference, Stanley manufacture a range of secateurs which represents both types.

The hedge around your garden will give you seclusion and shelter for your plants. It has many clear advantages over fencing for this purpose, but in order to maintain it properly it needs occasional trimming. Although you may elect to purchase a mechanised hedge trimmer, you will almost certainly need a pair of hand shears for final trimming (and for a variety of other tasks in the garden). The best hand shears are still assembled individually by craftsmen and their performance reflects the amount of hand-work involved - and so, obviously, does the price. The most useful shear is one with blades approximately 8½ in/20 cm long with a cutting notch for dealing with heavy twigs. Smaller shears with approximately 6 in/15 cm blades are made for lady gardeners. Both patterns are available in stainless steel, carbon steel or anti-friction coated carbon steel. Stainless steel has the advantage of not being affected by sap and moisture which obviates the cleaning and oiling process which is essential to keep carbon steel in pristine condition. One additional shear to the Stanley range made from carbon steel has contoured cutting edges which prevent twigs riding out of the blades as they cut. These shears complete a range which has been classed as perhaps the finest in the world.

Your garden equipment will not be complete without a garden barrow. The Stanley barrow has a one piece deep-drawn pan with rolled edges for rigidity and safety, a wide section wheel set well under the load for ease of control (and to obviate tyre marks on your lawn) and the ability to stand upright without support. This makes the barrow easy to empty and easy to store in the minimum of space.

Tool maintenance

All tools perform better if they are maintained in good condition and garden tools are no exception. Wear will take place, cutting edges will become blunt, and the surfaces of most tools will be affected by corrosive chemicals in the soil. More and more chemical fertilizers are now being used and steps must be taken to combat the effects which these chemicals can have upon your garden tools.

Stainless steel has a very much higher resistance to corrosion than does carbon steel, but even so, after use, stainless steel garden tools should be thoroughly washed. Remember carbon steel tools must also be wiped over with an oily rag to prevent them rusting.

The heaviest tasks in your garden will fall to your spade and fork. Both will perform better if their surfaces are smooth and polished, another advantage of stainless steel tools whose surfaces are polished to a mirror-like finish during manufacture. Carbon steel spades and forks only achieve a degree of polish during use but the better this polish can be maintained, the less friction will be created as the tool is used. This makes penetration of the soil easier and avoids the clogging effect of it sticking to the tool. The tines of a fork are self-sharpening as they wear; a spade, however, will tend to become blunt during use. To help it to maintain its performance you must resharpen the cutting edge occasionally. The best quality spades have heat-treated blades which will resist the attentions of a file and you must use a sharpening stone on these. Do not sharpen your spade to a feather edge, as this will quickly be deformed by stones in the soil. Maintain an edge thickness of approximately $\frac{1}{16}$ in/1.5 mm, this being the most suitable for all conditions.

If your spade or fork is fitted with a wooden handle, care must be taken to preserve it. The original protective lacquer will eventually weather and it will be necessary either to re-lacquer or to treat the wood with linseed oil.

The affects of sun and rain may cause the grain to swell and leave splinters protruding from the handle itself. If this happens make sure that the wood is well smoothed down with glass paper before applying a preservative. Storage in extremely dry conditions will reduce the moisture content of the timber, leading to shrinkage and to loss of strength. In order to overcome these disadvantages, top quality spades and forks are now fitted with tubular reinforced moulded polypropylene handles, which are stronger and lighter than wood and quite impervious to the conditions that cause the deterioration of wooden tools. They require no maintenance and will give trouble-free service for a life-time.

The general term 'cultivating tools' includes weed forks, trowels, hoes, rakes, edge knives etc., and as with spades and forks, these are manufactured basically either in stainless steel or carbon steel. The head of the tool should receive the same care as recommended for spades and forks and those tools which have a cutting edge, i.e. trowels, hoes, edging knives, perform better if the cutting edge is maintained with a fine file or sharpening stone. Wooden handles need the attention already discussed but most manufacturers produce a range of lightweight cultivating tools fitted with aluminium alloy tubular handles with PVC sleeving. These require no maintenance whatsoever.

Cutting tools such as shears and secateurs require routine maintenance to retain their maximum efficiency. After use, their blades should always be cleaned of sap, oiled and sharpened with a honing stone as necessary. The pivot bolt will require occasional oiling.

Tidiness and cleanliness go hand in hand - establish storage positions for all your garden tools and a routine for their maintenance. This will give you the incentive to make sure that they are always stored in good condition, suitably protected against corrosion and ready for immediate use when they are next needed.

If you have difficulty in selecting or obtaining the products you require, contact the garden tool experts - they will be happy to help you. Their address is:

Stanley Garden Tools Limited
Woodhouse Mill
Sheffield S13 9WJ

To bring soil into the right physical condition it must be cultivated as well as manured. It is worth pointing out that the word 'manure' has the same derivation as 'manoeuvre', in other words the moving about or working of the soil was traditionally regarded as a way of enriching it.

Cultivations are deep or shallow, digging or hoeing, and have different functions.

Digging

The reasons for digging are to break up the topsoil, to make root development easier and permit surplus water to drain away and moisture from below to be drawn up in dry weather, to bury annual weeds and remove the roots of perennial ones, to leave a rough surface which will weather down into a tilth for sowing and to incorporate manure or compost.

The right way to dig Use a spade if possible, though on very heavy land you may have to use a fork. Choose a tool with the right length of handle to suit you and with a smaller blade or tines if the standard size is likely to prove tiring. In this, as in all gardening operations, the right tool is essential to an efficient job.

Except on the lightest land, dig when the surface is dry or slightly frozen. Most digging is done in the winter and a surface just crusted with frost provides excellent conditions. Don't worry about turning in the frost, it will make no difference to soil temperatures at sowing time.

Start at one end of the plot to be dug, at the left-hand corner. Aim to turn over a strip not more than 6 - 8 in / 15 - 20 cm wide with each row of digging. If you try to dig too wide a strip you will find each spadeful very heavy to lift and your rate of work may actually be slower.

Drive the spade in by resting a foot on the shoulder of the blade and transferring to it the weight of the body. Don't try to force it down by pushing the handle or by a chopping stroke as though you were using a pickaxe. Insert the blade vertically so that it reaches its maximum depth.

Pull the handle back to loosen the clod. Slide the left hand down the shaft of the spade to the point of balance, lift the soil and throw it gently forward, inverting the blade so that it slips off.

Repeat this with a steady, deliberate rhythm, keeping the spade cuts in line to form a small regular trench, with the dug soil thrown clear of your operations. When you reach the far side of the plot clean the spade with a trowel or flat piece of wood kept there for the purpose, walk leisurely back to the starting point, and begin another row.

If you want to leave a perfectly executed job you can barrow all the soil from the first row to the point where you will finish and use it to fill the trench which will be left there.

Digging grassland for the first time This is a problem of the brand new garden. There are several ways of tackling it but the most effective is to remove a layer of turf.

Begin by cutting down and removing tall grass and weeds. Then pare the turf off a narrow strip with a sharp spade or a mattock, taking off only a thin slice and leaving the fibrous grass roots. Dig in the usual way, picking out roots of perennial weeds and the long white runners of twitch or couch.

Remove the turf only from the area you expect to dig immediately, you will find that even in wet weather the soil just uncovered can be dug

without difficulty, whereas if the entire plot is turfed you may be held up by wet conditions before it can be dug.

The turf should be stacked grass downwards and eventually used to make potting compost or for the soil layers in the compost heap.

What about the subsoil? First, take care not to bring any of it to the surface. Second, if there is poor drainage, with water ponding after heavy rain, the subsoil may be to blame. It may be naturally impervious or it may have been compacted into a 'pan' by past ploughing.

Breaking up the subsoil nearly always does good. Dig in the usual way, but throwing the topsoil far enough forward to leave a trench about 8 in wide with the subsoil exposed. Dig the subsoil with the fork, breaking it up but leaving it in place. Then, with the spade, complete another row of digging in the normal way, covering the broken-up subsoil and exposing another strip of subsoil. This is a modified form of trenching or double-digging, and although it doubles the time taken over the work it is justified by results on badly drained heavy land. Try it on a small area and compare crops.

Digging in manure The amount to be used depends on how much is available. Use it on ground where you do *not* intend to grow root crops (See Making Plans/Vegetables, pages 22/23).

Don't spread manure or compost over the ground before digging. It makes things difficult in the event of rain and loses nutrients through exposure to air. Use it direct from the barrow or from small heaps strategically placed on the plot to be dug.

On completing each row of digging shake out the manure over the soil already dug so that it is just covered by the next row of digging. Don't leave it in a compact mass at the bottom of the trench. Plants like organic matter distributed through the soil, not jammed between topsoil and subsoil like the filling in a sandwich.

Hoeing

The hoe is probably the oldest implement of cultivation. Its basic modern forms are the draw hoe, which the operator pulls towards him while walking forward on ground already hoed, and the Dutch hoe, which is used with a forward-pushing stroke while the operator walks backwards, leaving the hoed ground untrodden.

Many recent improvements in design, especially in the Dutch hoe, have improved the efficiency of the tool. Both forms are essential pieces of equipment, the draw hoe for cultivation and taking out drill, the Dutch hoe also for cultivation and especially for controlling weeds. One should also mention the short handled onion hoe, a wonderful little tool too seldom seen. Although it entails stooping - or getting down on one's hands and knees - it is perfect for cultivating close to small seedlings or between closely-spaced rows.

Using the hoe Use both types with long strokes and the edge of the blade just below the surface. Don't chop with the draw hoe or jab with the Dutch hoe, especially close to seedlings.

Hoe regularly when the surface is dry throughout the growing season. Hoeing aerates the soil, destroys seedling weeds, and creates a 'soil mulch', the layer of loose soil which conserves moisture by reducing evaporation.

The more often the hoe is used, the easier the work, the blade slipping effortlessly through a friable tilth. Time spent in hoeing apparently clean ground is never wasted. Weed seeds are always germinating below the surface and the best time to kill weeds is before you see them.

The general layout of a new garden is worth considering in advance. There is a temptation to get cracking, to cultivate the easiest-looking patch and wallop in a tree or some seeds. That way the garden is apt to grow haphazard. With experience you find things in the wrong places, time and energy being wasted and crops not coming up to expectations.

You may, of course, take possession of a garden perfectly laid out and fully stocked with equipment and permanent crops. If so, the next couple of pages are not for you.

A 'new' garden, in the present context, means either an uncultivated plot attached to a new house or a cultivated garden which has been neglected or is purely ornamental. We shall not put forward elaborate plans, because they seldom fit the reader's requirements. But there are general considerations for the kitchen garden planner to bear in mind.

Clearing the ground

The uncultivated garden A major problem is often the disposal of builder's rubble and subsoil excavated from footings and trenches.

If possible, contact the builders before completion of the work and get both removed entirely from the site. Rubble is apt to get buried in shallow pits, and subsoil to be spread evenly over the whole garden. On heavy land this is a disaster. At the very least, try to have the subsoil deposited in one place. It will grow hardy ground cover plants, shrubs and spring bulbs, but it will not grow vegetables.

Find out if any piped land drains run under the garden and if so whether they have a clear outlet, usually into a nearby ditch.

The neglected garden Initial clearance here is largely a matter of coping with perennial weeds, docks, nettles, thistles and twitch.

If you take possession in the summer begin by cutting down the top growth and burning it or using it as the foundation of the first compost heap.

Dig a small area at a time, shaking out the weed roots and burning them. Alternatively, destroy the weeds by applying sodium chlorate and delaying sowing and planting until the following spring, when winter rains will have washed the chemical out of the soil.

Take care when clearing not to destroy anything worth saving. Derelict soft fruit bushes and canes recover marvellously if pruned and cleaned up. Top fruit will also need pruning, but this should be done in stages over a year or two. Herbs may be found lurking in a weed forest and should be uncovered by careful hand weeding and digging.

Apply no organic manure to the neglected garden until the weed growth is under control. Natural fertility usually builds up when a garden runs wild and vigorous nettles and thistles indicate a food reserve for the first year's crops.

Light and shade

When it comes to planning actual layout, remember the importance of light.

Try to avoid trees, tall hedges or boundary fences on the south-east, south-west or south of the plot. On the north and east, trees and hedges are a valuable windbreak, but trim back branches that overhang cultivated areas.

Don't plant fruit trees in the vegetable beds, the only exception to this rule being the planting of cordon or espalier trees on north or east margins. Fruit trees among vegetables not only shade them and take more than their share of soil foods, they grow too vigorously and may fruit less quickly and less regularly.

The question of light must be considered particularly in relation to winter crops in greenhouse, frame, and under cloches. On a summer's day the whole garden may be filled with sunlight, but remember that in midwinter, when crops under glass most need light, the sun is only 30% above the horizon at noon. Then even a moderately high fence to the south casts a very long shadow.

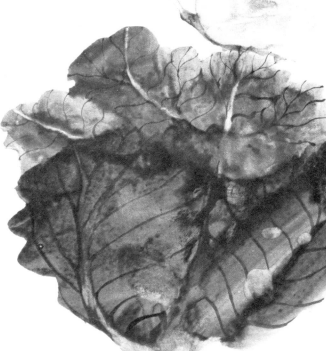

Beds and paths

The vegetable-growing area, unless very small, is best divided into separate beds with intersecting paths. This may seem a waste of precious space, but paths are necessary in harvesting crops, carting manure and other activities. The vegetable garden cultivated as a single plot gets a lot of temporary paths made across it during the season.

The best shape for individual beds is the rectangle, with the crop rows running across the shorter dimensions. It is a slight advantage to have these rows running north and south so that during the growing season they get equal sunlight on both sides, but this is not vitally important. Winter crops under cloches do better in east/west rows, since the greater area of glass is then turned to the south, the only direction from which appreciable sunlight is received.

Paths need only be 24 in/60 cm wide, but must have an all-weather surface. Gravel or clinker needs attention in the matter of weeds and are not ideal for the wheelbarrow after rain or frost. Grass is far worse, time-wasting, a haven for pests, and bare and muddy in winter. Best is on-site concrete or matt-surfaced concrete slabs, laid level on a bed of sand.

Don't forget paths to the shed, greenhouse and compost heap and from the kitchen door to the herb bed.

Garden structures

These may include greenhouse, cold frame and tool shed. The first 2 may depend on available space, operating time, and finance. The last, however small it may be, is almost a necessity.

The garden shed not only has to accommodate tools - and leaving tools lying about in the open is very nearly criminal - it also has to serve as a store for fertilisers, herbicides and seeds, the drying of herbs, beans and onions, the storage of roots in winter and a miscellany of other purposes. It should be as dry and substantial as possible.

A useful and practicable building for the small garden is the combined shed and greenhouse. It is a span roof structure divided down the centre, one half having board or asbestos cladding, the other being glazed to form a lean-to greenhouse. Greenhouses and their siting are discussed more fully in Crop Protection/Greenhouses, pages 36/37.

Most garden structures, whether sectional or not, require planning permission from the local authority, usually obtainable without difficulty.

Water supplies

A standpipe is useful in the garden where a hose is in use - attaching it to an indoor tap is often unpopular.

All garden planning is in a sense contingency planning, or at least it must be flexible. In a climate as variable as ours you cannot say with certainty when a crop will be planted and harvested or what the yield will be.

Despite this, you must have an annual cropping programme for the vegetable garden because you cannot make out the seed order until you decide what to grow. We shall come back to the seed order again, the point to remember here is that unless you get it in early in the New Year you may not get the varieties you want. About Boxing Day, therefore, take a look round, estimate the space available and decide what you will grow, how much, and where.

Rotational cropping

This simply means not growing the same crops on the same ground year after year, which when you come to think of it is no more than common sense.

To grow the same crops, or crops of the same type, continuously in the same soil leads to a build up of pests and diseases peculiar to those crops. As some crops make heavier demands on particular soil nutrients than others it also means that the soil is depleted of some foods faster than of others. Finally, leguminous crops (peas and beans) leave the soil richer in nitrogen, and crops needing special manuring, like marrows, cucumbers and celery, also leave a lot of residual fertility. So it is sensible to succeed them with other crops which make use of it.

In planning a rotation divide the growing area into 3 plots or beds and the crops into 3 groups.
Group/1 Root crops Potatoes, carrots, parsnips, beetroot, turnips.
Group/2 Brassicas Brussels sprouts, cabbages, cauliflowers, calabrese, sprouting broccoli, kale.
Group/3 Miscellaneous crops Other vegetables and salads.

Grow 1 group in each of the 3 plots changing the plot each year so that the rotation is completed in 3 years.

Manure the plot according to the crops to be grown on it.

For root crops No manure when winter digging. No lime, compost or peat in potato trenches. Compound fertiliser before sowing for all crops.
For brassicas Manure in winter. Lime after digging if necessary. Compound fertiliser before planting. Nitrogenous fertiliser as top dressing.
For miscellaneous crops Some compost or manure if available.

Compound fertiliser before sowing. Prepared sites for marrows, squashes, cucumbers and celery.

THREE YEAR ROTATION

Plot 1
First year Root crops. Fertiliser. No manure or lime.
Second year Brassicas. Manure. Lime if needed. Fertiliser.
Third year Miscellaneous crops. Manure or compost if available. Fertiliser.

Plot 2
First year Brassicas. Treat as Plot 1, second year.
Second year Miscellaneous crops. Treat as Plot 1, third year.
Third year Root crops. Treat as Plot 1, first year.

Plot 3
First year Miscellaneous crops. Treat as Plot 1, third year.
Second year Root crops. Treat as Plot 1, first year.
Third year Brassicas. Treat as Plot 1, second year.

A rotational plan is a guide, not a blueprint. Its intention is to have the bulk of crops moved around in sequence and to use manures and fertilisers to the best advantage. It cannot be followed in detail because crops overlap, and with successional plantings any one plot may carry crops from different groups in one season. But the broad principles are sound enough.

Maximizing yields
One object of planning is to make the most of your ground. In addition to cultivation and manuring, your returns are going to be affected by how many productive plants you can get into a given area.

One thing is certain. You cannot increase yields by increasing the plant population beyond certain limits. There are optimum plant spacings, varying somewhat with conditions. But avoid extremes. If you thin a row of carrots to 6 in/ 15 cm apart you will get large carrots and a smaller total weight than if you thinned to 4 in/10 cm. And if you leave them unthinned you will get nothing usable at all.
Row and plant spacings The distances between plants and rows advised for individual crops later in the book are fair averages derived from most gardeners' practical experience. But don't follow them too rigidly.

If, for example, you find there is space for only 3 rows of onions at 12 in/30 cm apart, and you doubt if this will accommodate all the sets you have bought, reduce the row spacing to 9 in/22.5 cm. You will then have room for 4 rows and a larger crop. But inter-row weeding will be more tricky and you will have to take care that the crop is not overgrown.

Another factor to be considered in estimating the possible numbers of rows is the space between different crops. Where a crop with widely spaced rows is next to one more closely spaced, the distance between them must be the wider spacing. Thus, if you have 3 rows of potatoes 24 in/60 cm apart next to 2 rows of beetroot at 12 in/ 30 cm distance, the last row of potatoes must be 24 in/60 cm from the first row of beet, otherwise the latter will be overshadowed by the more vigorous crop.

The way to maximum production is not through overcrowding crops but by ensuring that ground is used to its full capacity and not left vacant or bearing only weeds and the remnants of old crops.
Successional crops When crops finish in summer, clear them away, hoe or fork the soil lightly and work in a dressing of compound fertiliser.

A variety of crops may be sown from early June to early August. Water drills before sowing in dry weather and water seedlings to get them started as quickly as possible.

After early potatoes, early peas, broad beans and dwarf beans, sow:

In June Swedes, turnips, beetroot, carrots, winter cabbage and cauliflower (planted), sprouting broccoli (planted or sown where to grow), lettuce, radishes, perpetual spinach.

In July Hungry Gap kale, turnips, early stump-rooted carrots, beetroot (in the first fortnight), lettuce, radishes, salad onions, perpetual spinach.

In August Turnips for spring greens, prickly-seeded spinach (first fortnight), radishes, lettuce Tom Thumb to mature in open and Kwiek, to mature under cloches.

By September and October, crops of maincrop potatoes and runner beans will be cleared, releasing ground for spring cabbage plants, sowings of lettuce for spring harvesting and of broad beans for cloching or wintering in the open.

Successional cropping, 2 harvests instead of 1, is the surest way of making the most of your vegetable plot. Waste no time in getting the old crop out and the new one in. Every day makes a difference to a crop with only half a season in which to mature.

Provide for your late sowings when making out the seed order. Trying to buy seeds in midsummer is no fun at all.

Fruits are divided into 2 classes. *Top fruit* grows on trees of various shapes and sizes and includes apples, pears, plums, peaches, nectarines and apricots. *Soft fruit* grows on bushes, canes and plants and includes gooseberries, currants, raspberries, loganberries, blackberries and strawberries. Grapes grow on vines and figs on trees of a sort; their classification is doubtful.

We shall not offer any detailed plans for a fruit garden. What you decide to grow and where in the garden you decide to grow it are matters of personal choice. But a newcomer to the business needs a few basic facts before making a start and we list some of them here.

Soils The top fruits succeed in most soils, but it is worth remembering that the most fussy are dessert apples and the most tolerant are cooking apples and plums. Whatever the soil, good drainage is essential, and on heavy and chalky soils the subsoil should be broken up as much as possible. Very rich soil is not needed for top fruits, and certainly not for apples.

Soft fruits, which reach maturity more quickly and produce heavier and rather more consistent crops in relation to the size of the plants, benefit from a regular use of fertilisers on poor soils. Their main requirement is for plenty of humus in the soil, and with good soil preparation and annual mulching with organic material any garden can be induced to yield its quota of summer berries.

Climate The southern and south-eastern regions of England produce the best dessert apples because of their dry summers and high sunshine records. But the Midlands, the South-West, the North-West and East Anglia all have commercial fruit-growing areas, and it can be assumed that top fruits will succeed in most parts of England. Peaches and apricots are normally grown on walls for the easier protection of their blossom from spring frosts, not because the trees themselves are not hardy.

Spring frosts are the most damaging climatic feature. Some districts are particularly at risk because of a low-lying position; cold air flows downhill and in a spring radiation frost the lowest temperatures are reached at the lowest points. If you are in such a 'frost hollow' it may be advisable to concentrate on later-flowering fruits.

Top and soft fruits flower from March to June more or less in the following order: peaches, plums, cherries, pears, apples, strawberries, gooseberries, currants, raspberries, loganberries, blackberries. The last three are normally safe from frost. The top fruits all flower during a crucial period from March to early May, and in a known frosty district you should consider planting late-flowering varieties.

Finding space: top fruit
In most gardens this is a tougher problem than soil or climate. You have to consider, not the somewhat tiddly little specimen to be planted, but its eventual size. The 2 important factors are the shape of the tree and the type of rootstock on which it is grafted.

Tree forms Avoid those like the standard which make large orchard trees and are slow to come into full bearing. Choose from:

The bush It has a very short stem or trunk and main branches growing in an open-centred cup-shaped form. Used for apples, pears and plums. Easily accessible for pruning and picking. Plant 12 - 15 ft/3.5 - 4.5 m apart.

The single-stemmed cordon One main stem with short laterals kept pruned back. Used for apples and pears, not for plums which resent hard pruning. Fine for growing on walls in narrow spaces between windows, and for growing in rows supported by posts and wires. Cordons are planted in an oblique position so that the stem starts off slanting, even though it grows vertically later. This discourages too rapid growth and promotes earlier fruiting. Plant 2½ - 3 ft/75 cm - 1 m apart.

The fan-trained tree A very short stem from which evenly-spaced branches radiate fan-wise and are trained to a wall. Used for peaches, nectarines, apricots, figs, Morello cherries and, in colder districts, plums. Both cordons and fan-trained trees should be planted with the stem about 9 in/22.5 cm from the base of the wall. Horizontal space required per tree, 12 - 15 ft/3 - 4 m. The closer planting is permissible when there is more vertical space and the branches can be led up higher.

The espalier This is another trained tree consisting of a vertical stem with long straight horizontal branches arranged in tiers. It is low-growing in relation to its overall size and may be planted on the northern border of the vegetable garden. Used for apples and pears. Space at least 16 ft/5 m apart.

The family tree Several varieties - usually 3 of apple or pear are grafted on 1 root. Intended for those who want a choice of varieties but have room for only 1 tree. Perfectly satisfactory but care must be taken to see that 1 member of the family does not take over the whole tree.

Fruit trees in pots For those with the smallest gardens, or with only a balcony, courtyard or patio, pot-grown apples, pears, plums, peaches and citrus fruits are a practical proposition. The technique is not new, the largest sellers of potted trees introduced it in Victorian times so that fruit-laden trees could be borne into the dining room for the delectation of guests. Repotting and general care are simple (see The Care of Growing Crops/Fruit, pages 34/35).

Buy 3 - 4-year-old bush trees, fans with 6 - 7 branches and espaliers with 2 - 3 tiers. Older and larger trees move less satisfactorily and take longer to establish.

Pollination Many varieties need pollen from another variety to fertilise them. They are described as 'self-sterile' while those needing no pollinator are called 'self-fertile'. If you can have only 1 tree choose: Dessert apples, Ellison's Orange or Laxton's Superb. Plums, Victoria or Czar. Pears, Conference or Williams' Bon Chrétien.

Remember that even self-fertile varieties crop better with other varieties nearby, and that a family tree is a selected mixture of varieties.

Rootstocks Fruit trees do not grow on their own roots but are grafted on roots which greatly affect the ultimate size of the tree and the time it takes to reach maturity. A tree which is to crop well while remaining small must be grafted on a 'dwarfing' stock, and for the 3 main fruits the following stocks are suitable:

Apples On fertile soils, M9. On poorer soils M26 or M11.

Pears These are offered on Quince A and sometimes also on Quince C. Choose Quince A because some stocks of Quince C carry a virus infection.

Plums Specify St. Julien A for most plums and Common Plum rootstocks for the gages. St. Julien A is also the one for peaches.

There is at present no dwarfing stock for sweet cherries and the trees are not suitable for the small garden. The acid Morello cherry can be kept within bounds if fan-trained on an east or north wall.

Finding space: soft fruit
The problem here is altogether simpler. Soft fruits are self-fertile and need no pollinators. They grow on their own roots and attain their natural size, though planting distances and training can affect yields from a given area.

Gooseberries As bushes, plant 5 ft/1.5 m apart. As single-stem cordons on walls, 1 ft/30 cm apart. As triple-stem cordons, 3ft/1 m apart. This method of growing is worth considering where space is limited.

Blackcurrants As separate bushes 5 - 6 ft/1.5 - 2 m apart. As a continuous hedge, 4 ft/1.2 m apart. The latter method provides a profitable demarcation hedge in any part of the garden.

Raspberries Plant canes 1½ ft/45 cm apart, with 5 - 6 ft/1.5 - 2.0 m between rows. Close planting between rows is permissible if canes are kept strictly trained and not allowed to spread laterally.

Loganberries and blackberries These are normally planted 10 - 12 ft/3 - 4 m apart, but the less vigorous blackberries may be spaced at 6 - 7 ft/2 m. Rather closer planting is possible where the canes can be trained upwards on a tall fence or trellis, but the fruit is then more difficult to net against birds.

Strawberries Summer fruiting varieties are planted 12 - 15 in/30 - 37.5 cm apart, with rows 2 ft/60 cm apart. The 'matted row', in which runners are allowed to root and form a wide, closely planted strip, has a high yield/space ratio, though it looks untidy. Perpetual varieties require a 50% wider spacing than the summer fruiters.

The necessity of ordering seeds early in the year has already been mentioned. Even the largest seedsman cannot hold an unlimited stock of every variety and as the season advances the choice inevitably narrows.

Apply for catalogues from the major firms if you are not already on their mailing lists and place your order before the end of January.

The choice of varieties Some guidance on this is given in the part of the book dealing with individual crops, and the varieties recommended are those likely to succeed in a wide range of conditions. Gather any suggestions you can from local gardeners.

Well established varieties are identifiable in catalogues by more or less straightforward descriptions. New introductions are sometimes announced with excessive enthusiasm which may or may not be justified. A seedsman may rely on the plant breeder's description, and a variety imported from the Continent or the United States may not live up to its reputation here. If, however, a variety carries an Award of Merit or a Highly Commended from the Royal Horticultural Society (**A.M. RHC** or **H.C. RHC**) you will know that it has been successful in trials in the United Kingdom.

It is a sound rule to rely for the most part on well-tried favourites but to make limited sowings every season of a few new introductions. Many of them represent very real improvements in yield and quality and become permanent additions to the annual list.

Seed prices may appear high, but in terms of combined time and cash the cost of seeds is almost the smallest part of one's gardening investment. Good seed, true to type, is not produced cheaply and the seedsman's prices are a greater bargain than is sometimes realised.

Seeds of F_1 hybrids are dearer than other varieties because the stocks are hand-pollinated under strictly controlled conditions. They cost more per packet or the packets contain less seed.

Pelleted seeds An increasing range of varieties is available in pelleted form, each seed being enclosed in a protective coating which makes it much larger. This enables small seeds to be handled individually and spaced out when sowing, so reducing the work of thinning. Pelleted seeds are naturally more expensive than non-pelleted but are far more economical in use. They are often marketed in plastic dispensers which protect the coating from damage.

Storage of seeds It is essential to store them in dry conditions. Temperature is unimportant and even extremes will do no harm in a dry atmosphere.

The viability of stored seeds, the length of time for which they may be kept without losing the power to germinate, is not something on which a definite ruling can be given. In general, it may be said that seeds of the cabbage family, swedes and turnips

remain viable for several years and many other varieties for more than 1 year. Peas and beans are generally viable for a couple of years, but to save the possible waste of time caused by a germination failure you should test a sample before sowing. Place 10 or 20 seeds in moist peat in a warm place such as an airing cupboard for a week and check the number that germinate. If it is about 80% the seeds are worth sowing.

Home-saved seeds Peas and beans which have become too old for culinary use may be harvested for seed. Leave the pods on the vine until dry, then shell out the seed and leave it spread thinly in a dry, airy place for a week of further drying. Store it in envelopes bearing the name of the variety.

Seeds of marrows and courgettes may be saved if

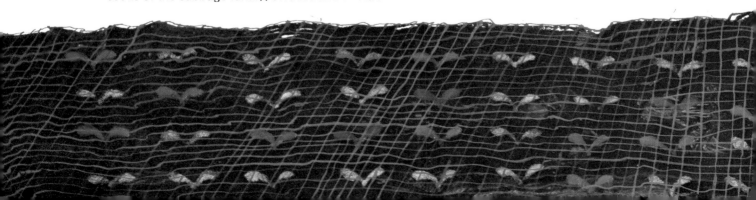

the fruit has been allowed to ripen, but the plants may not be entirely true to type. It is not advisable to save seed of the same crop for several years in succession because standards are only maintained by expert yearly selection. Small seeds are simply not worth the trouble of saving. And 2 special warnings:

Don't save seed from any of the cabbage family. It cross-fertilises easily, and you may end up with bizarre and quite useless plants.

Don't save the seed of F_1 hybrids. They are produced by the crossing of 2 separate and specially bred parent lines and cannot reproduce their own characteristics.

Seed potatoes and onion sets Buy only certified seed potatoes. Order them early in the year and when delivered stand them on end in shallow boxes or seed trays in a light, cool but absolutely frostproof place to sprout. They will make sturdy green shoots which give the crop a good start when the tubers are

planted. If left in the dark they produce long, white shoots which get broken off in planting.

Buy heat-treated onion sets. They too should be unpacked and spread out thinly in a light place to prevent the formation of long weakly shoots. The worst thing that can happen to them is to be left in a cupboard in the polythene bags in which they are usually sold.

Preparing the seed bed
As used here, the expression 'seed bed' means any area of soil in the right condition for sowing. It can also mean a small plot set aside for raising plants such as cabbages and leeks which are later to be transplanted to their permanent quarters.

Starting in the spring Don't be impatient. Keep off the soil until it no longer sticks to your boots. Sooner or later there will be days of warm sun and drying wind. Then the soil will become lighter in colour and the clods will break down into a fine tilth at the touch of a rake.

The most effective agent in producing a good tilth in heavy and medium soils is frost. Water inside the clods freezes and expands, pushing the soil particles apart. The lumps disintegrate when raked into a layer of soil finer than you could obtain by any mechanical means. If you tread on the soil while it is still wet you compress the particles together again and the work of the frost is undone.

Fertiliser should be applied before raking down on ground where you intend to sow within the next week or 2. Rake the surface level, removing any large stones. Leave the surface to dry again before sowing.

2 rules for a good start in the spring. Finish the winter digging early. Be guided by the soil and the season rather than by the calendar.

The seed bed in summer Different problems arise when you replace a crop with successional sowings in the warm, dry months.

If the old crop was of peas and beans, cut off the tops at ground level, leaving the roots with their accumulated nitrogen to enrich the soil.

Don't dig the site deeply. This results in a loss of moisture which should be conserved. Hoe the surface to a depth of 2 in/5 cm removing weeds. On light soils this may give you a tilth for sowing, but on heavy land it may leave only small lumps, especially if the ground has been much trodden in gathering the preceding crop.

To reduce the nobbly soil to a tilth, leave it to dry *completely* - only a matter of a day or so in midsummer. Then soak it thoroughly from hose or watering can. Leave it to dry a little and it will rake down into a tilth good enough for small seeds. The process is similar to that of freezing, the soil lumps contract as they dry and when they absorb water expand and fall to pieces.

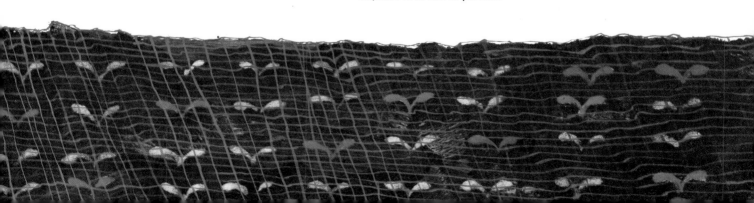

We have seen that for successful germination a seed must have warmth, moisture and air. The first is ensured by not sowing before the soil has warmed up. The second by covering the seed with moist soil. The third by not burying it too deeply.

Making drills

A drill is a miniature trench in which seeds are sown so that they come up in a straight row. The tool used for making drills is the draw hoe, and with it are made both wide and narrow drills.

The wide drill is made by pulling the hoe towards you with the edge of the blade flat to the ground, scraping out a flat-bottomed trench as wide as the blade. It is normally 2 - 3 in/5 - 7.5 cm and is used for sowing large seeds such as peas and beans which are individually handled and spaced.

The narrow drill is made with the corner of the draw hoe, leaving a V-shaped furrow up to 1 in/ 2.5 cm deep, though often it should be only about half that depth. It is used for sowing small seeds which cannot be placed individually and also pelleted seeds.

Always use a garden line when taking out a drill in order to achieve a straight row. Straight rows are not just a matter of appearance but are necessary for optimum spacing of the crop and crooked rows of very small seedlings are liable to damage when you are hoeing between them. When using a rotavator for inter-row cultivation they are a sure recipe for disaster.

Stretch the line taut and walk backwards along it, keeping the hoe blade just in contact with it. On completing the drill move the line into position for the next one, measuring the distance between rows at both ends. A measuring stick is handy for this purpose, a piece of wood such as a plaster lath about 3 ft/1 m long. Mark it at 6 in and 12 in/15 cm and 30 cm intervals with bands of black paint, so that when it is lying on the ground the distances are easily read.

Sowing

Small seeds should be sown thinly to make thinning easier, but not so thinly as to leave an incomplete row if germination is patchy. It is better to err on the side of generous sowing than to be faced with blank spaces. In pea and bean rows this may be rectified by sowing additional seeds at the end of the row and transplanting the surplus seedlings to the gaps when they are an inch or so tall, but root crops and many other small-seeded varieties cannot be transplanted.

Whether you sow thickly or thinly, the vital thing is to sow as evenly as possible. Several gadgets for sowing are on the market but are not in general use. When sowing small seed, tip a little from the packet into the palm of the hand and dribble it into the drill between thumb and forefinger, keeping the hand close to the ground, especially when sowing small, light seeds in windy weather.

Cover the seeds by drawing the soil over them from the sides of the drill with the draw hoe or the back of the rake. Firm lightly by tamping with the back of the hoe blade.

With practice, you can fill in the drill with the feet, shuffling along it, one foot on each side, pushing the soil towards the centre and gently pressing it down. Most beginners, however, find it easier to use a tool for the purpose.

Sowing pelleted seeds The pellets should not, as sometimes suggested, be sown at the final spacing of the crop. That is to say, if you are sowing carrots intended ultimately to be spaced 4 in/10 cm apart you should not space the pelleted seeds at that distance. Space the pellets 1 in/2.5 cm apart and you will have a margin against possible failures while still having little thinning to do. Where the tilth is poor or there are other unfavourable factors space the pellets at half this distance.

It is important that pelleted seeds of all crops should be covered as lightly as possible, the drill being made very shallow. After sowing, the soil must be kept moist and in dry weather may have to be watered daily until the seedlings emerge. Lack of moisture is a frequent cause of failure of pelleted seed.

Raising plants for transplanting As already noted, vegetable plants for planting out later in permanent positions, cabbages, sprouting broccoli, leeks, etc., are grown in a small seed bed set aside for the purpose.

Choose a site accessible from a path, rake the soil to a fine tilth and work in 2 oz per sq yd/66 g per sq m of superphosphate. Have ready a piece of nylon netting large enough to cover the bed and some wooden pegs on which to support it. Some of these seedlings, especially brassicas, are all too attractive to birds early in the season.

Sow in short, shallow drills 6 in/30 cm apart. Sow thinly and thin the seedlings to 1 - 2 in/2.5 - 5 cm apart as soon as they are large enough to handle. Or sow pelleted seeds an inch apart and don't thin.

Water the seedlings when necessary and give them a good soaking the day before you intend to lift them for planting out.

Emergency sowings Plants normally grown in a seed bed and transplanted can if necessary be sown where they are to grow.

Take out a drill on the site intended for plants, water it if the weather is dry, and sow a few seeds in a group, spacing the groups as far apart as you would have set plants. Reduce the seedlings at each 'station' as it is called until there is only one.

With no check from transplanting, the crop can make up for a late sowing and the method is useful when seed bed sowings have failed or plants have proved impossible to buy. Most of the cabbage family may be started in this way in an emergency.

Broadcast sowing Seeds sown broadcast are distributed over an area instead of being concentrated in rows. Broadcasting is the oldest form of sowing, its greatest disadvantage being the difficulty of controlling weeds in the crop. There is some interest in it now for a few limited purposes.

The broadcast sowing of a late crop of carrots or turnips is a worthwhile experiment and may produce a bigger yield of small roots in the autumn than the conventional row crop sowing.

Prepare a strip of ground 24 in/60 cm wide, rake it to a level tilth a week or two before you intend to sow, and if annual weeds germinate remove them by hand or treat them with a contact herbicide (Weedol).

Scatter seed very thinly and evenly over the strip and rake it in. Use the rake with short backwards-and-forwards strokes which cover the seeds without displacing them from one part of the strip to another. Alternatively, prepare a bucket or two of fine soil and sprinkle it thinly over the strip. Firm it gently with the back of the spade.

When the seedlings appear, thin any seriously crowded groups and remove weeds. Otherwise leave them to grow until the first roots reach a usable size. Pull them as fast as they develop and others will grow in the space created.

The difference between sowing and planting is that one sows seeds but plants plants. True, one also plants potatoes and other things that are only parts of plants, but there remains a real distinction between sowing a seed, which is in a state of suspended animation, and moving a developed organism like a plant or a tree.

In practical terms one has to transplant vegetable plants which are in active growth, and plant fruit trees, bushes and canes, which are dormant, about the only fruit not moved in a dormant state being the strawberry.

Vegetable plants

This includes salads. The crops fall into two categories, hardy varieties like Brussels sprouts, and tender varieties grown in the open but started under glass like marrows and tomatoes.

Hardy varieties If you have grown your own plants in a seed bed they will be ready for their permanent quarters by early summer. Ideally they will have short stems, spreading leaves of a healthy green and plenty of fibrous root. Plants that have been grown in crowded conditions will have long, spindly stems, small, widely spaced leaves and tap roots without much fibre to hold the soil.

If possible, select a cloudy, showery spell for transplanting. In dry weather, water the plants the day before lifting. Lift with a trowel or hand fork, retaining as much soil round the roots as possible. Give this soil a gentle squeeze to keep in position as each plant is lifted. Lay the plants in a trug or similar carrier and when you have enough for a row plant them immediately.

Put down the garden line on the planting site and make the planting holes with the trowel at the required distances. The holes should be deep enough for the plants' lower leaves to be just clear of the soil without the exposure of a lot of stem. Make the soil firm round the roots with the fingers and before the planting hole is completely filled in give the plant a good watering. When the water has sunk in, complete the levelling of soil round the plant.

If you have to plant in persistently dry weather take out a wide drill about 2 in/5 cm deep where the row is to be planted, and flood it with water the day

before planting. Plant in the usual way, making the planting holes in the drill which is left uncovered for a time after the completion of planting. Further watering of the newly transplanted crop can then be effected by flooding the drill every three or four days from the hose or watering can. When the plants are well established, soil is pulled back into the drill and the ground left level.

The plants flag in hot sun for some days after planting and overhead sprinkling with water in the evening is a help.

Tender varieties Tomatoes, marrows, courgettes, squashes, cucumbers, melons, sweet corn and peppers can only be planted outdoors when there is no longer any risk of frost.

Select a sheltered and sunny position for these crops. Make sure they are properly hardened off before planting out. Use any spare cloches as protection for the first week or so.

Water plants in pots or boxes several hours before removing them for planting. Avoid root disturbance as much as possible, especially when planting marrows, cucumbers and melons. If you raise the latter yourself grow them in small peat pots and plant in the pot, the rim just below the surface. Make sure

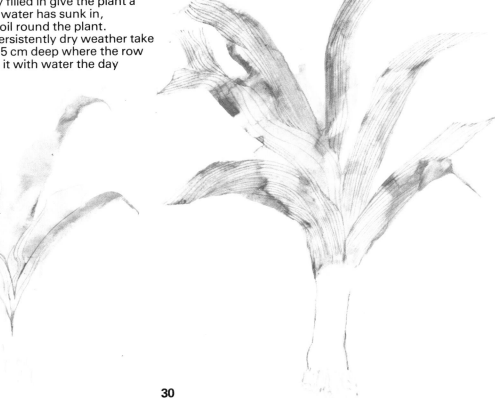

that the pot is thoroughly soaked, so that the roots will have no difficulty in penetrating the sides.

When the plant is in a clay or plastic pot it is 'knocked out' in such a way that the soil ball around the roots remains intact. Rest the pot upside-down in the hand with the plant projecting down between the fingers. Tap the rim of the pot smartly on a hard surface and plant and pot will separate without damage to the soil ball.

Buying plants When buying, order in advance from a local nurseryman and say when you would like to take delivery. If you buy from ordinary retail sources avoid the tall, overgrown specimens, tomatoes with bluish foliage, hard stems and trusses of bloom, and marrows turning yellow. They have been around too long and are half-starved.

Planting fruit

Fruit trees, bushes and canes are planted when dormant - which means 'sleeping' - usually from October to March. Autumn planting while the soil is still warm is preferred. Never plant when the soil is frozen hard or is waterlogged, even though you may have to wait weeks for the right conditions.

Treatment on arrival When the trees or bushes are delivered leave them wrapped up if they are to be planted within a matter of days. Keep them in a cool place and on no account bring the packages into a centrally heated house.

If, because of weather conditions you are going to be unable to plant for some time, the trees should be 'heeled in'. Take out a trench long enough to accommodate them laid side by side and deep enough to cover the roots. Lay them in this, leaning at an angle against one side, and fill in the trench, heaping plenty of soil over the roots. Here they can stay for weeks or even months until conditions improve.

Planting trees Prepare the planting site during summer by digging in rotted manure or compost and a good dusting of coarse bone meal. A few barrowloads of fine soil placed under cover to keep dry are a help when filling in.

Approximate planting distances for trees and bushes are given elsewhere (see Making Plans/Fruit pages 24/25). Prepare the planting hole only when ready to plant, not in advance. If the tree roots are dry, soak them in water for 12 hours before planting. Cut back damaged roots beyond the point of damage with sharp secateurs.

Get someone to hold the tree upright in position with the roots spread out flat. Mark the perimeter of the roots to get the size of the hole. Dig it deep enough to cover the roots up to the soil mark on the stem. Loosen the subsoil with a fork.

With the tree held upright and the roots spread out, fill in gradually, sifting fine soil between the roots and ramming it carefully with a piece of wood. Continue to the surface and level off. Trees not planted against a wall or other support must be staked at planting, with a stout wooden stake or an angle iron, otherwise the wind will rock them and the roots fail to take hold. Insert the stake while filling in, when its point can be guided between the roots without damage to them and it is easy to drive into the subsoil. It should be 4 - 6 in / 10 - 15 cm from the

stem, which should be secured with an adjustable tree tie.

Planting bushes and canes The same general rules apply, though of course planting distances and the size of planting holes are very different.

Most soft fruits are planted up to the soil mark (the depth at which they grew in the nursery), but blackcurrants should be planted several inches deeper to encourage the development of basal shoots and more stems.

Thinning

If you sow small seeds thickly enough to ensure a complete row the seedlings will stand too thickly to reach a useful maturity. Begin to thin them out as soon as they are large enough to handle.

Thin when the soil is moist to make withdrawal of the seedlings easier and lessen the upheaval caused to those that remain. In dry weather water the seedlings before thinning but give the tops time to dry - wet tops make it a messy job.

Pay attention to 'singling'. Seedlings often appear in a close cluster looking like 1 plant; it is essential to pull out all but 1, however tedious the process. Beetroot and perpetual spinach are the worst offenders because their 'seed' is really a dried capsule containing several seeds and they naturally come up in bunches.

Thin carrots and onions in the evening, when carrot and onion flies are less likely to be on the wing. They are attracted by the scent of crushed seedlings to come and lay the eggs which produce their destructive larvae. Remove carrot and onion thinnings from the bed.

Always thin by stages, first to about 1 in, then to 2 in/2.5 cm and 5 cm, then to the final distance. The actual intermediate distances are not important, the thing is to give each plant room to grow and to thin again as the row fills up. The reason for not doing it in one fell swoop is that some losses may be expected from pests or weather and if they occur when the seedlings are at their maximum spacing there are going to be some nasty gaps.

In some crops the final thinning may be delayed until the thinnings are large enough to use. This applies to turnips, carrots, beetroot, lettuce (if you only want leaves) and spinach.

Weed control

When crops are growing vigorously the weeds naturally do likewise, competing for space, soil nutrients and water. If the crop is to do well, they must be kept in their place - on the compost heap.

Hoeing The value of regular hoeing has already been emphasized. Ground hoed frequently in dry weather remains weed-free, the weeds being

Between the establishment of a crop by sowing or planting and its coming maturity and harvest lies the routine work that takes up much of the gardener's time. The great thing is to keep abreast of these little jobs and not allow them to build up into a major headache.

destroyed as seedlings. In showery weather hoeing is less effective but should be continued whenever possible, because in this condition weeds grow most quickly.

Hoed-up weeds need not be raked off if the soil is dry, though some gardeners do it as a matter of course and to augment the compost heap. In showery weather they should always be removed as the small ones re-root themselves and start all over again.

Hand weeding Weeds growing in the crop rows or in broadcast strips can only be removed by hand. If they are to come up and not break off the soil must be moist. In weeding among small plants press down the soil on either side of the weed with the fingers of one hand as you pull it out with the other. This prevents a lot of soil and possibly some of the crop coming up with the weed roots.

To remove large annual weeds such as sow thistles from a crop row use a pointed trowel and cut off the weed just below ground level, leaving the roots in the soil. A trowel, especially a stainless steel one, is an effective weeding tool, dealing equally well with long-rooted creeping thistles and the spreading mats of chickweed.

Herbicides Certain herbicides or weedkillers may be used to control weeds on cultivated ground as well as on paths and in lawns. 3 types are used for different purposes. A well known trade name is given where appropriate.

Contact herbicides Paraquat and diquat (Weedol). The herbicide is absorbed through the leaves and green parts of the plant. On reaching the soil it breaks down and leaves no toxic residue. It may be used between rows and around fruit trees and bushes so long as it is not splashed on stems and foliage. Very rapid and effective in warm sunny weather and against annual weeds. Apply from a watering can fitted with a rose or sprinkler bar held close to the ground to prevent drift.

Follow the makers' instructions in the use of this and other herbicides.

Selective herbicides 245,T. (brushwood killer, nettle killer). This is related to the 24,D. used to control broad-leaved weeds on lawns. It is very effective in dealing with nettles, docks, thistles and even shrubby growth and brambles. It cannot be used on ground already bearing crops but does not kill grass or taint the soil for very long periods. Take care not to let it drift on to crops and do not use it in the vicinity of tomatoes or store it in a greenhouse where they are growing. Another selective weed-killer is dalapon (Dowpon) useful in controlling twitch or couch and other grasses.

An example of a total poison is sodium chlorate. Used at a strength of 6 oz per gallon of water/200 g per 4.5 l it will clear most grasses and weeds from a neglected or uncultivated plot. Applied in September the ground may be planted in the spring when the poison has been washed out by winter rains. If applied in spring or summer the soil will not be safe for planting for 9 - 12 months.

Keep a watering can solely for use with herbicides and label it to that effect. Never store unused herbicide solutions **AND ESPECIALLY NOT IN**

SOFT DRINK BOTTLES.
Watering and mulching
Lack of moisture is a limiting factor in summer growth. The soil is a sort of sponge, soaking up rain in the winter for use later on. The better it is cultivated, the more organic matter it contains, the more effective it is as a reservoir and the greater its reserves of moisture. But in the growing season soil moisture is lost very rapidly, partly by evaporation from the surface, but even more by transpiration by the crops. The larger the plants the more water they transpire, so that when growth is at a maximum a lack of moisture affects them at a crucial time.

How much water is needed? This depends on how much falls between spring and autumn to bolster the vanishing reserves. Something like 2.5 in/6.25 cm a month would be a summer average. An inch of rain is equal to rather more than 4 gallons of water per sq yd/18 l per sq m. For every fortnight with little or no rain, therefore, you would need to apply this amount just to make up for the rain deficit. To maintain the soil moisture at the levels of early spring you might reckon on 9 gallons per sq yd/40 l per sq m for every dry fortnight.

In wholly practical terms, it is just no use dishing out little drops of water. Far better to concentrate on a small area or one crop at a time and soak it. Peas, runner beans, carrots, spinach, lettuce and sometimes early potatoes all benefit greatly from plenty of water and might be considered priorities.

Another point is that you cannot slightly moisten the soil to a considerable depth. Only when the topmost layer is saturated does the water extend downwards; saturation is the only way to get it down to all the roots. To moisten the top layer may entice the roots upwards, where they will be more vulnerable to sudden drying out.

Water should be applied as gently as possible from a rose or spray nozzle, or, better still, through a length of layflat polythene tubing with small holes, which enables a whole row to be watered slowly and gently.

Mulching
A mulch is a layer of material applied to the soil surface to reduce moisture loss by evaporation. It also helps to suppress weeds and if composed of organic matter such as peat, compost or rotted manure, benefits the soil when eventually dug in.

The mulch should be spread along both sides of the row to a depth of about 3 in/7.5 cm and a width of some 18 in/45 cm. The soil should be moist when it is applied.

The soil mulch formed by regular hoeing has already been mentioned. A layer of loose soil looks dry because no moisture is being drawn up from below to be evaporated. A useful inorganic mulch is black polythene sheeting. Held in position by stones and kept close to the row, it keeps the soil remarkably moist and is an effective suppressor of weeds. Treated with care, it lasts for years.

Although the herbicide 245,T. is generally approved for garden use some doubts have recently arisen over its complete safety. Ask when buying if any new recommendations as to its use have been made.

Fruit trees and bushes need less attention than vegetable crops. They are long-lived and do not have to be started afresh and nursed through infancy every year. They will produce a crop of sorts if completely neglected but for satisfactory results they must have care in such matters as pruning.

Reliable tools are essential to efficient pruning. For young trees and for soft fruits a good pair of secateurs may be all you need, but for established trees, and especially for overgrown and neglected ones a suitable saw, knife and possibly a long-handled pruner are well worth their cost. Jagged cuts and split branches not only look deplorable, they are too often entry points of disease.

The object of pruning is to produce as much fruitful growth as possible to limit excessive, unfruitful and dead growth, and to maintain the proper shape of the tree. The pruning of individual fruits is briefly summarised elsewhere, here we can look at the general principles applying to the pruning of various groups of top and soft fruits.

Apples and pears

Prune in summer if you have time, and also in winter, preferably before Christmas and never during severe frost.

Cordons Prune in summer by nipping out the growing points of laterals (side-shoots) when they have 3 clusters of leaves, usually in July. Do not stop the leader or new growth of the main stem in this way; allow it to continue growing and if possible train it at a 45° angle. In winter cut back any new laterals that have grown to the same length as the summer pruned ones. The idea is to get the stem thickly covered with fruiting spurs, the short growths bearing a number of fruit buds. Also in winter, shorten the season's growth of the leader by a third.

Espaliers Treat each branch in the same way as a cordon. To increase the number of branches allow conveniently placed laterals from the main stem to grow and train them in a horizontal position.

Bush trees Treat each main branch basically as though it were a cordon, keeping the laterals well pruned back and the centre of the bush open. If there is room for more branches allow laterals growing in the right direction to develop, but remove inward-growing and criss-crossing ones. The more sunlight a branch receives the more fruit buds it develops, hence the need to prevent the tree becoming a dense mass of growth.

Plums

Prune the plum family as little as possible. Prune only in summer, when cut surfaces heal rapidly, to reduce the chances of infection by silver leaf disease. Pruning cuts of more than ½ in/1.25 cm diameter should be coated with bituminous paint.

Bush trees may as a rule be left to grow naturally, though diseased branches and those which cross and chafe against others must be cut out. Fan-trained forms on walls may be summer-pruned by stopping the laterals when they have 6 leaves. If this is not done the space between the main branches will become choked with untrained growth. When the main branches begin to reach the limits of their allotted space they may be checked by stopping the extension shoots (the leaders of each branch) in the same way.

Peaches

The fruits are borne on shoots of the previous year's growth, a peculiarity which makes their pruning different from that of other top fruit.

From the base of each fruit-bearing shoot several new shoots grow in summer. Nip out all but 1 of them, leaving that 1 to grow on. It is known as the 'replacement shoot'. When the fruit has been gathered, cut out the old fruiting shoot and tie in the replacement shoot. The fan-trained tree thus produces more fruiting shoots each year as its branches extend, but without overcrowding of the space between them.

Neglected trees

Begin by cutting out dead and diseased branches. Make clean saw cuts in sound wood well beyond the affected portion, pare off rough edges with a sharp pruning knife, and paint the wound.

Thin out tangled and overcrowded branches in the centre of the tree. Spread the work over several seasons, too-drastic cutting, especially of a vigorous tree, leads to over-production of new wood. Once the tree has been brought back into shape you can begin to restrict the smaller laterals by summer and winter pruning and induce the formation of more fruiting spurs.

The first winter of operations is a good time to apply a tar oil wash, a good soaking will clean off mosses and algae and eliminate many long-established pests.

Cane fruit

The distinguishing feature is that fruits are borne on canes of the previous year's growth, the old canes being cut out immediately after fruiting so that the new ones can grow and ripen before the winter.

Blackberries, loganberries and hybrid berries

Cut out old canes close to the ground after fruiting. Canes are thick, tough and sometimes very prickly, a heavy-duty pruner and a pair of leather gloves are a great help. Avoid damage to the young canes and if the old canes are entangled with them cut the latter into sections and remove them piecemeal.

Raspberries Cut out the old canes of summer-fruiting varieties in August and tie in the new ones. If the latter are very crowded thin them out by removing poor and weakly ones. Autumn-fruiting varieties have all the canes cut back close to the ground in late February. The fruit is then borne on the young canes which grow during the summer. It is usual to cut raspberry canes back to within 6 in/ 15 cm of the topmost training wire to which they are tied, leaving the top of the row level.

Bush fruit

Blackcurrants New wood carries the most fruit. Every year, in late summer or autumn, cut down about a quarter of the branches to soil level, choosing the oldest and woodiest ones. New branches grow up to replace them. Old, neglected bushes get a new lease of life if all the growth is cut down to a few inches above ground level.

Red and white currants Unlike the blacks, they

surprise d'Automne

Lancashire Lad

Victoria

Laxton's Superb

King of the Pippins

Beauty of Bath

Blenheim Orange

are produced on fruiting spurs on mature wood. Cut back all the laterals on the main branches every winter to within about 2 in/ 5 cm of the base. Shorten the leader of each main branch by at least a third. The bush is on a short 'leg' or stem and all growths from this and suckers from the ground must be removed.

Gooseberries They too grow on a leg and must not be allowed to send up a thicket of growths from the ground. Cut back laterals to about 3 in/7.5 cm in winter and cut back the leading shoots of main branches by about half of the year's new growth. The aim is to produce strong branches, not overcrowded but thickly set with short laterals and fruiting spurs.

The Care of Potted Trees
Full details of the culture of pot-grown trees are always supplied by the nurseryman from whom you buy them, and only a summary can be given here.

Except for the citrus fruits, which require slightly different treatment from ordinary top fruit and are not dealt with here, they are perfectly hardy. They must stand outdoors in the growing season, with the pots plunged to the rim in soil if you have any, or standing in a courtyard or on a balcony if you have not. The vital requirement is that they must be in full light, not necessarily in sunlight, but not covered by an opaque roof.

In winter the trees may be left outside, but the pots must be covered with some protective material to prevent the soil freezing solid.

Alternatively, they may be placed in an unheated shed or garage. They must never be kept in a place warm enough to start them into premature growth. In the spring, however, they may be taken temporarily into a cold greenhouse when in flower to protect the blossom from frost.

The pots must be watered at all times, very frequently in summer, just enough to keep the compost moist in winter. The trees are usually repotted annually, a practice which encourages a mass of fibrous root and fewer large, thick roots which are not wanted in pots. Pot size is gradually increased over the years.

All forms of protection by glass or transparent plastics have as their object the extension of the growing and cropping season of hardy things like strawberries and lettuce and to obtain more consistent results from those crops, like cucumbers and tomatoes, for which our climate is not ideal.

Frames, cloches and the completely unheated greenhouse are known as 'cold glass'. A greenhouse with a heater able to keep temperatures just above freezing - a 'cool' house - is more valuable for the kitchen gardener, as it is for the grower of decorative plants.

Types of Greenhouse

The lean-to structure stands against a wall and is a useful choice where a south- or west-facing wall is available. It is more easily heated than a free-standing house, especially if erected against the dwelling house. Its disadvantage is that it receives light mainly from one direction. Very narrow lean-to structures, not more than 3 ft / 1 m wide are now on sale for sites with very limited space.

The span-roof structure comes in many different designs. One way of making a choice is through advertisements in the gardening press, the manufacturers' literature and, if possible, inspection of some of the products at their showgrounds.

If you intend to plant crops - tomatoes, for instance - in a border on the floor, the sides should be glazed to ground level to ensure adequate light. If everything is to be grown in pots on staging you may prefer the plant-house type, with the sides covered with board or other cladding up to the level of the staging. You may, of course have a glass-to-ground

structure with portable staging to be removed when plants are to be grown in the border. At least one large firm supplies a combined house, glazed to the ground on 1 side and boarded up to the staging on the other.

Construction and siting

In the construction of the framework the choice is between timber and aluminium. Timber structures are initially less expensive but more costly in upkeep, and painting a greenhouse is not everyone's idea of fun. Metal greenhouses are now on the whole well designed; it is not true that they are colder than timber structures, heat loss occurs through the glass, not the framework.

Things to look for are features making for ease of erection, such as accurately drilled bolt holes and putty-less glazing, a wide door without a high step to permit the entry of a barrow, reasonable height to the eaves and adequate means of ventilation.

The site should be level and approached by a good path. The nearer it is to the dwelling house the better if plants have to be attended to in the winter. If the greenhouse is rectangular in plan, it will receive more light over the entire year if the long axis runs north and south. On the other hand, it will gather more winter sunlight if it runs east to west, with the long side exposed to the south.

If the site is small and square-shaped, there is everything to be said for a hexagonal structure. This design, glazed to the ground, admits an absolute maximum of light from all directions and provides a lot of usable floor space relative to its overall size.

Greenhouse equipment

Heaters Current fuel costs rule out the possibility of maintaining a growing temperature in the amateur greenhouse during the winter. It is still possible, however, to exclude frost without running up large fuel bills, to maintain a minimum of 40° - 45°F/5° - 7°C in February and March to raise seedlings of summer cabbage and cauliflower, celery and other semi-hardy crops, and of the more tender subjects in April and May.

When using the greenhouse for plant-raising early in the year it must be remembered that it is the minimum temperature that counts. On a sunny April day the temperature may run up to 80°F/27°C under glass, but if it is allowed to fall to near freezing at night you cannot sow things like tomatoes. Some form of heating is therefore advisable if the greenhouse is to be really useful in the kitchen garden.

The fuels principally used are paraffin, gas and electricity. In absolute terms paraffin is the cheapest and electricity the dearest.

Blue flame paraffin heaters are quite satisfactory for small structures. They give off no harmful gases but increase the moisture and carbon dioxide content of the air, which is beneficial to plants. A storage tank can now be connected to this type of heater to eliminate the need for frequent filling.

The greenhouse gas heater is safe and efficient, but for the small house its purchase and installation costs are disproportionately high.

Electricity is expensive but has the advantage of thermostatic control and the most economical use of fuel. A 2 kilowatt fan heater with a built-in thermostat is usually adequate for the small greenhouse. Never use a domestic fan heater for the purpose, it has no thermostat and is not meant to operate in humid conditions. All greenhouse electrical equipment must be properly installed and effectively earthed.

Containers and composts Pots and seed trays are best made of plastic. Plastic pots are lighter than clays and dry out less quickly, plastic seed trays outlast the old-fashioned wooden ones, are more easily cleaned and unlikely to carry disease. Peat pots are made of compressed horticultural peat and are planted with the plant in them, the roots soon penetrating into the surrounding soil with none of the usual transplanting check. Although only used once, they are well worth the extra cost compared with ordinary pots for those crops that particulary dislike root disturbance.

Plants grown in containers require special soils, and these are known as sowing and potting composts, not to be confused with the composted vegetable matter used as manure. Most amateurs buy ready-mixed composts, and they are of 2 main types, loam-based and soil-less.

The John Innes (JI) composts are based on sterilised loam, peat and sand, to which are added plant nutrients. There are four grades, JI Seed, and JI1, JI2 and JI3 Potting, the last three for different sizes of pots and plants. The JI range are not standardised products and are apt to vary with the quality of the loam.

The soil-less composts, typified by Levington, are proprietary products based on peat. They are light, clean to handle, and give excellent results, especially in the quick growth of young plants.

Raising plants in the greenhouse

Sowing Fill a seed tray with the correct grade of compost. Brush it off level with the rim, then firm it gently with the fingers, leaving the surface well below the rim. Level it and sow the seed very thinly. Cover with not more than 1/3 in/1 cm of compost, firm the surface, and water from a fine rose. Label with the name of the variety and date of sowing. Cover with a sheet of glass to reduce evaporation or slip the tray into a polythene bag. Exclude light with a piece of brown paper or cardboard, but remove this immediately the first seedlings appear.

Large seeds such as marrow and sweet corn should be sown 2 or 3 to a small pot, removing all but the strongest seedling if more than 1 germinates. These seeds should be covered to a depth of 1/2 in/1.25 cm, those of the marrow and cucumber type being pushed edgeways into the compost rather than laid flat and covered.

In using soil-less compost, whether for sowing or potting, it is important never to let it dry out, peat is a difficult substance to moisten again once this happens. The composts are sold in a moist condition and the plastic bags in which they are packed should be kept closed to retain the moisture.

Pricking out Small seedlings have to be given room for development by being transplanted singly to pots or by being moved from the seed tray to a deeper one and spaced about 2 in/5 cm apart. This pricking out process should take place while the seedlings are very small, before the true leaves have developed and, above all, before stems and roots have become intertwined.

Fill the pots or tray to which the seedlings are being transferred with compost and make it quite firm. Lift a seedling by inserting the point of a penknife or small plant label under it, holding it by a seed leaf, not by the stem which is susceptible to crushing. Make a hole in the potting compost with the label, drop the seedling in so that the leaves are just clear of the surface, and firm the compost gently around the stem. Water from a fine rose and keep the pricked-out seedlings in shade for a few days.

The use of pelleted seed makes pricking out a lot easier and can in some cases eliminate it altogether. The important thing is to see that seedlings do not suffer from being left over long in the seed tray. It has been shown experimentally that tomatoes, for instance, pricked out in the seed leaf stage are likely to grow and perform better than those pricked out after the development of the first true leaves.

The garden frame

The traditional cold frame is a large box with sides of brick, timber or asbestos and a sloping glazed top. New designs have hinged instead of sliding top lights and glazed sides to admit more light, but the basic idea is the same.

In a limited way, the frame is a substitute for the cold greenhouse. It may be used for growing winter lettuce and for cucumbers and melons in summer. It is most useful in producing early brassica plants such as Brussels sprouts and summer cabbage, since they can be sown in the ground and thinned out as in an outdoor seed bed, eliminating the work of pricking out into seed trays.

The frame is also used for hardening off glass-raised plants before they are planted in the open, the lights being at first opened during the day, then on mild nights, so that the change of environment is gradual. In this way too, the frame is handy for those who like to start marrows and other tender plants on a warm window-sill. These seedlings have to be moved to a position in full light before they become drawn, and in a frame they may be grown on for several weeks before it is safe to plant them out, provided the lights are covered over on cold nights. Under these conditions a frame is warmer at night than a cold greenhouse, the sun-heat absorbed by the soil during the day being radiated back and trapped in a relatively small space. Frames were at one time covered with special straw mats which had the advantage of drying quickly when they got wet; an effective modern substitute is plastic bags, such as those used for peat or soil-less compost, loosely stuffed with crumpled newspaper and tightly sealed against the wet.

Cloches

The original cloche, as its name implies, was a bell-jar, used by French market gardeners to protect single plants or small groups. The continuous cloche now in use is designed to cover any length of row. It will not accommodate tall plants, but it is otherwise the most adaptable form of crop protection. It shelters autumn-sown crops through the winter, brings forward the sowing dates of many spring-sown crops and is used in many ways to lengthen the growing and cropping season at both ends.

Types of cloche Glass tent cloches consist of 2 sheets of glass held in a wire framework in the shape of an inverted V. The converging sides give plants little head-room, and although effective on a single row of fairly short plants they are not the most economical form of protection.

Barn cloches are made up of 4 sheets of glass, 2 vertical at the sides and 2 sloping to form the roof. The most popular type of barn is 24 in/60 cm long, about the same width, and 9 in/22.5 cm to the eaves. The barn is the most useful of glass cloches, covering 1 row of a crop like early peas up to flowering, or at least 2 rows of smaller-topped crops like lettuce or beetroot.

Rigid plastic cloches of moulded PVC and similar materials are available in many designs. Their advantages over glass are lightness and freedom from breakage. Because the material is so much lighter than glass, plastic cloches may be made up to 4 ft/1.2 m in length. Disadvantages are a high initial cost, some lack of stability in exposed positions, and the fact that if damage does occur they cannot be repaired simply by replacing a broken sheet of glass.

The polythene tunnel is the cheapest form of cloche. It consists of stout wire hoops covered with polythene sheeting and may be of any desired length. Tunnels may be bought ready-made, or made at home. The hoops are of 6 or 8 gauge galvanised wire bent so that the hoop is 24 in/60 cm wide at the base and 20 in/50 cm from base-line to top of the curve. The legs of the hoop are pushed 8 in/20 cm into the ground on either side of the row, giving a height of 12 in/30 cm from ground to apex. The hoops are spaced 3 ft/1 m apart and polythene sheeting is stretched tightly over them being gathered together and pegged down at each end. The edges are let into a shallow trench and buried so that the wind cannot get underneath and rip off the sheeting. The initial cost of tunnelling is very low and it is widely used commercially. Its drawbacks are that the polythene needs frequent renewal and that attending to the crop takes longer than with conventional cloches.

Using cloches

Soil preparation Successful cloche cultivation demands plenty of humus in the soil. The crop is more dependant on artificial watering than if grown in the open and a moisture-retaining soil is a great asset.

For early spring sowings cloche the site at least a week and preferably a fortnight beforehand to warm up the soil.

General management In attending to a crop under ordinary (not tunnel) cloches, remove a cloche from the end of the row, deal with the plants that it covered and move the next cloche into its place, uncovering the next section of row. On reaching the end, finish off with the cloche first removed.

Keep the ends of the row always closed, a through draught reduces the protective effect of the cloches. For ventilation in hot weather space them ½ in/1.25 cm apart. In very hot sun the fruit of cloched strawberries suffers severely and may be literally cooked, apply a light coating of limewash to the roof glass.

Window-sill plants

In the absence of a greenhouse it is quite possible to start some of the more tender crops on a warm, well lighted window-sill.

Marrows, courgettes, melons, cucumbers, sweet corn and even tomatoes may all be sown in small pots as already suggested, and grown on in them until planting-out time.

Peat pots are preferable, not only from the plants' point of view but because they are usually square and stand more closely together than the conventional round ones.

Window-sill culture of kitchen garden plants most often goes wrong in the intermediate or hardening off stages. In the average room there is plenty of warmth for germination and enough light for the initial growth of the seedlings. Later, however, they become drawn from lack of overhead light, and it is when this begins to happen that transfer to the lighter and cooler environment of a garden frame is advisable.

Powered implements have a place in the larger gardens, and many gardeners own or hire machines. Their functions are concerned with basic cultivation, and most other gardening operations cannot be mechanised.

In the private garden the machine takes second place to the hand tool. No machine can dig a planting hole for a tree,

Rotava

Rotavators

The rotary cultivator or rotavator is the most widely used garden machine after the lawnmower. It is employed for deep cultivation in place of digging, surface cultivation in place of hoeing, and mixing manure, compost or the remains of spent crops into the soil. By fitting special attachments it has secondary uses in such things as hedge trimming.

The design of rotavators Basically, the machine consists of tines or hoe blades revolving about a horizontal axis and driven by a small petrol motor.

There are 2 variants. In one, the rotor carrying the tines is mounted in front of the engine, under which are two wheels carrying the weight of the machine. They are not powered, and the rotavator is propelled, or, rather, dragged forward by the action of the tines. There is no gearbox and the forward speed of the machine is controlled by the throttle and the speed of rotation of the rotor or tiller. This type of machine is rather lacking in speed and depth control but is relatively lower in price than other models because of its mechanical simplicity. It is also efficient in that the entire engine power is applied to the tines.

The other type of rotavator has the rotor mounted behind the engine, with a pair of powered driving wheels between. It has a clutch and gearbox, so that the forward speed can be varied in relation to the rotary speed of the tiller. This enables the machine to travel more slowly when more power is required on heavy land or when tilling to maximum depth. Depth of working is usually controlled by an adjustable skid at the rear of the machine.

Most machines are now equipped with 4-stroke engines and modern recoil starters. They are as mechanically reliable as the motor lawnmower. Most garden models are in the 2 - 3½ hp range, through commercial types are more powerful. Low-grade petrol is used and fuel consumption is low in a properly maintained engine.

Subsidiary equipment supplied as extras includes fixed cultivating tools, rotary lawnmowers, hedge trimmers, small circular saws and garden trucks. The cost of these attachments may in many cases be justified but hitching them to the basic machine is sometimes time-consuming and they do not as a rule do the job as efficiently as a purpose-built machine.

Acquiring a rotavator You either buy new, buy second-hand, or hire.

The purchase of a new machine is financially justifiable only if there is more ground to be cultivated than you have time or energy to cope with and paid labour is unobtainable or too expensive.

Begin by getting the sales literature of several makers and selecting the sizes and types most likely to suit your pocket and your garden. Contact local dealers and ask for demonstrations of alternative models on your own ground. Note how the machines handle, whether they are likely to be tiring to use in restricted space, whether they have adequate power to work your soil to a good depth and whether routine maintenance in things like the replacement of worn out tines or blades is easy.

The buying of a used machine is tricky unless you have personal knowledge of it and the seller. Reconditioned models are sold by several large firms and these should not run you into large repair bills. In rural districts a bargain is sometimes picked up in the local auction market, but you must be very wary of machines showing obvious oil leaks and still more wary of those that have been freshly painted.

The hire of a machine is an economical alternative to purchase, the main drawback being that you often cannot take advantage of a few hours of perfect conditions because there is no machine on hand. Hire firms exist everywhere. See 'Garden Machinery Services' in the Yellow Pages.

take out a celery trench, build a compost heap, prune a currant bush or plant an onion set. For innumerable routine jobs the gardener must depend on good tools and a certain minimum of manual skill. A good thing too, if gardening is to maintain its attraction as a hobby.

weeds.

Space between the rows must be wide enough to accommodate the machine. The width of the strip cultivated is from 10 - 18 in/25 - 45 cm by most garden-sized rotavators, but the overall width of the machine may be greater. It is not safe to cultivate mechanically between rows less than 24 in/60 cm apart. Nor can you work too close to small seedlings without the risk of burying them in soil flung sideways.

The machine has in fact no advantage over hand tools in the small garden and where every foot of ground is potentially valuable.

Effects on soil Mechanical cultivation is particularly useful in taking advantage of short spells of fine weather and dry conditions. It encourages the less energetic gardener to prepare ground for successional crops in summer when hand work is less attractive. And it is very effective in mixing organic manures and green manure crops into the soil.

Two possible disadvantages of rotavation as compared with digging should, however, be considered, both most apparent on heavy soils. The first is that ground rotavated in autumn is left with a relatively level surface instead of the rough lumpiness which aids the penetration of frost. Winter rains tend to compact this into a sodden layer which dries more slowly than the rough surface of hand-dug soil and does not crumble into a friable tilth. Paradoxically, by breaking up the soil more finely, rotavation makes it harder to obtain the fine tilth so desirable in spring. Possible remedies are to attach a small ridging plough to the machine and leaving the soil in exposed ridges, to obtain the same effect by pulling the draw hoe through it, leaving a succession of deep drills, or lightly to stir the surface with the fork when it is frozen, leaving it roughened.

The other unwanted effect of regular rotavation is the formation of a 'pan', a layer of compacted soil which in time may impede drainage. If the cultivation is always to the same depth the action of the blades in pressing down the soil below them at the bottom of their sweep solidifies this impervious layer further with every cultivation. In light soils with a gravelly subsoil it is never a serious problem, but on clay you may find increasing waterlogging in the topsoil. Hand digging a part of the area each year is then advisable, it moves the soil a little more deeply than mechanical cultivation and breaks up the pan.

Pros and cons of using machines

Digging by hand is the slowest and physically hardest work in the kitchen garden, although, as already pointed out, it need not be regarded as an exhausting chore. With a rotavator the work is done much more quickly, but it should be realised that some people find using the machine more tiring than a spell of digging. A time-saver, then, but in a strict sense not necessarily a labour saver. Hence the need to try out a machine in your own garden before reaching a decision.

Most machines have handles that swing to either side, so that the operator can always walk on the uncultivated ground as the machine moves to and fro across the plot. At the end of each pass the machine must be turned and this can become tiring if only a short distance is worked. Whatever the overall size of the garden a plot with 1 fairly long dimension is advisable for a rotavator to be worked efficiently and easily.

Adequate working space becomes even more necessary if the machine is to replace hand hoeing between rows, at which it is quick and efficient if set just to skim the surface. A bare headland about 6 ft/ 2 m wide is needed to turn the machine without danger to oneself or damage to the crop. This headland cannot be planted and must be kept free of

Cabbage White

A comprehensive list of the pests and diseases to which crops are theoretically subject is enough to scare anyone off gardening for life. Most of the possible troubles never materialise, but a few of them are part of every gardener's experience.

Hygiene and environment
The living conditions of plants cause crop losses greater than all the specific pests and diseases. Vigorous, well cultivated crops have great natural resistance and powers of recovery. The spade, the compost heap and the hoe are better guarantees of health than an armoury of pesticides and fungicides.

Garden hygiene Remove and burn immediately diseased potato haulm, cauliflower stumps infested with cabbage root fly larvae, broad bean tops with blackfly and other sources of infection.

Clear away remnants of winter cabbage and Brussels sprouts as the crops finish, they are favourite winter quarters for aphids even though you cannot see them.

Keep trimmed all grass that could form a refuge for slugs. Cultivate or clear with herbicides patches of perennial weeds such as nettles.

Functional disorders Troubles not due to disease are often recognisable by the symptoms.

Yellowing leaves and flabby stems of crops in winter. Unless an immediate consequence of hard frost this is due to poor drainage and destruction of roots by waterlogging. Attend to it later by breaking up the subsoil or, in extreme cases, putting in a pipe drain or soakaway.

Generally poor results from pea and bean crops, despite adequate manuring, and the presence of large numbers of plantains and daisies among the garden weeds. Probably due to lime deficiency. Test if possible, and apply finely ground limestone after winter digging.

Failure of hardy crops to survive winter frosts. If this occurs on well-drained light soils it is probably due to lack of potash or too much nitrogen. Grow such plants 'hard', not encouraging exuberant growth with nitrogenous fertilisers. Top dress in summer with sulphate of potash or a compound fertiliser with a high potash content.

Generally slow and stunted growth when growing conditions are favourable. Most probably shortage of nitrogen, as in cabbages in early spring when nitrogen has been washed out of the soil. Top dress with nitrogenous fertiliser.

PESTS

Insect pests

Using pesticides The persistent chlorinated hydrocarbon insecticides like DDT are now either forbidden or not recommended. Safe and reasonably effective pesticides based on derris and pyrethrum are available as aerosols and as dust in blower packs. For most purposes and for the smaller garden these are the simplest forms of application. The same types of pesticide may also be obtained in ordinary liquid form to be used in a sprayer. An effective and non-toxic (but evil-smelling) spray for use against resistant pests such as cabbage aphids is Malathion. As a preventive soil dressing for root flies and wireworms Bromophos is satisfactory, but consult your garden centre and get the latest recommendations. The pesticide scene is always changing and the tendency is towards safer and more thoroughly tested products.

Commonsense pest-killing
Pesticides are not magic potions. Use them as soon as trouble is diagnosed and before the pest gets a firm foothold. Remember that the most harmless chemical substance is potentially harmful if misused. The following are the commonest enemies.

Aphids Blackfly on broad beans and occasionally on runner beans. Grey aphids on brassicas. Pick out the tops of broad beans when blooms have set, spray immediately fly colonies are seen. Inspect brassica crops from midsummer, looking for greyish patches of aphids in sheltered crevices. Spray thoroughly and frequently. Remember that aphids multiply very rapidly, laying eggs or producing live young according to conditions.

Caterpillars Those of the Cabbage White butterfly eat the leaves of all the cabbage family. Spray repeatedly if necessary, paying particular attention to the undersides of leaves, and hand-pick the caterpillars if you have time. Pea Moth caterpillars are the familiar 'maggots' in pea pods. Early varieties are seldom affected. Spray maincrops when in flower at 10-day intervals. Spraying the pods after flowering is ineffective.

Flea beetles These little wretches are specialised feeders, attacking the seedlings of brassicas, swedes and turnips. They may be seen hopping about when disturbed, and the seedlings will at first show punctured leaves but may soon disappear altogether. Spray or dust repeatedly with derris. Keep the seedlings watered and growing quickly, the flea beetles damage only the seed leaves and the crop is safe when the true leaves develop.

Root flies The larvae of these insects prey on particular crops. The Carrot Fly and Onion Fly can cause serious damage to these roots in light soils. As advised elsewhere, take precautions not to attract the flies when thinning the crops. Treat the soil with Bromophos before sowing. Cabbage Root Fly prefers cauliflowers as a host. Dig up and burn affected plants with adhering soil and the white maggots that eat the roots. As a precaution, dust the soil round each plant with Bromophos or 4% calomel dust immediately after planting out.

Slugs Some eat the green parts of plants and other, smaller species burrow into roots and potato tubers below ground. They move about freely in wet conditions and shelter in weedy, neglected areas. Put down metaldehyde slug pellets near crops being damaged, covering them with up-tilted tiles or something of the sort to stop birds eating them while allowing access to the slugs. Water the ground with metaldehyde solution to inhibit the below-ground species.

Wireworms Tough, yellowish soil pest capable of boring right through a potato. Mainly troublesome in newly-dug grassland and usually disappear with cultivation. Treat the soil with Bromophos, grow only early potatoes, scoop up the soil under suddenly wilting seedlings and dispose of any wireworms found.

Non-Insect pests

Birds Seedling peas, brassicas, beetroot and spinach beet are the chief sufferers. Cover with cloches or nylon net. Protect with black cotton strung criss-cross along the row on short pegs. It must be black, its frightening effect depending on its invisibility.

Field mice They eat pea and bean seeds, leaving small round holes along the row where they have excavated. Warfarin or one of the newer poisons are effective mixed with a cereal base. Break-back traps, baited with cheese, chocolate or soaked broad bean seeds, according to local taste, are probably even more so. They must be so sited that mice can get at them, but not birds.

DISEASES

Very few where vegetables are concerned.

Club root This is the only serious disease affecting the cabbage family, turnips and swedes, occuring in poorly-drained, lime deficient soils. Rotate crops and apply lime when necessary. If the disease is present, as shown by stunted growth and swellings on roots, lime the ground heavily, giving about 1 lb per sq yd / 0.5 kg per sq m, followed by light dressings in the 2 succeeding years. Dip the roots of brassica plants in a thin paste of 4% calomel dust before planting out.

Potato blight A disease of humid weather and maincrop potatoes. Spray in July with Dithane or Bordeaux Mixture if the season is wet. Haulm badly affected with blight should be cut off and burnt before the spores are washed down to infect the tubers.

Mildew Swedes are badly checked by mildew in hot weather. Sow them late so that maximum growth comes in the cooler days of early autumn.

Onion neck rot This occurs in stored onions, which may look perfectly sound on the outside. Insist on certified heat-treated onion sets and onion seed guaranteed free of infection.

Virus diseases Several occur in potatoes, causing deformed leaves, stunted growth and a negligible crop in individual plants. Buy only certified seed potatoes. Similar virus symptoms occur in marrows, the plants failing to grow and blotches appearing on the leaves. This should not be confused with the natural grey markings on the foliage of Zucchini and some other varieties. Pull up and burn affected plants. The only precaution is to grow enough plants to allow for the possible occasional loss.

Hygiene and environment
Start with healthy stock bought from reputable nurserymen. Provide conditions for healthy growth, and deal promptly with symptoms of trouble.

General hygiene Clear up and burn top fruit prunings. Prune with sharp tools and paint wounds. Cut out the old wood of cane fruits immediately fruiting is over so that new canes receive maximum light and air to ripen the wood.

Keep trees free of mosses and algae. Winter spraying with a tar oil wash achieves this in addition to dealing with insect pests.

Thin overcrowded top fruits and remove badly scabbed, rotten or mummified fruits from contact with healthy ripening ones.

Pollination troubles Abundant blossom followed by failure to set fruit may, as suggested elsewhere, be due to lack of pollinating variety in bloom at the same time. Where neighbouring gardens have a selection of fruit trees, or in a commercial fruit-growing area, this is not likely to be the cause.

Late frosts are frequently responsible. High winds or persistent damp, cold weather, limiting the flight of pollinating insects, are equally harmful though this is not always recognised. Windbreaks to the north and east make a lot of difference to the working conditions for bees and other insects in blustery spring weather. Among the soft fruits gooseberries and blackcurrants in particular set more fruit in a sheltered situation.

Chlorosis Soil conditions sometimes produce abnormal states in fruit trees. One of these is lime-induced chlorosis, which occurs in trees on chalk soils if planted in cultivated ground. The leaves become increasingly pallid and eventually almost white, growth and fruiting being badly affected. The trouble is caused by the intake of too much calcium, which prevents the normal formation of chlorophyll in the leaves. The remedy is to grass down the area around trees, those growing in grassland are not liable to chlorosis. When the grass is established, give it an occasional light dressing of compound fertiliser and keep it trimmed. Drop the fertiliser dressings when the trees regain normal coloration.

Over-vigorous trees It is a fairly common complaint that trees are growing like mad and producing little fruit. There are several possible reasons. The tree may have been grafted on a rootstock that produces a large, slow-maturing tree, and in that case it will eventually yield heavy crops provided it has enough room and you have enough patience.

It may have been pruned too hard after a period of neglect, causing all the buds to form shoots instead of blossoms in an effort to replace the lost wood. Stop all winter pruning for 1 - 2 years and restrict growth by summer pruning laterals, pinching out the growing points of shoots in July and again in late August if fresh growth is evident.

A common cause of lush growth in garden trees is planting in a too-fertile soil. Trees of several years' growth may be checked and induced to fruit by root pruning. Take out a trench surrounding the trunk in a circle of 2 ft/60 cm radius. Dig carefully, cut thick roots and try to leave fibrous feeding roots intact. Fill in the trench, ramming the soil well. Stake and tie the tree if its original stake is no longer there, it may become unstable with loss of its main anchoring roots. Small trees may actually be induced to start fruiting by being dug up and having thick roots trimmed back before replanting.

PESTS
Insect pests
Maggots in apples Chief offender is the codlin moth. It lays eggs on the leaves in June, they hatch and the caterpillars burrow into the apples and grow there. In August they emerge and spend the winter wrapped in cocoons under rough bark. Small trees may be thoroughly sprayed with Malathion when the petals fall and again 3 weeks later. Large trees are difficult to spray, but many caterpillars may be caught in bands of sacking or corrugated cardboard wrapped round the trunk in late July and removed and destroyed in winter.

The apple sawfly is another source of maggots, which tunnel into the fruit earlier in the season than the moth larvae. When the apples fall they burrow into the soil for the winter. Spray with Malathion at petal-fall, cultivate the soil around the trees in autumn to disturb the caterpillars, pick and destroy any apples seen with small holes about midsummer and do the same with punctured windfalls. Eliminating maggotty apples is a long-term exercise requiring persistence.

Aphids on plum trees If allowed to persist they get worse each year, swarming on young shoots and the undersides of leaves and covering everything with a black sticky deposit known, most inappropriately, as 'honeydew'. Destroy their eggs by thoroughly soaking previously affected trees with tar oil wash in December or January. Finish off survivors by spraying with Malathion just before the flowers open.

Gall mites on blackcurrants Minute creatures which feed on the inside of buds, destroying flowers and producing the swollen 'big bud' by which their presence is identified. Pick off and burn these big buds whenever noticed. Spray with lime sulphur when the flowers open.

Gooseberry sawfly and magpie moth The caterpillar of these two feed on gooseberry leaves in spring and can defoliate bushes if not dealt with. Inspect bushes in early May, pick off and destroy caterpillars and spray or dust repeatedly with derris. The pest is easily controlled, but if given a free run for a week may ruin the season's crop.

Raspberry maggots They are the grubs of the raspberry beetle. In some gardens they appear to be endemic, in others they are rarely seen. The grubs hatch at just the right moment to feed on the ripe fruit, and the time to catch them is when the first fruits show a tinge of pink. Spray thoroughly with derris at this time and you will get maximum control without in any way affecting the crop.

Protection from birds
To the grower of soft fruits damage by birds poses a greater problem than all the insect pests. The only way to be sure of

Tiger Moth

gathering a crop is to net the bushes or canes.

Modern nylon netting is far superior to the repaired fish net formerly used and is good temporary protection where there is no permanent fruit cage. Place stout canes, slightly taller than the bushes, along both sides of them and stretch the net over them, pegging it down firmly at the bottom and keeping it clear of the bushes at all points. Cover the tops of the canes with small jam or fish paste jars so the net slides easily over them and does not catch when erecting it. The same method may be used to protect strawberries, using stakes about 24 in/60 cm high. It is no use simply slinging the net over the bushes or plants so that it rests on them.

The permanent fruit cage should have sides of wire netting of ¾ in/ 2 cm mesh and a top of nylon net, removed in winter. A permanent wire netting top may cause the cage to collapse if it becomes overloaded with wet snow, and the cage should be open to birds except in the fruiting season.

DISEASES

Apple canker Starting as a sunken area on a branch it develops into a cankered mass which will kill the branch if it encircles it. Cut out small branches showing the symptoms. On larger ones, pare away the cankered part down to clean wood with a sharp pruning knife. Paint the wound with a special canker paint obtainable from the garden centre. Check up on drainage, canker is a disease of wet soils.

Apple scab Brown patches on fruit, spreading and cracking in severe cases. Spray twice with lime sulphur, once when the flower buds are still green and again when they are just showing pink.

Silver leaf disease in plums Branches die back from the tip, the leaves turning a distinctive silvery colour. The inner wood of the branch is affected by a deep brown stain. Cut back the diseased branch in section until you reach a point 6 in/15 cm beyond the last trace of stain. Paint the wound with bituminous fungicidal paint. Prune only in summer when the wounds heal quickly and the disease spores are less likely to gain access.

Peach leaf curl The leaves develop red patches which swell into white blisters. Eventually the diseased leaves fall and the crop may be affected. Spray trees which have suffered with Bordeaux mixture in January or February. Collect and burn fallen leaves.

Grey mould on strawberries This disease, caused by the fungus Botrytis, can destroy a large part of the crop in a wet season. The berries rot just as they are ripening and become covered with a greyish furry mould. As a preventive measure, spray with benamyle (Benlate) when the first flowers open, and repeat 10 days later. Or spray twice with captan, but not if the fruit is to be bottled, jammed or frozen. The plants must be sprayed when flowering, spraying the berries is useless. Pick and remove infected berries as soon as they are seen.

The mere gathering of a crop may look the easiest part of the exercise, and certainly it is the most satisfying. But it is quite possible to spoil the work of months by carelessness at a critical time.

Correct harvesting of vegetables and fruits has 3 aims. To pick the crop in perfect condition for immediate consumption, freezing, jamming or other forms of preservation, as in the case of peas or raspberries. To gather it in perfect condition for natural storage, as in the case of potatoes or keeping apples. And to promote further development of the crop where some of it is still immature.

Vegetables not stored naturally
Brussels sprouts Pick from the base of the stem, working upwards as sprouts develop. Pick and use tops when most of the crop has been gathered. Open or 'blown' sprouts are useful as greens but cannot be frozen.
Cabbages If cabbage hearts are cut so as to leave a few leaves on the stem, young shoots are produced which can be cooked as greens. Pull up the plants, however, if they begin to develop colonies of aphids. The variety

Winter White is exceptional in that it will store naturally for weeks if cut and kept in a cool place.
Cauliflowers A close watch must be kept on summer varieties, which spoil quickly in hot weather. Bend leaves over the curd to protect it from the sun and select those in perfect condition for freezing. The curd remains usable for up to a fortnight if the entire plant is pulled up and hung upside-down in a cool, dark place.
Globe artichokes and asparagus These 2 are among

the few permanent vegetable crops. They must be treated with a thought for their performance in future years. The large central heads of artichokes are gathered first and the smaller buds as they develop. Avoid damage to the large leaves and harvest the heads before the scales begin to turn purple. Asparagus is cut below ground level, care being taken not to injure the roots. Cut all the shoots, including thin and deformed ones, during the cropping period. Stop cutting in

June and encourage maximum growth of 'fern' to build up the crowns for next year's crop.

Peas and beans Garden peas are picked while the pods are smooth and green, without wrinkling or loss of colour. The peas themselves should also be bright green, not whitish, and with no obvious skin when cooked. Sugar peas are picked while still flat, with no apparent bulges from developing seeds inside. Broad beans are gathered before the seeds are fully grown and covered with a tough skin. Dwarf and runner beans are picked before the seeds develop, runner beans should be almost flat and tender enough to snap when bent. It is essential for all these crops to be gathered young if required for freezing.

The systematic harvesting of peas and beans affects the total yield. The plant's objective is to produce seed, and if the pods are allowed to grow old and seeds to mature the objective is achieved and the production of further pods ceases. Pick closely and regularly and the later pods will develop. Runners especially should be thoroughly picked over at least 3 times a week in hot weather.

Sweet corn Delayed harvesting can spoil the crop. Pick when the kernels contain a thin cream, before it thickens into dough with the conversion of sugar into starch. Use or freeze within a few hours of picking.

Tomatoes Fruit may be picked when it acquires a yellowish tinge and will ripen without serious loss of quality. Outdoor tomatoes must be brought in before autumn frosts. Pull up the entire plant and hang it in a warm place with the fruit on it, or pick the fruit and lay out in a single layer. It is immaterial whether they are in light or darkness, but warmth is essential for ripening.

Vegetables stored naturally
Beetroot Pull or lift in October, taking great care not to damage the roots. Twist off the tops (do not cut them as this causes bleeding). Store in shallow boxes, lightly covered with peat so that they can be easily inspected, in a cool but frost-proof place.
Carrots Lift in October, carefully levering long roots out of the

ground with fork or spade. Lay out to dry for a few hours and brush off soil with the fingers. Twist off tops and store as advised for beetroot. Keep the roots completely covered with peat.
Celeriac Lift in late autumn. Trim off roots and side-shoots. Store in a very cool place - a degree or so of frost will not hurt.
Jerusalem artichokes Leave in the ground and dig as required. When cutting down the tops about a foot of stem should be left so the position of the row is clearly visible throughout the winter.
Onions Harvest shallots in July, set-grown onions in August and seed-grown varieties in September. Dry the bulbs thoroughly, outdoors in fine weather or spread out in a shed if it is wet. Store so that air circulates round them, hanging in bunches or string, or in make-shift bags of netting.
Parsnips Lift as required. Mark the rows by covering them with a narrow strip of peat.
Potatoes Lift carefully when the tops die down and the skin on the tubers is set and cannot be rubbed off. Leave for a few hours to dry and rub off soil. Discard diseased or damaged tubers. Store in boxes in complete darkness and cool but absolutely frost-free condtions.
Turnips and swedes Lift any time in late autumn. Store as advised for carrots, first trimming off leaves and tap-roots. Slight frost will not harm the stored roots.
Marrows and squashes These are the only vegetables other than roots to be stored for any length of time without artificial preservation. The fruits must be allowed to ripen until the skins are nearly as hard as plywood, then brought indoors before there is any danger of frost. Lay them out in a frost-proof place and inspect them frequently. Although normally keeping until after Christmas they occasionally decay from within and cause a sudden and unexpected mess.
Fruits not stored naturally
Blackberries and loganberries Harvested from July to September. Pick when fully ripe, blackberries are useless if hard and green at the tips and loganberries must be purple and not bright red.
Blackcurrants July is the main

picking month. If the berries are to be used immediately they may be stripped from the stalk or strig, but they are less messy and remain in better condition if the strig is picked with the berries.
Gooseberries If there is a heavy crop start thinning the berries as soon as they are large enough to cook or freeze. The remainder will have a better chance to grow.
Peaches and nectarines Test for ripeness by taking the fruit in the palm of the hand and pressing very gently with the fingertips near the stalk. If the flesh 'gives' the fruit is ripe and will come away without pulling. Collect the fruit in a basket lined with soft material and keep in a cool place until used.
Plums Pick when fully ripe if the fruit is intended for dessert. For cooking, jamming and bottling it should be slightly unripe. Some of the best dessert gages split in wet weather and they too must then unfortunately be picked unripe if much of the crop is not to be lost.
Raspberries Pick only when the fruit is dry, it goes mouldy quicker than any other soft fruit. The berries should be quite ripe and come cleanly away from the white core, leaving it on the cane.
Strawberries For all purposes the berries should be fully ripe, without unripe shoulders or tips. Handle the berries as little as possible, holding them by the stalk. Pick over the plants once a day in hot weather.
Fruits stored naturally
Apples Approximate picking dates for different varieties are given in the catalogues. The test for ripeness is to lift the fruit up gently until the stalk is horizontal, if ripe it will come away with very little pull. Store in a cool place - the ideal temperature is 40°F/5°C - and away from contact with any strong-smelling substance like fresh paint or creosote. They are best wrapped individually in squares of oiled paper sold for the purpose, squares of newspaper, or polythene bags with ventilation holes. The last method also helps to reduce shrivelling.
Pears Test for ripeness as advised for apples. Store in the same conditions but laid out singly and not wrapped. Dessert pears ripen very suddenly and must be kept open to inspection.

BRASSICAS They like: Good, firm soil. An open, unshaded position.
Plenty of water in summer. Fresh ground every year.

BRUSSELS SPROUTS

Characteristics
Very hardy and one of the most important winter greens. Likes a long growing season and should be sown and planted early. Resists the hardest frost but tall varieties suffer in winter gales - grow the more compact varieties on exposed sites.

Best soil
In good heart, heavy rather than light, not too recently manured, and very firm. Rotted organic manure or garden compost may be applied during winter digging, but this should be done early to allow the soil to settle. If at all acid, apply garden lime at the rate of 6 oz per sq yd/200 g per sq m immediately after digging. Just before planting, rake in 3 oz per sq yd/100 g per sq m of general fertiliser.

When to sow
As early in March as conditions permit. Sow in a seed bed in shallow drills 6 in/15 cm apart. Sow thinly and thin to 1 - 2 in/2.5 - 5 cm apart, or sow pelleted seeds 1 in/2.5 cm apart and don't thin. Protect from birds with net or black cotton if necessary, or the seed bed may be cloched.

When to plant out
In May or June. Water the seed bed before lifting, lift carefully, retaining soil round the roots, and plant with a trowel. Space between plants and between rows, 24 in/60 cm. Compact varieties may be spaced at 18 in/45 cm in the rows. Plant with the lower leaves just above the surface, water after planting and continue watering until established. If unable to raise plants, order from a local nurseryman for delivery in May.

Quantity of seed
Seedsman's packet contains several hundred seeds, though fewer of F₁ hybrids than other varieties. If you have space for several rows sow a packet each of an early and a late variety. Surplus seed remains viable for several years.

Time to germination
10 - 14 days when sown in March.

Season of use
September - March.

Storage life in freezer
1 year. Only small, high quality sprouts should be frozen.

Crop for average family
A yield of 1 lb/500 g per plant may be expected from F₁ hybrids and half that from non-hybrids. 2 30 ft/9 m rows should yield 20 - 30 lb/10 - 15 kg spread over the winter months.

Reliable varieties
Focus (early hybrid), Peer Gynt (early/midseason hybrid), Siltrex (midseason for light land), Cambridge No 5 (non-hybrid late), Early Dwarf (for the smallest garden). Best all-rounder for the small garden and good for freezing is Peer Gynt.

Caring for the crop
Hoe regularly until leaves meet in the rows. Remove yellowing leaves and if necessary support tall varieties by pushing in a bamboo cane against each plant. Not a demanding crop once established.

For culinary applications see page 109

CABBAGES, SUMMER AND AUTUMN

Characteristics
These cabbages are less hardy than the winter and spring varieties and mature more quickly. Summer types are sown early under glass or late in an outdoor seed bed, those for use in autumn are only sown outdoors.

Best soil
All types of soil are suitable if dug and manured well in advance of planting. These crops benefit from organic manures and from the usual dressing of compound fertiliser raked in before planting. Firm soil produces solid hearts, if you plant immediately after digging and manuring the cabbages will be soft and leafy.

When to sow
For early summer crops sow in greenhouse or frame in a pan or seed tray when a temperature of 40° - 50°F/5° - 10°C can be maintained. Prick out the seedlings into trays of potting compost, grow on until about 3 in/7.5 cm high, harden off and plant out in March or April. If unable to do this, order plants for delivery in late March.

For late summer and autumn crops sow in a seed bed as advised for Brussels sprouts in April. If pelleted seed is not used, thin early and aim at getting stocky, broad-leaved little plants.

If early plantings fail sow a fast-growing variety in situ, taking out a drill, dropping a pinch of seed or a few pelleted seeds every 18 in/45 cm and reducing to one plant per station. This may be done as late as early July with the prospect of an autumn crop.

When to plant out
From March to June, as plants become available. Space plants 18 in/45 cm apart in the rows, with the rows 24 in/60 cm apart. The early summer varieties may be spaced 3 in/7.5 cm closer in the row and the rows 6 in/15 cm closer.

Quantity of seed
Small packet each of 2 varieties. F₁ hybrids like Hispi have many fewer seeds per packet than non-hybrids, but still plenty for the average garden.

Time to germination
7 - 14 days.

Season of use
June - November.

Storage life in freezer
Same as for winter and spring varieties.

Crop for average family
Two 30 ft/9 m rows or 40 plants should yield 2 cabbages a week from midsummer until autumn if at least 2 varieties are grown. Remember that many other vegetables are available in summer.

Reliable varieties
Early sowing under glass or in the open   Greyhound, Hispi (outstanding F₁ hybrid), Derby Day.
Late sowing   Winningstadt, Primo, Autumn Monarch.
Red pickling cabbage   Ruby Ball. Treated like other summer varieties, this is a superb cabbage for all purposes.

Caring for the crop
Little attention beyond hoeing and watering is needed. When harvesting, the heart of the cabbage may be cut and the stump and a few leaves left in the ground to provide tender green shoots. This should not be done if there is any sign of aphis on the leaves or the ground can be more profitably used.

For culinary applications see page 109

CABBAGES, WINTER AND SPRING

Characteristics
Hardy, being harvested between November and May.
Varieties fall into 2 distinct groups and it is important to make
the right choice for the purpose when buying seed. Winter
cabbages are sown in late spring, grow through the summer
and mature from autumn onwards. Spring cabbages are sown
in late summer, grow very little in winter and mature in spring.

Best soil
In good heart, and firm. Organic manure or compost should be
dug in and the soil given plenty of time to settle. Cabbages
planted on recently dug and manured soil run to outer leaf
rather than heart and suffer more in severe weather. Spring
cabbages are a good succession crop to maincrop peas or
runner beans. Rake in a light dressing of compound fertiliser
before planting winter varieties. Give no fertiliser to spring
varieties until March, then top dressing with 1 oz per yd/
33 g per m of sulphate of ammonia.

When to sow
Sow winter cabbage in May in a seed bed as advised for
Brussels sprouts. Sow spring cabbages, also in a seed bed, in
late July or early August. In both cases water the drills before
sowing in dry weather, protect from birds if necessary, and
water thoroughly before lifting the plants.

When to plant out
Plant out winter cabbages in July in rows 24 in/60 cm apart
with the plants 18 in/45 cm apart. Plant with the lower leaves
just clear of the ground and keep watered in dry weather until
established. Plant out spring cabbages in September or
October in rows 18 in/45 cm apart with the plants 9 in/22.5 cm
apart; when the plants are large enough in the spring every
other one is used as 'spring greens', the remainder being left to
make fully-hearted cabbages.

Quantity of seed
Smallest seedsman's packet contains several hundred seeds.
Surplus seed remains viable 2 - 4 years.

Time to germination
6 - 10 days.

Season of use
Winter varieties, November - March. Spring varieties, March -
late May.

Storage life in freezer
6 months. Only solid hearts should be frozen.

Crop for average family
Yield should be 20 - 30 lb/10 - 15 kg per 30 ft/9 m row. Ideal
would be 1 row each of early winter, late winter, and spring
varieties.

Reliable varieties
For early winter (sown in May)   Drumhead, Christmas
Drumhead.
For late winter (sown in May)   January King, Ice Queen, Best
of All.
For storage in winter (sown in April)   Winter White. This
variety may be cut when hearted and stored for weeks in a
cool place indoors as an insurance against very severe
weather.
For spring (sown in August)   Harbinger, April, Ellams Early.

Caring for the crop
Winter cabbages must be kept growing steadily through the
summer. Hoe regularly and water freely when the foliage takes
on a bluish tinge from lack of moisture.
    Spring cabbages need little attention during the winter but
should be hand weeded when necessary in spring if the
ground is too wet to hoe. Inspect the plants after frost and
re-firm any that have been lifted out of the soil.

For culinary applications see page 109

CALABRESE

Characteristics
A green sprouting broccoli, more tender than the white and
purple forms, sown in spring and maturing in late summer and
autumn. Available in two types, one forming a large central
curd followed by a few lateral sprouts, the other with a smaller
central head and a succession of useful sprouts.

Best soil
Calabrese succeeds on light soils better than many brassicas
provided they contain enough organic matter not to dry out
badly. The crop must not go short of water and benefits from a
peat or compost mulch. Rake in a dressing of compound
fertiliser before planting.

When to sow
In April in a seed bed as advised for Brussels sprouts.
Alternatively, where the plants are to grow in May or early
June, taking out a drill and sowing a pinch of seed or a few
pelleted seeds at the right planting distance. This is a good
method as calabrese is often checked by transplanting in hot,
dry weather.

When to plant out
In June or early July, watering the seedlings well before lifting
from the seed bed and on planting. Space 18 in/45 cm apart in
the row, rows 24 in/60 cm apart. It is difficult to buy plants but
consult your local nursery early if you hope to do so.

Quantity of seed
1 packet will produce upwards of 100 plants. Seed remains
viable for 2 - 4 years.

Time to germination
10 - 14 days in April, 7 - 10 days in May and June.

Season of use
August - November. Possibly later in mild weather.

Storage life in freezer
1 year. Calabrese is increasingly popular for freezing.

Crop for average family
1 row of about 20 plants. More than that might crowd out
more important winter crops.

Reliable varieties
Green Comet (for a large cauliflower-like head but few
sprouts), Atlantic, Express Corona, Autumn Spear.

Caring for the crop
Hoe regularly and keep the crop moving by watering when
necessary and giving an occasional feed of liquid fertiliser. The
crop is ready when the head or shoots are a mass of tight
green buds. Keep the sprouts closely picked when they reach
this stage.

For culinary applications see page 108

CAULIFLOWERS, SUMMER AND AUTUMN

Characteristics
These cauliflowers are only half-hardy, and will not stand hard frost. Early summer cauliflowers are the most delicately flavoured of the whole family.

Best soil
These cauliflowers repay the most generous treatment you can give them. Dig in as much organic manure or compost as you can spare and supplement it with peat on dry sandy or chalky soils. Before planting, rake in a dressing of 3 oz per sq yd/100 g per sq m of compound fertiliser.

When to sow
Sow an early variety in the greenhouse or frame when you can maintain a temperature of around 50°F/10°C preferably in February or early March. Sow thinly in a pan of seed compost and prick out into potting compost 2 in/5 cm apart. Better still, prick out individually into small peat pots. Harden off ready to plant out when 3 in/7.5 cm tall.

Sow late summer or autumn varieties in April in a seed bed as advised for Brussels sprouts. Rake the soil to a very fine tilth and sow in shallow drills. Pelleted seed, well spaced, ensures that the seedlings grow without a check, but remember to keep them watered.

When to plant out
Plant early varieties in April, choosing a mild, damp spell and handling carefully to minimize root disturbance. Checks cause the plants to 'button' or form small, premature heads. Space them 18 in/45 cm between plants and rows.

Plant later varieties in May or early June, watering well before lifting from the seed bed and when planting. Space them 24 in/60 cm both ways. Cauliflower plants are available from nurserymen from March onwards.

Quantity of seed
Average packet provides up to 70 plants under glass, rather fewer in outdoor seed bed.

Time to germination
7 - 14 days.

Season of use
June - July for earlies, August - November for others.

Storage life in freezer
6 months. Small earlies may be frozen whole, larger curds as sprigs.

Crop for average family
Not more than 20 plants each of early and later varieties. Cauliflowers are apt to mature simultaneously, causing a glut.

Reliable varieties
Early Snowball, Snow King (for early crop), All the Year Round, Delta (for late summer). Majestic, Canberra, South Pacific (for autumn).

Caring for the crop
Never allow cauliflowers to suffer from lack of water. In hot weather bend the outer leaves over the curd to prevent scorching and discoloration. If too many mature at once lift the plants with their roots and hang upside-down in a cool shed, where they will remain in good condition for a week or 10 days.

For culinary applications see page 109

CAULIFLOWERS, WINTER

Characteristics
Reasonably hardy, but in a very severe winter may be entirely destroyed. Some varieties mature in early winter and others in spring. In favoured districts such as the South-West the crop may also be harvested in midwinter.

Best soil
Good but not over-manured. Winter cauliflowers must make satisfactory growth during the summer but have more time to do it than summer varieties and the growth must not be soft. They can be planted on ground manured for a previous crop with a dressing of compound fertiliser raked in before planting. The soil must be well drained.

When to sow
In April or May in shallow drills in a seed bed as advised for Brussels sprouts. The soil should be as fine as possible and the seed sown thinly. Keep the seed bed watered and hand weeded if necessary to avoid any check to the seedlings.

When to plant out
When the plants are about 4 in/10 cm tall, usually in June or early July. Water thoroughly before lifting from the seed bed. Plant 24 in/60 cm between plants and rows. Water the plants in and continue watering until established, choosing a cloudy, unsettled period for planting if possible. Winter cauliflower plants are on sale in June.

Quantity of seed
A packet contains over 100 seeds, sometimes twice that number. Seed remains viable for 3 - 4 years.

Time to germination
6 - 10 days. Watch for bird damage as seedlings emerge.

Season of use
November - May, but seldom harvested in January and February in colder districts.

Storage life in freezer
Same as for summer and autumn varieties.

Crop for average family
About 20 plants each of 2 varieties, 1 early winter and 1 spring.

Reliable varieties
Veitch's Self-Protecting (for late autumn and early winter), St. George, Reading Giant (for spring). These varieties are of proven hardiness, which is of first importance. The 'Roscoff' varieties offered in many catalogues should only be grown in mild coastal districts.

Caring for the crop
Established plants need little summer attention other than hoeing and an occasional watering in dry weather. The habit of growth is different from that of the summer cauliflower, the curd being protected by tall, incurving leaves. You may have a glut with the advent of warm spring weather; the development of an almost-mature head can be slowed by cutting the roots close to the stem on one side of the plant and gently bending it into a semi-horizontal position facing north.

For culinary applications see page 109

KALE

Characteristics
The hardiest of winter greens, surviving the severest frost and starting into growth when the weather improves. Tender and mild-flavoured when cooked but, like most leafy things, not suitable for freezing.

Best soil
The crop succeeds on poorer soil than any other brassica. It should be well dug, not waterlogged and not short of lime, but no manuring or other preparation is necessary.

When to sow
Kale is best sown where it is to grow. That way you are saved the trouble of transplanting from a seed bed and can sow any time from mid-May to mid-July. Sow a few seeds at 18 in/45 cm intervals in a drill ¾ in/2 cm deep, reducing the seedlings to 1 at each station as they grow. Or sow thinly along the entire length of the drill and thin by stages. Water the drill before sowing in dry weather and keep watered until seedlings emerge. Rows should be spaced 18 in/45 cm apart.

Quantity of seed
Small packet provides over 100 plants. Seed remains viable for 3 - 4 years.

Time to germination
5 - 10 days.

Season of use
January - April.

Crop for average family
In districts with average winters one 30 ft/9 m row is enough. In colder districts 2 rows provide insurance against loss of other winter greens.

Reliable varieties
Dwarf Curled (for winter and early spring), Hungry Gap (for late spring).

Caring for the crop
Because it can be sown late, kale is a good crop to succeed summer vegetables such as early potatoes. Once established, it needs no attention other than hoeing and if growth seems slow during summer it continues late into the autumn.

For culinary applications see page 110

SPROUTING BROCCOLI

Characteristics
Hardy. Survives most winters but likes some shelter from north and east winds. Date of first harvesting varies with temperature.

Best soil
Firm, containing some manure but not too rich. Does well in succession to early peas or potatoes.

When to sow
In a seed-bed in April or May in drills 6 in/15 cm apart and ¾ in/2 cm deep. Thin to 2 in/5 cm as soon as possible.

When to plant out
When the plants are 3 in/7.5 cm tall. Space plants 18 in/45 cm apart with 24 in/60 cm between rows.

Quantity of seed
1 seedsman's packet provides 50 - 100 plants.

Time to germination
7 - 14 days. Protect seedlings from birds immediately following germination.

Season of use
February - May. In mild winters and favoured districts the first pickings may be earlier.

Storage life in freezer
1 year. The crop freezes well.

Crop for average family
20 - 40 plants per 40 - 60 ft/12-18 m of row. In warm weather the crop develops very quickly and this number of plants should yield a surplus for freezing.

Reliable varieties
Purple Sprouting, White Sprouting. Varieties described as 'Early' and 'Christmas' may indeed be so, but will not crop in hard weather.

Caring for the crop
Water the seedlings after planting out until well established. Hoe between plants regularly until leaves begin to meet.

If the first sowing fails and time has been lost, sow again where the plants are to grow. Take out a drill the full length of the row, sow a pinch of seed every 18 in/45 cm cover and firm the soil. Water in dry weather. Thin each group of seedlings by stages to 1. This may be done up to late June in cold districts, early July in mild ones.

Harvesting
Keep the shoots closely picked to prevent the plants running to seed. High quality shoots are small with minimum of stalk.

For culinary applications see page 108

CHIVES

Characteristics
A hardy perennial member of the onion family, non-bulbous and growing in clumps of slender tubular leaves. Useful wherever a mild onion flavour is required and as a substitute for salad onions.

Soil and situation
A soil that has received a fair amount of organic matter and does not dry out in summer or become waterlogged in winter guarantees a long picking season, though chives are tough enough to survive adverse conditions. Plant in full sun or partial shade.

Propagation
Start by buying a few plants and setting them 9 in/22.5 cm apart any time between September and March when soil conditions are suitable. Every 3 or 4 years the clumps will need dividing. Lift in March or April, break the clump into small groups of about a dozen stems each, and replant. To be on the safe side, do not divide all your clumps in the same year.

Preservation and storage
Chives are among the best herbs for freezing. If no freezer is available they may be pot-grown indoors for a winter supply. Wait for at least 2 months after the tops have died down, then lift a complete clump and pot up in John Innes or soil-less potting compost. Choose a pot large enough to take it without disturbing the roots. Keep watered and grow in the greenhouse with a little warmth or on a window-sill. A rest period seems to be necessary before the plant is brought into warmth and December is early enough to start.

Species or varieties
Allium schoenoprasum   There are no distinct varieties.

Caring for the crop
The globular purple flowers begin to appear in June and from then on the leaves begin to look tatty. Remove the flowers as soon as they are noticed and in July cut the clumps hard back. Keep well watered at this time and give a little weak liquid fertiliser to promote new growth. Hand weed the clumps when the tops die down in autumn and cover with a very light layer of well rotted manure or garden compost.

For culinary applications see page 110

MARJORAM

Characteristics
2 types are grown. Pot marjoram is a hardy perennial. Sweet marjoram is a half-hardy shrubby perennial which may survive the winter but is best grown as a half-hardy annual. Both grow to a height of 18 - 24 in/45 - 60 cm. The leaves of both are used for the same purposes but those of pot marjoram are inferior in flavour and often bitter.

Soil and situation
A deeply dug soil, preferably well manured for a preceding crop, produces the leafy growth required. The position should be in full sun and for sweet marjoram should be as sheltered as possible so that the seedlings can be planted out early and have a long growing season. Pot marjoram may be planted in the herbaceous border, though it is not particularly ornamental.

Propagation
Buy plants of pot marjoram and divide clumps in autumn or early spring. Sow sweet marjoram under glass in March or April when a minimum temperature of 50° - 55°F/10° - 13°C can be assured. Sow in a pan of seed compost, covering the seed only lightly. Prick out the seedlings singly into small pots of potting compost and harden off before planting out in late May or early June.

Preservation and storage
Marjoram leaves are suitable for drying.

Species or varieties
Sweet marjoram, Origanum marjoram, which is the most worth growing, will be found in the seed catalogues under sweet or knotted marjoram.

Caring for the crop
Keep seedlings of sweet marjoram regularly weeded and watered if necessary after planting out. If growth appears to be slow give a fortnightly feed of liquid fertiliser. Pickings of fresh leaves may be prolonged in autumn by cloching, and it is worth while leaving cloches with ends in position over a few plants in the hope that they may come through the winter.

For culinary applications see page 110

MINT

Characteristics
A hardy perennial, available for picking from April to October. It has a vigorous root system of spreading rhizomes and may become an invasive nuisance when grown with other herbs. It can be produced out of season in pots in the greenhouse or on the window-sill.

Soil and situation
A moisture-retaining soil containing compost or peat. The plant is affected by drought, especially in late summer when fresh growth is needed to prolong picking into the autumn. Unlike most herbs, it succeeds in partial shade as well as in full sun.

Propagation
Propagate by root division between October and April, preferably in February or March. Dig up roots, cut the white rhizomes into 4 in/10 cm lengths and replant 2 -3 in/5 - 7.5 cm deep a few inches apart. Mint beds should be remade every 3 years, old woody roots being scrapped. Buy new roots in October or November or in February or March. Bunches of mint bought at the greengrocers will sometimes develop roots if kept in water in a light place. These rooted cuttings may be planted out in pockets of really good soil or potting compost and watered daily from a fine rose until well established.

Preservation and storage
Mint may be frozen, dried or preserved in vinegar. Out of season it may be grown in the greenhouse or on the window-sill. Dig up roots from November onwards, cut into 2 in/5 cm lengths and plant thickly 1 in/2.5 cm deep in potting compost. Keep damp and in a temperature above 50°F/10°C. Plantings after Christmas, when roots have been exposed to cold, are usually the most successful.

Species or varieties
The 2 usually grown are spearmint Mentha spicata and apple mint M. rotundifolia. Spearmint has the smaller leaves, is the more manageable, and is thought by some to be the better flavoured. Apple mint is extremely vigorous, growing to a height of 30 in/75 cm and having long, tough rhizomes which can burrow under a concrete path and throw up new shoots the other side. It succeeds in poor conditions and has a long season of use, often providing pickings well into November.

Caring for the crop
Clear away dead stems and weed the bed in autumn. Top dress it with an inch of well rotted manure or garden compost. Remove flower heads in summer and cut back apple mint to 6 in/15 cm in August to encourage young shoots for autumn picking.

For culinary applications see page 110

PARSLEY

Characteristics
A hardy perennial usually grown as an annual or biennial. It hails from southern Europe and does not always survive severe winters in Britain unless protected by cloches. This protection is also valuable in an average winter in maintaining a supply of fresh leaves.

Soil and situation
A fertile soil in a sunny or partially shaded position produces the leafy growth required in parsley. Dig and manure the site during the winter and bring the surface to a fine tilth for sowing in the spring. Rake in a pre-sowing dressing of 1 oz per sq yd/33 g per sq m of sulphate of ammonia. Remember that parsley is one of the most frequently used herbs and, if you do not have a herb bed, sow it alongside an all-weather path not far from the kitchen.

Propagation
Parsley is grown only from seed. Sow between March and June, the best time being from mid-April to mid-May. It is very slow germinating, taking 3 - 4 weeks, and if sown later than June will not be properly established by winter. If sown in March a lot of annual weeds will germinate ahead of the parsley and swamp the emerging seedlings. It is therefore best to prepare the site, allow the first crop of annual weeds to appear, remove them, and sow the parsley in a shallow drill. Thin the seedlings by stages to 6 in/15 cm apart.

Preservation and storage
Although not suitable for drying, parsley, like other soft-leaved herbs, freezes well. With some protection a year-round supply should be maintained from the garden. Seedlings from an outdoor sowing may be potted up, 3 - 5 in/12.5 cm pot, grown on in the open through the summer, and wintered in the greenhouse or on the window-sill.

Species or varieties
The type usually grown has closely curled leaves. Varieties are called Double Curled, Giant Curled or Moss Curled, but differences are not substantial. An excellent compact form is Bravour. Some seedsmen now offer the flat-leaved Continental type, reputedly better flavoured.

Caring for the crop
Keep seedlings hand weeded. Water freely in dry weather, drought seriously affects parsley, browning the foliage and stunting growth. In their second year the plants will throw up flower heads and these should be cut back while still small. To assure continuity of supply a fresh sowing should be made annually.

For culinary applications see page 110

ROSEMARY

Characteristics
An evergreen shrub, originating in southern Europe and the Eastern Mediterranean. Although hardy in the British Isles it may be badly scorched by severe frost, especially by freezing winds.

Soil and situation
Soil must be well drained and preferably light, but heavy land is satisfactory if deeply dug and opened up by the addition of peat, bonfire ashes or sand. The position should be in full sun and sheltered from north and east winds. The ideal position is against a south-facing wall, and here the shrub may grow 6 - 7 ft/2 m high with an almost equal spread.

Propagation
A single plant is enough for culinary purposes when established. It may be bought from a nursery and planted in autumn or early spring. Spring planting is often best for evergreens, but the shrub must be kept well watered and the foliage sprayed in hot weather. Propagation is by cuttings. Remove some lateral shoots about 6 in/15 cm long in August or September. They should be of new but ripened wood. Pull them from the branch with a 'heel' or cut just below a leaf joint. Take out a narrow trench 3 in/7.5 cm deep, line the bottom with coarse sand, place the cuttings in it a few inches apart, and fill in, making the soil firm. You will not know if the cuttings have rooted until the following spring. Those that begin to grow should be left at least until autumn before being planted in permanent quarters.

Preservation and storage
Fresh rosemary leaves are always available. It is not a suitable subject for freezing, but a supply of dried leaves is useful. After thorough drying they may be crumbled into powder for storing.

Species of varieties
The species is Rosmarinus officinalis. The variety Albus has very pale blue, almost white, flowers, and Pyramidalis is of erect, pyramidal habit of growth.

Caring for the crop
Practically no attention is needed apart from regular watering of transplants. Any pruning of over-large bushes should be done in spring.

For culinary applications see page 110

SAGE

Characteristics
Hardy evergreen shrub, rather straggly in form and growing to a height of 18 - 24 in/45 - 60 cm. A member of the large genus of salvias and originating in southern Europe, it is sometimes damaged in severe winters. The spikes of tubular purple flowers in June and July are decorative enough to warrant its inclusion in the shrub border.

Soil and situation
Any garden soil suits it if well dug and well drained. No manurial treatment is called for. Like most of the shrubby herbs it needs full sun to develop the essential oils in its aromatic and strongly flavoured leaves.

Propagation
Sage is easily raised from seed. Sow thinly in a pan of seed compost in the greenhouse or cold frame in April. Cover the seed lightly, keep moist, and it will germinate in about 14 days. Prick out the seedlings singly into 3 in/7.5 cm pots of potting compost, grow on under glass for a few weeks and then stand outside, sinking the pots in the ground to minimize watering. When the seedlings have made sturdy little plants 3 - 4 in/ 10 - 12.5 cm high plant them in their permanent quarters.

Alternatively, buy plants from the nursery and plant in March or April. Planting distance, 18 in/45 cm.

Preservation and storage
Sage is better stored dried than frozen. There should in theory always be fresh leaves available, but it is worth having dried ones in reserve.

Species or varieties
The botanical name is Salvia officinalis - 'officinalis' crops up frequently in the names of culinary herbs and of some other plants used as herbs in the past. It means 'used in the offices' in other words - in the kitchen. There are no distinct varieties though plants grown from seed may be found rather variable in habit.

Caring for the crop
Sage needs virtually no attention apart from trimming back dead flower spikes and pruning overlarge or straggling bushes in spring or summer.

For culinary applications see page 110

THYME

Characteristics
Hardy, evergreen, shrubby plants, dwarf or semi-prostrate, with tiny leaves and wonderfully spicy scent and flavour. It is one of the most widely used herbs.

Soil and situation
Soil must be well drained, preferably sandy or even stony, and the position in full sun. The thymes come from hot, dry Mediterranean lands and are happy in the poorest soil if it is not wet. They are decorative little plants, smothered with lilac flowers for much of the summer and, in some species, having colourful foliage. They may be used as path edgings, planted in the rock garden or in cracks in paving, and are one of the best herbs for the window-box or for container-growing on the patio.

Propagation
Grow from seed exactly as advised for sage. A packet of seed provides more seedlings than you can find room for and the only objection to the method is that you cannot acquire the less ordinary species in this way. Plants bought from the nursery may usually be increased by division in March, but sometimes it is difficult to detach a section of plant with enough root to start an independent life. An alternative is to take cuttings 2 in/5 cm long in June and insert them in a mixture of equal parts of peat and coarse sand in the cold frame or under a cloche. Water them overhead daily, pot up rooted ones into small pots and grow on outdoors until finally planting out in the autumn.

Preservation and storage
Thyme is very suitable for drying, retaining its scent and flavour well.

Species or varieties
Common thyme, Thymus vulgaris, is the ordinary culinary species and the one grown from seed. Lemon thyme, Thymus citriodora, is lemon-scented and has gold or silver variegated foliage. Thymus fragrantissima has a distinctive orange scent. Thymus herba-barona is a tough prostrate species from Corsica with a scent and taste generally likened to that of caraway seed. The more uncommon species may be bought from a specialised herb farm if unobtainable from a general nursery.

Caring for the crop
Thyme needs no attention other than clipping back after flowering and occasional trimming of straggly plants.

For culinary applications see page 110

ASPARAGUS

Characteristics
A hardy perennial requiring a year to get established after planting but thereafter producing its semi-luxury crop of edible stems for up to 20 years. It may be grown from seed, but this involves waiting 3 years for the first crop and the amateur gardener is advised to buy plants.

Best soil
The soil must be well drained, and for this reason asparagus used to be grown on raised beds. It is now usually planted on the flat, perhaps as a single permanent row across the vegetable plot, though on heavy land drainage is most important. Prepare the planting site in autumn, eradicating perennial weeds by digging or the use of a herbicide. Dig deeply and break up the subsoil. Dig in a barrowload of manure or compost for every 10 ft/3 m of row. Concentrate the manure on the planting site, putting down a line and digging it all into a 2 ft/60 cm wide strip. Mark the ends of the strip and leave the surface rough until spring. Then apply 3 oz per sq yd/100 g per sq m of compound fertiliser and rake it in.

When to plant
Order 2-year-old plants early in the year for delivery in late March or early April. The roots are then dormant but just about to start into growth. Plant immediately on arrival and at no time leave the roots lying about exposed to sun or wind.

Take out a trench 9 in/22.5 cm deep and 12 in/30 cm wide. Scrape the soil on the bottom into a ridge about 4 in/10 cm high. Set the crowns on this ridge, 12 in/30 cm apart with the fleshy roots spread out and pointing downwards. Fill in the trench, leaving the tops of the crowns several inches below the surface. Allow for a path or alleyway about 3 ft/1 m wide along both sides of the row. Spacing at 12 in/30 cm is closer than recommended for a conventional bed, but in a single row the roots have room to spread laterally and closer planting is permissible.

Season of use
April - June. Cutting should cease by the last week of June to allow the foliage to develop and build up strength for the next year's crop.

Storage life in freezer
9 months.

Crop for average family
Crowns are sold by the dozen. 2 - 3 dozen is usually as much as the average garden can accommodate.

Reliable varieties
The name of the variety is less important than the strain or breed. Find a specialist grower and ask for all-male plants which produce no berries but more stems.

Caring for the crop
Hand weed the row and take care to get rid of seedling perennial weeds. Once established, they are difficult to control without injuring the asparagus roots. During the harvesting period cut all shoots including thin and deformed ones. After cropping, water the 'fern' in dry weather to encourage growth. Cut it down when it turns yellow in autumn and clean up the row. Cover with 2 in/5 cm of well rotted manure or compost and over this 1 in/2.5 cm deep layer of soil from the adjoining paths.

For culinary applications see page 110

AUBERGINES

Characteristics
The aubergine or egg-plant is tender and in most summers cannot be relied on to crop outdoors in Britain, though it may do so in a warm and sheltered spot and especially if cloched. Normally, however, it is grown in the greenhouse in pots or in the border. It is an uneconomic plant from the point of view of space, producing only 4 fruits from the area required for a tomato plant. Not for the average garden or family.

Best soil
Open-air and cloche plantings need a humus-rich soil and good drainage. The south side of a wall is the best position. Use a soil-less potting compost or John Innes Potting No 3 for pot-grown plants in the greenhouse. For border plantings, dig in some peat and apply a light pre-planting dressing of compound fertiliser.

When to sow
Sowing cannot be later than March if the plants are to crop outdoors. For under-glass work seed may be sown in April. A night minimum temperature of 60°F/16°C is needed for germination and the same minimum must be maintained on sunless days for the seedlings to grow. Some form of heating or a heated propagator is therefore essential.

Sow in a tray of seed compost, covering the seed only lightly. Prick out singly into small pots and grow on close to the glass. Begin hardening off seedlings for outdoor planting when 3 in/7.5 cm high.

When to plant out
Plant under cloches in early June and in the open a week or so later, 18 in/45 cm apart. Plant in the greenhouse when the plants are 3 in/7.5 cm high, either 15 in/37.5 cm apart in the border or in 8 in/20 cm pots. Water the plants in and spray daily with tepid water.

Quantity of seed
Average packet is good for up to 50 plants.

Time to germination
18 - 25 days. Slowness of germination is one reason for an early start.

Season of use
August outdoors and under cloches, July - September in the greenhouse.

Storage life in Freezer
1 year.

Reliable varieties
Long Purple bears the largest fruit. Early Long Purple and New York may have a slightly better chance outdoors.

Caring for the crop
Nip out the growing points when the plants are 8 in/20 cm high. Allow 2 laterals to grow and when each carries 2 developing fruits stop them also. Remove all further side-shoots and fruits. Feed weekly with liquid fertiliser after the fruits have set.

For culinary applications see page 111

GLOBE ARTICHOKES

Characteristics
A large, half-hardy, perennial but short-lived plant grown for its edible flower buds. It takes up a lot of room in relation to the actual crop but is sufficiently decorative to be grown in the herbaceous border or as a specimen plant in odd corners of the flower garden. Although it may be raised from seed this is a slow process and not worth while. Buy plants and propagate from the suckers they produce.

Best soil
Dig the planting site deeply in winter, breaking the subsoil to improve drainage. Dig in well rotted manure or other organic material. Leave the soil rough until spring, then apply 3 oz per sq yd/100 g per sq m of compound fertiliser and lightly fork it in, getting a reasonable tilth for planting to a depth of several inches.

When to plant
Order plants early and ask for delivery in April. Plant immediately. Although they may look small they should be spaced 3 - 4 ft/1 m apart if grown in a row or in groups. If planted singly as decorative 'dot' plants, each should be conspicuously labelled to prevent it being hoed up as a thistle. As soon as the young plants are settled and beginning to grow give them fortnightly feeds of liquid fertiliser.

Season of use
July - September.

Storage life in freezer
1 year. Heads deteriorate rapidly after cutting and should be frozen as soon as possible.

Crop for average family
This depends on available space and the popularity of a crop far better known on the Continent than in Britain. On the heaviest clays and in very cold northern and eastern districts it is hardly worth growing.

Reliable varieties
There is usually no choice, but if possible get Gros Vert de Laon, outstanding for flavour and size of the heads.

Caring for the crop
Flower buds or heads are small in the first year but may be picked and used. In subsequent years pick the large heads before the scales begin to turn purple and smaller secondary buds will develop for later use. When the top dies down in autumn the root must be protected against hard frost. Cover it with straw or peat or, better still, with dry peat or leaves over which is placed a cloche with ends in position. This keeps the root warmer and drier than any other method.

Plants only last 3 - 4 years. In the third season propagate by taking suckers from the base in April, planting them in pots of soil-less compost until fully rooted and then planting them out. Suckers produced in November may be rooted in the same way and overwintered in the greenhouse for April planting.

For culinary applications see page 111

LEEKS

Characteristics
The mildest-flavoured of the onion family, very hardy and responsive to generous treatment, though yielding a crop of some sort in the poorest soil and bleakest situation.

Best soil
The only soil on which leeks fail is one completely waterlogged in winter. For size and quality in the stems, though, a soil well dug in winter and containing some organic manure is essential. A high-nitrogen source such as poultry manure is a recipe for plump, tender leeks. Apply a dressing of compound fertiliser before planting out.

When to sow
Mid-March - late April. Sow in a seed bed brought to a fine tilth, in shallow drills 6 in/15 cm apart. Sow very thinly and further thinning may be unnecessary.

When to plant
Plant in June or July, when the seedlings reach a height of 8 in/20 cm. If the weather is dry, water the seed bed some time before lifting the plants, lift carefully, keeping some soil round the roots, and trim an inch or so off long, straggling leaves. Make planting holes with a dibber, 6 in/15 cm deep and 6 - 9 in/15 - 22.5 cm apart, according to whether you want medium-sized leeks or are out to grow monsters. Rows should be 18 in/45 cm apart. Drop a seedling in its hole, fill the hole gently with water, and leave it. Enough soil will be washed down to cover the roots. The holes are not otherwise filled up and the stems have room to expand in them.

Quantity of seed
Average packet yields up to 100 plants. Seed remains viable for 3 years.

Time to germination
21 days.

Season of use
October - March.

Storage life in freezer
6 months. Leeks are dug from the ground as required in winter and frozen only if wanted in summer.

Crop for average family
Few families need more than 30 ft/9 m of row, and where space is limited winter greens should have priority.

Reliable varieties
For autumn use   The Lyon, Marble Pillar, Early Market.
For winter use and in cold districts   Musselburgh, North Pole.

Caring for the crop
Water freely in dry weather, the planting holes make this easier while the plants are young. As they get larger, increase the amount of white stem by gradually earthing them up. Never try to pull leeks when harvesting them, the roots are tenacious and the stems break easily. Lift carefully with a fork.

For culinary applications see page 111

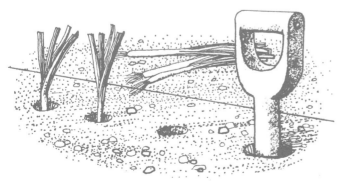

MARROWS

Characteristics
This includes the courgette and the pumpkin. They are tender and must not be planted outdoors while there is any danger of frost. The pumpkin bears the largest fruits, of a flattened spherical shape, and the courgette is the smallest. Small marrows may be used as courgettes. All have separate male and female blooms, the latter carrying a small fruitlet just behind the flower. The fruits do not grow unless the female bloom is fertilised by the transfer of pollen.

Best soil
Prepare individual planting sites of rich soil. Take out a hole at each site, mix the soil with half its volume of compost, decayed manure or other organic matter, refill the hole and raise the soil into a low mound. Distance between sites, 30 in/75 cm for bush (non-trailing) marrows and for courgettes, 4 ft/1.2 m for pumpkins and trailing marrows.

When to sow
Sow under glass in late April - early May. Don't be too early or the plants may be pot-bound and yellowing before it is safe to plant them out. Sow 2 seeds to a 3 in/7.5 cm peat pot, planting the seeds edgeways ½ - ¾ in/2 cm deep, and if both germinate remove the redundant one.

Alternatively, prepare pockets of seed compost on the planting sites and sow 3 seeds in each in late May or early June. Reduce to 1 seedling.

When to plant out
Plant out glass-raised plants in the first half of June. Water them in and see that the soil is kept moist. Place slug pellets around transplants and seedlings for a few weeks.

Quantity of seed
A small packet. Although the seed is supposed to remain viable for several years this cannot be relied on.

Time to germination
7 - 10 days.

Season of use
July - September fresh cut. October - January ripened and used from store.

Storage life in freezer
6 months. Courgettes and young marrows may be frozen, mature fruit is best ripened on the plant and stored naturally if freezer space is limited.

Crop for average family
4 plants provide enough fruits for immediate use and storage.

Reliable varieties
Bush varieties   Green Bush, White Bush, Zucchini, Golden Zucchini.
Trailing varieties   Long Green, Long White, Long Green Stripes (good for storage), Table Dainty (small, early).
Courgettes   Courgette Hybrid, Zucchini (cut while small).
Pumpkin   Hundredweight.

Caring for the crop
Keep the plants well watered in dry weather. Cut the fruits as soon as they are usable to encourage further cropping, leaving some towards the end of the season to grow large and ripen for storage. Hand pollinate if fruits fail to develop; pick a male flower when it first opens in the morning, strip off the petals and insert the pollen-covered stamens into the female flower.

For culinary applications see pages 112/114

MUSHROOMS

Characteristics
The mushroom is an edible fungus which feeds on decaying vegetable matter, mainly straw in the case of cultivated varieties, and is propagated from dormant spores called 'spawn'. As a crop it is unreliable but interesting. As a food it is richer in protein than almost any other vegetable.

Making mushroom compost
Compost for growing mushrooms commercially is usually made from strawy stable manure mixed with poultry manure and repeatedly turned until the straw breaks easily and is brown in colour. The amateur gardener may use straw and a chemical activator.

Place 3 or 4 bales of wheat or barley straw in a sheltered spot in the garden and thoroughly soak them with water. If this is done in the summer they will become warm inside in a few days. Then open them, spread a 4 in/10 cm deep layer in the form of a small square, sprinkle it with the activator, add another layer, and so on. After a few more days the heap will warm up again and is then turned, dry straw from the outside being placed in the middle and damped. Repeat the turning process until the straw is brown, breaks easily when a handful is twisted and smells like leaf-mould. It is then ready for making up into beds.

The activator may be of the type used in making garden compost or a special one called 'Boost'. Full instructions are supplied with the latter.

The mushroom bed
The site for the bed should be indoors, in a garage, shed or cellar, ideally where a temperature of 50° - 60°F/10° - 16°C can be maintained, though considerable variation from this will do no harm. The bed must be out of direct sunlight, though complete darkness is unnecessary. Make the bed 10 in/25 cm deep. Firm the compost and be sure it is uniformly moist. Cover it with newspapers to retain moisture. The area of the bed will depend on the size of the bales, but 4 bales should provide enough compost for one of about 12 sq ft/1 sq m, which is suitable for a small packet of spawn. If you want to grow mushrooms in cupboards or the attic, pack the compost into boxes 10 in/25 cm deep and leave a 2 in/5 cm space at the top for a 'casing' of soil or peat.

Spawning
A week or so after preparing the bed or boxes, test the compost with a thermometer. If the temperature is 70°F/21°C or below it may be spawned. Make holes 2 in/5 cm deep and 8 in/20 cm apart in all directions. In each hole put a walnut-sized piece of spawn and press the compost firmly back over it. About 2 weeks later the white threads of mycelium, the vegetative part of the mushroom, will be found spreading through the compost. At this point the bed is 'cased' with a 2 in/5 cm layer of sifted subsoil (not topsoil) or of peat mixed with a handful of ground limestone. Make the casing smooth and level. Keep it always moist but never so wet that water penetrates to the compost below.

Time to harvesting
In moderately warm conditions the mycelium soon spreads into the casing and forms clusters of tiny mushrooms called 'pinheads'. These develop into full-sized mushrooms, not all at once, but in 'flushes' of production. Gather the mushrooms by gently twisting the stems out of the casing, leaving the remaining pinheads as undisturbed as possible.

Storage life in freezer
6 months.

Buying spawn
Mushroom spawn is stocked by all seedsmen. Although it remains viable for some time you should buy only the quantity needed for immediate planting. There is no real varietal choice; all brands are pure cultures of the spores of the cultivated mushroom, though attempts are being made to reproduce the flavour of the wild species.

For culinary applications see page 112

PEPPERS

Characteristics
The sweet pepper or capsicum is a tender plant best cultivated in the greenhouse. It succeeds in a cold house under much the same conditions as the tomato. One variety is recommended for growing outdoors, but in an average summer results may be disappointing unless cloche protection is available.

Best soil
For outdoor or cloche growing the soil should be dug in winter and enriched with compost or rotted manure unless it has been well manured for a previous crop. Drainage is important and heavy land should be dug deeply. Choose a position in full sun and with shelter from cold winds. In the greenhouse, grow in soil-less potting compost or John Innes Potting No 3.

When to sow
Sow in the greenhouse in April if some warmth or a heated propagator is available, or in early May in a cold house, 4 or 5 seeds in seed compost in a 3 in/7.5 cm peat pot. Reduce to 1 seedling per pot. Keep as warm as possible until germination and grow on close to the glass, moving the seedlings further away from it on cold nights or covering them with newspaper. Begin hardening off seedlings intended for outdoor planting when they are 4 in/10 cm high.

When to plant out
Plant outdoors in early or mid-June, 18 in/45 cm apart. If you have cloches to spare, cover the plants until mid-July, when they will reach the glass. In the greenhouse, plant in 8 in/20 cm pots, leaving a 2 in/5 cm space at the top for the addition of more compost later.

Quantity of seed
No choice in size of packet.

Time to germination
10 - 14 days.

Season of use
August-September outdoors, July - October in greenhouse. Green and red peppers are not separate varieties; the green are unripe, the red and yellow ripe and therefore ready a little later.

Storage life in freezer
1 year.

Crop for average family
Not to everyone's taste. 6 plants outdoors and 3 in the small greenhouse for a trial run.

Reliable varieties
The older varieties, Bull-nose Red and Bull-nose Yellow are only suitable for the greenhouse. The new hybrid Canape is the best bet for outdoors and excellent for the cold greenhouse.

Caring for the crop
Allow the plant (really a short-lived shrub treated as an annual) to grow naturally, supporting it if necessary when fruiting with several thin canes. Feed both indoor and greenhouse plants weekly with liquid fertiliser after the first fruits have set. Spray indoor plants with tepid water when in flower and add more compost to the pots when fruit begins to swell.

For culinary applications see page 113

Special note
At least two major national seed firms now supply complete mushroom-growing outfits, a truly labour-saving development. All you have to do is to remove the cover from a container filled with ready-spawned compost, water it and await the mushrooms.

SEAKALE BEET

Characteristics
Related to perpetual spinach and having the same habit of growth, the green part of the leaf may be used in the same way. The main edible part, however, is the broad, white, succulent leaf stem and midrib. The plant is not fully hardy and is primarily a late summer and autumn crop. It deserves to be more widely grown.

Best soil
The better the soil, the better the size and quality of the edible stems. Dig in any available organic matter and apply a pre-sowing dressing of compound fertiliser. Given good cultivation and a fine tilth for sowing the crop does best on heavy soils. Where space is limited it, and especially its red variant, Ruby Chard, may be grown in clumps in the flower or shrub border as a fairly decorative foliage plant.

When to sow
Sow in late April in a narrow drill 1 in/2.5 cm deep, dropping a few seeds at 12 in/30 cm stations. Reduce each group of seedlings to 1 by stages. Although less subject to bird damage than perpetual spinach it may need protection.

Quantity of seed
Small packet when trying to crop for the first time.

Time to germination
10 - 14 days.

Season of use
Late summer and autumn.

Storage life in freezer
1 year.

Crop for average family
If the crop is unfamiliar to you, start by growing a short experimental row. 12 plants will provide about that number of pickings.

Reliable varieties
No named varieties, listed variously as Seakale Beet, Leaf Beet, Silver Beet, Swiss Chard. The red form is listed as Ruby or Rhubarb Chard.

Caring for the crop
Plants need plenty of room to develop and should be kept clear of weeds. Water generously in dry weather and give a fortnightly feed of liquid fertiliser from June to September. Begin harvesting when the leaves are about 15 in/37.5 cm high. Cut the outer stems carefully close to the ground, getting the full length of stalk. Take care not to injure the stems still growing in the centre of the plant. Finish the crop before the coming of hard frosts.

For culinary applications see page 113

SPINACH, ANNUAL

Characteristics
Summer or round-seeded spinach is a fast-growing summer vegetable sown from March - July. Similar to it but hardier is winter or prickly-seeded spinach sown in August for use in autumn and early winter.

Best soil
These leafy crops require good soil containing abundant nitrogen. Summer spinach especially also needs plenty of water, poor, dry soil causes it to bolt. Dig in manure, compost or peat, and before sowing rake in 3 oz per sq yd/100 g per sq m of compound fertiliser.

When to sow
Sow summer spinach at monthly intervals from mid-March to mid-July. Take out a wide drill - the full width of the draw hoe and ½ - ¾ in/2 cm deep and sow the rather large seeds thinly, giving the seedlings room to develop without early thinning. If this is done the first thinnings are large enough to use. Sow winter spinach in narrow drills of the same depth in the second half of August. Thin the seedlings by stages to 6 in/15 cm apart. Drills of both types should be 12 in/30 cm apart. Summer spinach likes partial shade and does well adjacent to tall crops. Winter varieties must have a sunny, sheltered position.

Quantity of seed
Large packet sows a 30 ft/9 m row. Buy fresh seed every year.

Time to germination
8 - 21 days according to time of year and soil temperature.

Season of use
Summer types, May - September. Winter types, October - December.

Storage life in freezer
1 year. Only young leaves without large stalks or midribs should be frozen.

Crop for average family
As every cook knows, the volume of spinach is enormously reduced in cooking. Allow 2 ft/60 cm of row, well grown, to provide 4 helpings.

Reliable varieties
Round-seeded summer varieties   Longstanding Round, Monarch.
Winter varieties   Greenmarket, Virkade.

Caring for the crop
If summer spinach is sown thinly in a wide drill it may be left to grow unthinned until about 6 in/15 cm high and then thinned to 4 in/10 cm between the plants. At this stage the thinnings are tender enough to be cooked entire if the roots and lower parts of the stems are snipped off. Winter spinach should be given space to make large, leafy plants while growing weather lasts. Finish the crop before Christmas, it is not immune to frost damage and becomes tougher with cold weather. For late winter and spring use rely on perpetual spinach.

For culinary applications see page 113

SPINACH, PERPETUAL

Characteristics
Also known as spinach beet or leaf beet, the plant is a hardy biennial. Sown in summer, it makes a large tap-root with a usable crop of leaves by autumn. It continues to produce leaves during the winter in open weather or if covered by cloches. In spring it grows vigorously, but eventually runs to seed and should then be dug up and another sowing made.

Best soil
Any soil in good heart gives good results if well dug to permit development of strong roots. It is a useful crop to succeed early potatoes. Rake in a light dressing of compound fertiliser before sowing.

When to sow
Sow between mid-May and mid-July in narrow drills 1 in/2.5 cm deep and 18 in/45 cm apart. For a quick start soak the seed for 12 hours before sowing. Also soak the bottom of the drill if the weather is dry and continue watering until emergence of the seedlings. Thin by stages to 9 in/22.5 cm apart. Protect from birds with black cotton or netting immediately on emergence, the seedlings, like those of beetroot, are sweet and apt to disappear in a day.

Quantity of seed
Large packet or ½ oz/15 g sows a 30 ft/9 m row.

Time to germination
7 - 12 days.

Season of use
September - May.

Storage life in freezer
See Spinach, Annual.

Crop for average family
A 30 ft/9 m row is usually enough. The crop lends variety to winter and spring menus but occupies the ground longer than most.

Reliable varieties
No named varieties. Usually listed as Spinach Beet.

Caring for the crop
Little attention is needed apart from routine hoeing and weeding. Once established it does not suffer in dry weather to the same extent as summer spinach. Cropping may be prolonged by cutting off flower stems as they appear and top dressing or feeding with liquid fertiliser, but a freshly-sown row is more worth having.

For culinary applications see page 113

SPROUTED SEEDS

Characteristics
The nutritional value of some germinated seeds with their shoots is far greater than that of the unsprouted seeds. Sprouted beans have long been used in Chinese cookery, and the conversion of starches in malted barley is another example. It is now realised that in sprouted seeds of certain species proteins may reach 30 per cent, with very high levels of vitamins.

Method of sprouting
Seeds are sprouted indoors at any time of year. An ordinary living room temperature, 60° - 65°F/16° - 18°C is about right, though it may be higher without damage to the seeds.

The simplest method of culture is to sprout the seeds in a jam or preserving jar. A piece of muslin is needed to cover the top, and an elastic band to hold it in place. Measure the quantity of seed required into the jar, a dessert-spoonful is enough in most cases, for the seeds with their sprouts may increase in bulk up to 10 times. Rinse the seeds with cold or tepid water and drain off. Cover the top with the muslin held by the elastic band. Thereafter, rinse the seeds with tepid, *not* hot, water, every morning and evening. Keep the muslin in place, pour the water through it, then lay the jar on its side for the liquid to drain off. Germination takes place quickly and the sprouts are ready in 3 - 8 days. They may be kept in light or dark conditions according to whether white or green sprouts are preferred.

Suitable varieties
The following are now available with cultural and cookery instructions.

Fenugreek   Ready in 3 - 6 days. Strong spicey flavour. Use in vegetable cookery and curries.

Mung beans   Ready in 3 - 6 days. Used in a wide variety of Chinese meat and fish dishes.

Alfalfa   Ready in 2 - 6 days. Used in soups and egg dishes. Each batch should be used or transferred to freezer within 8 days or its distinctive flavour of green peas will be lost.

Adzuki beans, Small Manchurian bean   Ready in 6 - 7 days. Used when the sprouts are about 1 ½ in/3.75 cm long it is probably richer in protein even than the Mung bean.

A number of other seeds, including lentils, may be sprouted, and it is possible to produce a succession of fresh vegetable and salad material with no more garden than a row of jam jars.

For culinary applications see page 112

SQUASHES

Characteristics
The squashes are closely allied to the marrows and require basically the same treatment. They are of American origin, very varied in size and shape, and appear to be better value than marrows in percentage of dry matter, food content and flavour. Our main reason for treating them separately from marrows is to draw readers' attention to them as worthwhile alternatives to marrows.

Best soil
Sites should be prepared as for marrows. The plants are generally less vigorous than marrows and maximum planting distances for trailing types should be 3 ft/1 m. The trailers may be trained up fences, trellis or tripods of 3 stout canes.

When to sow
Sow exactly as advised for marrows. When sowing in situ it is important for the soil to be warm and in late districts mid-June is early enough unless the sowing can be cloched. Glass-raised plants probably have a better start and if you have no greenhouse a few may easily be raised on the window-sill.

When to plant out
Plant out in the first half of June, choosing a warm spell. The squashes are bred for hot summers, and although they stand hot and even dry weather better than marrows they appear to suffer if exposed to cold conditions in the early stages of growth.

Quantity of seed
Buy the smallest packets obtainable and if possible try out more than 1 variety. Surplus seed should be good for at least 1 more year.

Time to germination
6 - 10 days.

Season of use
As for marrows, but the winter squashes may keep longer.

Storage life in freezer
6 months. It is better to grow a winter variety than to waste freezer space storing summer ones.

Crop for average family
Begin with 2 or 3 plants each of 2 varieties, treating the crop as an experiment.

Reliable varieties
Summer varieties   Baby Crookneck, Vegetable Spaghetti, Sweet Dumpling.
Winter varieties   Hubbard Squash, Butternut, Gold Nugget.

Caring for the crop
Growth is less robust in some of the squashes than in marrows and pumpkins and they do not smother the weeds so quickly. Young plants should be regularly hoed round and hand weeded. It is important for keeping quality that winter varieties should be allowed to ripen on the vine until the skins are as hard as wood. Cut them before the autumn frosts and store in a cool but frost-proof place.

For culinary applications see page 114

SWEET CORN

Characteristics
This is a tender crop once confined to the southern counties of England, but now more widely grown with the introduction of varieties maturing in a shorter season. A favourable site, sunny and sheltered from strong winds, is perhaps more important than the actual area.

Best soil
Not too rich and containing no fresh manure to encourage excessive growth. Dig in peat to conserve moisture and apply a pre-planting dose of compound fertiliser.

When to sow
Sow outdoors in late May, under cloches in late April, or in the greenhouse in mid-April.

Whether sown direct or raised under glass the plants should stand 18 in/45 cm apart in the rows with the same distance between rows. Grow in a block of several short rows, not in one long one. This is because the sticky 'silk' of the cobs must catch the wind-borne pollen from the male 'tassels' to effect fertilisation, from plants in a single row much of the pollen is blown away by a cross-wind.

Sow outdoors or under cloches in drills 1 in/2.5 cm deep, placing 3 or 4 seeds at 18 in/45 cm stations and reducing to a single seedling. Protect from birds for the first 4 weeks. Under glass, sow 2 or 3 seeds to a small peat pot, reduce to one, grow on close to the glass and harden off before planting out.

When to plant out
Late May or early June. Plant with the lower leaves just clear of the ground. Water in and, again, protect from birds until the leaves have toughened. Cloched seedlings may be left covered until they touch the glass.

Quantity of seed
A large, ½ oz/15 g, packet is enough for 30 ft/9 m of row, allowing for wastage of surplus seedlings. Seed remains viable for 2 years but it is safer to buy fresh every year.

Time to germination
10-14 days.

Season of use
July - October according to variety and sowing date.

Storage life in freezer
1 year. Cobs must be gathered at the correct sweet, creamy stage and frozen promptly.

Crop for average family
This depends on its popularity. It takes up a lot of space in relation to yield, though sufficiently ornamental to be grown at the back of the flower border in groups.

Reliable varieties
The following are all F_1 hybrids, mature earlier and have larger and sweeter cobs than the old varieties. North Star, Polar Vee (for colder districts), Earliking, John Innes Hybrid, Extra Early Sweet. The last should not be grown near other varieties as cross-pollination is said to reduce its sugar content.

Caring for the crop
Sweet corn grows tall and is shallow rooting, becoming unstable and liable to damage in a strong wind. In an exposed position, set the plants in a trench or drill 4 in/10 cm deep. In dry weather give the trench an occasional flooding, and fill it in with soil when the plants are about 2 ft/60 cm high. Additional roots are then produced from the base of the stem, giving the plant a firmer anchorage.

For culinary applications see page 114

PEAS AND BEANS They like: Good soil but no fresh manure. No shortage of lime. Lots of water when pods are forming. And, they gather nitrogen from the air and leave the soil richer.

BEANS FOR DRYING

Characteristics
Similar to dwarf or French beans and grown in the same way. The pods are not eaten green - although they can be - but are allowed to ripen on the plant, the beans being shelled and stored for use in winter. Beans are the richest source of vegetable protein. The best-known kinds, the Soya Bean, the Navy Bean (baked beans) and the Lima Bean (butter beans), are unsuccessful in our climate, but we have others which do well and are equally nutritious.

Best soil
Any good soil, prepared as for dwarf beans. A fine tilth for sowing, obtained by winter digging and weathering, makes all the difference to germination.

When to sow
Mid-May, not earlier because the crop has the whole summer to mature. Sow a single row in a narrow drill 1 ½ in/3.5 cm deep, watering it first if the weather is dry. Space the seeds 6 in/15 cm apart. More space is allowed than for dwarf beans picked green because a full load of pods is carried and overcrowding prevents them drying properly.

Quantity of seed
Average packet sows a 20 ft/6 m row.

Time to germination
About 14 days at that time of year.

Season of use
Autumn to following summer.

Crop for average family
A 20 ft/6 m row yields several pounds of dried beans. More space would only be justified in a large garden.

Reliable varieties
Comtesse de Chamborde, a true haricot bean and a heavy cropper, Granada, Purley King, Brown Dutch. The last was widely grown by amateur gardeners during the Second World War but is now not often listed.

Caring for the crop
Treat it as you would other dwarf beans but stop feeding and watering when all pods are full-grown. Prop up the pod cluster with twigs. When the pods are brown and the plants almost dead, pull them up and hang in small bunches to dry (hang them in an airy shed in wet weather). When the pods are completely dry, shell out the beans, spread them thinly for a few days' further drying and store for the winter.

For culinary applications see page 115

BROAD BEANS

Characteristics
Very hardy. May be sown in autumn, but this is a gamble without cloche protection. Early spring sowings, established while the weather is cool and damp, invariably do better than later ones.

Best soil
Does well on heavy soil if well dug and the surface is weathered to a good tilth for sowing. On non-chalky soils lime should be applied every third year for peas and beans. Broad beans can do without manure if given a standard dose of 3 oz per sq yd/100 g per sq m of compound fertiliser, raked in before sowing.

When to sow
Make an autumn sowing in October or early November. Sow Longpod varieties in spring from late February to late March and Windsors in March or April. Sow a double staggered row in a wide drill, seeds 6 in/15 cm apart, rows 24 - 30 in/ 60 - 75 cm apart according to available space. Sow extra seeds at the end of each row and transplant later to fill gaps. Drills should be 2 in/5 cm deep on heavy soils, slightly deeper on light soils.

Dwarf or 'fan types, suitable for small gardens, are sown in single rows, seeds 9 in/22.5 cm apart, rows 18 in/45 cm apart.

Quantity of seed
Small seedsman's packet sows 20 ft/6 m double row. Surplus seed may germinate following year, but is unreliable and should be tested.

Time to germination
14 - 24 days. Don't be alarmed if earliest sowing is slow to emerge.

Season of use
June - early August. Season is extended a week or so by cooking young pods whole before beans have fully developed, but this is not to everyone's taste.

Storage life in freezer
1 year. Beans must be frozen very young and before the skin toughens.

Crop for average family
A double row yields up to 1 lb per ft/500 g per m. One row is usually enough with other summer vegetables available.

Reliable varieties
For autumn sowing   Claudia Aquadulce (giant Seville). This variety is useless sown in spring.
For early spring sowing   Bunyard's Exhibition, Dreadnought, Imperial Green Longpod, Masterpiece.
For late spring sowing   Imperial Green Windsor, White Windsor, The Sutton (dwarf).

Caring for the crop
Pinch out the growing points when a reasonable number of pods has set to head off blackfly attack and hasten development of the pods. In an exposed position support tall-growing varieties by inserting stout canes at 6 ft/2 m intervals and stretching garden twine between them along both sides of the row.

For culinary applications see page 114

DWARF OR FRENCH BEANS

Characteristics
Tender. Unless protected by cloches must not be sown until a fortnight before latest expected spring frost. Not as productive as the runner bean but more reliable under drought conditions and in exposed northern districts.

Best soil
Succeeds on light soil better than any other leguminous plant. Dig in well-rotted manure or compost during the winter if you have it to spare and rake in a dressing of compound fertiliser before sowing. Remedy any lime deficiency.

When to sow
Under cloches in the first half of April, cloching the ground at least a week beforehand to warm it. In the open, sow at the end of April in early districts and the first week of May in late districts or in cold, late seasons.

Sow a double staggered row in a wide drill 1½ in/3.5 cm deep, spacing the seeds 4 in/10 cm apart. The drill is shallower than recommended for broad beans and the seeds closer. Germination is sometimes erratic if soil temperature is low and is improved if the beans are near the surface. Sow a batch at the end of the row for transplanting into gaps. Space rows of dwarf beans 24 in/60 cm apart and of climbing French beans 3 ft/1 m apart.

Quantity of seed
Large packet sows a 30 ft/9 m row. The sowing rate recommended is higher than that generally practised, the most common complaint about these beans being of poor results where the widely-spaced single row is sown. The crop from an over-full row is much larger than from an incomplete one.

Time to germination
14 - 21 days. After the latter period there is a chance that the seed may have rotted.

Season of use
June - August. Season may be prolonged to September by making a second sowing in June.

Storage life in freezer
One Year. A good subject for freezing if picked very young.

Crop for average family
A 30 ft/9 m row fills a midsummer gap between maincrop peas and runner beans. Don't sow more than this at one time unless you are prepared to deal with a glut of pods in hot weather.

Reliable varieties
For earliest sowing   Earligreen, Tendergreen (both recommended for freezing).
For heaviest crop   Masterpiece, The Prince, Glamis (the last was specially bred for cold northern districts).
Climbing French beans   Romano, Purple Podded, Earliest of All.
The climbing varieties are very productive if sown like dwarf beans and provided with canes about 4 ft/1.2 m tall.

Caring for the crop
Watch the emerging seedlings for slug damage and put down slug pellets. Hoe regularly and water in dry spells. When the pods form draw soil up to the stems to support the plants and prop up the pod clusters with branching twigs to keep them off the ground.

For culinary applications see page 115

GARDEN PEAS

Characteristics
The Garden or Green Pea is so called to distinguish it from the Sugar Pea or Mangetout. It is one of the most important summer vegetables and some varieties are hardy enough to be sown in autumn for an early crop. Tall varieties were formerly popular and were grown on 'pea-sticks' cut from hedges, but dwarf forms are now far more common and crop just as heavily.

Best soil
A medium to heavy soil, dug and manured early in the winter, gives the best results. The lighter the soil, the more organic material it needs for a really good crop. Rake in the standard dressing of compound fertiliser before sowing.

When to sow
Average dates are as follows: autumn, sow in October, cloche in November, or leave unprotected to take their chance. Early varieties in spring, under cloches in February and early March, in the open in March and early April. Maincrops, in April and May. Early variety for late cropping, in first half of June.

Sow in a wide drill 2 in/5 cm deep for early sowings and 3 in/7.5 cm deep for later ones. Scatter the seeds so that they lie about an inch apart but don't waste time placing them individually. Firm the soil gently after covering in the drill. Space rows 24 in/60 cm apart.

Quantity of seed
Average packet should sow a 30 ft/9 m row, but don't skimp on seed, a well-filled row gives a better return on time and cash than a gappy one. Seed may be viable in year following purchase but should be tested before sowing.

Time to Germination
10 - 17 days according to time of year. Protect from birds with black cotton or nylon netting.

Season of use
June - September from successive sowings.

Storage life in freezer
1 year. Only young peas can be successfully frozen.

Crop for average family
Reckon on ½ - 1 lb per ft/250 - 500 g per 30 cm of row, according to variety and season. Spread the season by choice of different varieties and allowing at least fortnightly intervals between sowings.

Reliable varieties
For sowing under cloches in autumn   Meteor, Feltham First, Sleaford Phoenix.
For spring sowing under cloches   Histon Mini, Hurst Beagle, Meteor.
For first sowing in the open   Any of the above, also Kelvedon Wonder, Pioneer, Pilot.
For maincrop sowings   Early Onward, Onward, Greenshaft, Victory Freezer.
For June sowing and sutumn crop   Kelvedon Wonder, Hurst Beagle.

Caring for the crop
In dry weather water thoroughly, driblets are worse than useless. Apply a peat or compost mulch while the soil is damp.

Varieties recommended are all dwarf, varying between 18 - 30 in/45 - 75 cm in height, but they need some support to prevent pods lying on the ground and rotting or suffering slug damage in wet weather. Place stout pegs or canes, of the same height as the peas are expected to reach, at intervals along both sides of the row. Stretch garden twine between them, enclosing the row in a string fence so that it cannot flop sideways. Three strings is usually enough, and canes and twine can be used for more than 1 season.

For culinary applications see page 115

63

RUNNER BEANS

Characteristics
Tender, must not be exposed to frost. Likes a sheltered position and is easily damaged by wind, which also discourages pollinating insects and delays setting of blooms. One of the most productive vegetables

Best soil
Treat runners generously. Mark off the site and dig in as much organic manure as possible during winter. Apply lime if necessary. Rake in the usual dressing of compound fertiliser when preparing the ground for sowing in spring.

When to sow
Sow in greenhouse or frame in April or early May if a temperature of 55°F/13° - 16°C is assured. Sow in seed boxes 3 in/7.5 cm deep in potting compost, beans 1 in/2.5 cm deep and 2 in/5 cm apart.

Sow under cloches in late April in narrow drills 12 in/30 cm apart and 2 in/5 cm deep. Space seeds 6 in/15 cm apart.

Sow in the open in mid-May, and for succession in mid-June, in the same way as under cloches. This produces a double row 12 in/30 cm wide, which is the most satisfactory when beans are staked. If more than one double row is grown the distance between them should be 6 ft/2 m for stick beans and 4 ft/1.2 m for 'ground' beans dwarfed by stopping the growths.

When to plant out
Plant out beans started under glass in late May or early June before they start to run up, spacing them as advised for seed.

Quantity of seed
Seed is expensive. A large packet sows a 20 ft/6 m row.

Time to germination
14 - 21 days.

Season of use
Late July - October.

Storage life in freezer
1 year. One of the best freezer vegetables.

Crop for average family
A 20 ft/6 m row can produce over 100 lb/45 kg but crop varies with the season.

Reliable varieties
Kelvedon Marvel (early but small), Streamline, Prizewinner, Enorma. A naturally dwarf form is Hammond's Dwarf Scarlet, which may be kept under cloches until almost in flower and produces long pods on a plant only 18 in/45 cm tall.

Caring for the crop
Water freely and feed with liquid fertiliser. Mulch with peat or garden compost. Spray flowers with water in the evening to encourage setting.
Method of staking   Use bamboos at least 6 ft/2 m tall and preferably 7 ft/2.5 m. They last for years if stored in the dry. Insert them in the ground 12 in/30 cm apart along both sides of the double row and about 3 in/7.5 cm clear of the plants. Bring each pair of canes from opposite sides together and tie them where they cross a few inches from the top. The row is now straddled by a series of canes forming inverted Vs. Lay horizontal canes along the top, resting on the point where the vertical canes cross, and tie them in position. At each end, run a length of twine from the end canes to a peg in the ground to act as a guy rope.

If you have no room for a continuous row, grow runners on 'wigwams' of canes in odd corners. 4 or more canes tied together at the top and 3 seeds or 2 plants set at the foot of each cane.

Ground beans are dwarfed by pinching out the growing point when about 12 in/30 cm tall. Laterals grow up and are similarly stopped, the row forming a bushy mass. In a dry season the method is satisfactory, though the pods are often short and curly. In wet weather they are affected by slug damage and decay.

For culinary applications see page 116

SUGAR PEAS

Characteristics
The edible-podded Sugar Pea or Mangetout is slightly more tender than the Garden Pea. It is not advisable to sow it too early or to waste cloches on its protection, since it is more of an 'extra' than a staple crop.

Best soil
The quality of Sugar Peas depends a lot on the quick growth of the pods, on poor soils they are often small and tough. On dry sands and chalks the plant is hardly worth growing, but on good soils and in districts with heavy summer rainfall it can produce a substantial crop. Prepare the ground as advised for garden peas.

When to sow
Any time in April. Sow in a wide drill 1 ½ in/3.5 cm deep, scattering the seed as advised for garden peas. Space rows 24 in/60 cm apart.

Quantity of seed
Average packet sows 20 ft/6 m row.

Time to germination
10-17 days. Protect seedlings with nylon net or black cotton, preferably just before they emerge. This is the crucial period for bird damage to both sugar and garden peas and prompt action is worth while.

Season of use
Late June - early August.

Storage life in freezer
1 year. Only flat young, tender pods are worth freezing.

Crop for average family
Even where the crop is appreciated, 1 row is sufficient.

Reliable varieties
Dwarf Sweetgreen, Carouby de Maussane. The latter, a French variety, is tall and needs the support of sticks or netting.

Caring for the crop
Treatment is the same as for garden peas. Correct harvesting is most important, especially in hot weather when the pods grow quickly. They must be picked while still flat and before the formation of seeds. Once the pods begin to bulge they acquire a tough lining and are uneatable.

For culinary applications see page 115

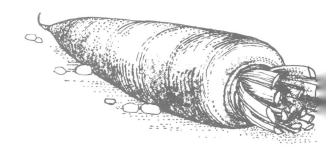

64

ROOT CROPS

They like: Deeply dug, well cultivated soil.
Lots of humus but no fresh manure.
Prompt thinning and proper spacing.
Careful harvesting for winter storage.

BEETROOT

Characteristics
Not fully hardy. Seedlings are damaged by spring frosts and cold spells cause bolting. Roots are also liable to frost damage and should not be left in the ground too late in autumn.

Best soil
Any soil in reasonably good heart. Peat or compost applied during winter digging is a great help on heavy and very light soils, but no fresh manure. Rake in a light dressing of general fertiliser 14 days before sowing.

When to sow
Late March under cloches, early April in early districts, late April in late ones. Don't be too early with these open air sowings. Late and successional sowings, May - early July. All in drills ½ - ¾ in/2 cm deep and 12 in/30 cm apart.

Quantity of seed
Average seedsman's packet sows about 25 ft/7 - 8 m of row.

Time to germination
10 - 17 days. Germination is quicker if seed is soaked for 12 hours before sowing.

Season of use
June - October from the ground, thereafter from store.

Storage life in freezer
8 months. Roots must be young and quite small.

Crop for average family
30 ft/9 m of row should yield 20 lb/10 kg of mature roots plus usuable thinnings. This is usually enough for the main sowing, with a small later one if desired.

Reliable varieties
Round varieties for first sowings   Boltardy, Avonearly, Early Bunch.
Good varieties for storage   Detroit, Crimson Globe.
For late sowing   Cylindra, Little Ball.

Caring for the crop
Beetroot seeds are in fact dried capsules each containing several true seeds so that the seedlings come up in little clumps, making singling a tedious finger-and-thumb job. It is now possible to buy monogerm seed producing only single seedlings.

The emerging seedlings are attractive to birds and an entire row may disappear very quickly. Keep watch for germination and protect with black cotton or nylon net.

Hoe and hand weed regularly and water when neccessary or the roots will be woody.

For culinary applications see page 116

CARROTS

Characteristics
Hardy. Survives spring frosts but is checked by severe ones. Valuable for late sowings in succession to main summer crops and for winter storage.

Best soil
Light land preferred if given adequate water. On heavy clays grow only stump-rooted varieties. Use no fresh manure but rake in general fertiliser at 3 oz per sq yd/100 g per sq m before sowing.

When to sow
Sow small quick-growing varieties in March under cloches and April in the open. Maincrops in April and May. Late crops in June and early July. All in drills ½ - ¾ in/2 cm deep and 12 in/30 cm apart.

Quantity of seed
Small seedsman's packet sows a row 30 ft/9 m long. Sow thinly or use pelleted seed spaced individually.

Time to germination
10 - 21 days. Rather slow in spring but quicker in summer if ground is kept moist.

Season of use
First pullings June onwards. Used from the ground until November and from store November to March.

Storage life in freezer
1 year. Only small roots are frozen.

Crop for average family
Equivalent of 2 30 ft/9m rows should yield enough for summer harvesting and storage. Don't make larger spring sowings in the medium-sized garden but sow after early potatoes or peas if more are wanted.

Reliable varieties
For earliest crops   Amsterdam Forcing, Early Nantes, Sweetheart, Chantenay.
On heavy soils   Early Scarlet Horn, Early Nantes.
Maincrop on deep soils   New Red Intermediate. James' Scarlet Intermediate.
For Freezing   Early Nantes, Sweetheart.

Caring for the crop
Thin the carrots by stages to 3 - 4 in/7.5 - 10 cm apart, starting as soon as the seedlings are large enough to handle. The later thinnings should be large enough to use or freeze. The destructive carrot fly is attracted to lay its eggs by the smell of the seedlings during thinning. Water the ground before starting, firm it round the remaining seedlings afterwards, and remove the pulled-up ones from the carrot bed. And, if possible, thin late in the evening when the flies are not around.

A late carrot bed may be sown broadcast and yield a large crop of small roots from a limited area. Mark out a strip 18 in/45 cm wide where a crop such as early potatoes was grown, rake it to a level tilth, and sprinkle the seed over it evenly and thinly. Rake the seed in or cover it lightly with fine soil. Keep watered, hand weed at least once, and start pulling the roots as soon as they reach usable size.

For culinary applications see page 116

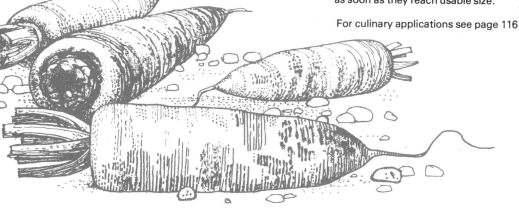

CELERIAC

Characteristics
An irregularly turnip-shaped root, celeriac has a strong celery flavour and is a useful celery substitute where celery is difficult to grow. It is used in cooking though less suitable for salads. It may be lifted and stored for winter.

Best soil
Quality depends upon soil fertility and moisture. Dig in manure, compost or even peat, and before planting rake in 4 oz per sq yd/133 g per sq m of general fertiliser. On thin chalk soils celeriac is not worth growing.

When to sow
In pans of seed compost in the greenhouse or frame when a temperature of 50°F/10°C minimum is obtained. Prick out as soon as seedlings can be handled and harden off in the frame or under cloches.

When to plant
May - July. Plant in wide, shallow drills 18 in/45 cm apart, with the plants 12 in/30 cm apart. Plant firmly with the little bulb at the base of the seedling just resting on the soil. Water, and keep watered.

Quantity of seed
Small packet yields at least 100 plants.

Time to germination
10 - 14 days in reasonable temperature.

Season of use
Autumn - spring.

Storage life in freezer
6 months. Useless as a salad when frozen.

Crop for average family
Not more than 1 row (20 - 30 good-sized roots) usually needed.

Reliable variety
The variety Globus is the only choice for performance and quality fresh or frozen.

Caring for the crop
The object of planting in a drill is to make watering easier, flood the drill frequently in dry weather. Give occasional feeds of liquid fertiliser if the crop 'stands still'. Remove all suckers and shoots arising from the root.

For culinary applications see page 117

JERUSALEM ARTICHOKES

Characteristics
Very hardy. Knobbly tubers and tall, fast-growing stems. Unfailing cropper and provides useful summer screen for shed or compost heap.

Best soil
Any soil will do but tubers are larger in a good one. Usually grown in an odd corner and not in main vegetable plot as small tubers are always left in the ground and come up year after year.

When to plant
Mid-February - mid-March. Plant in trench 4 in/10 cm deep, tubers 12 in/30 cm apart. If you want more than 1 row, space them 3 ft/1 m apart.

Quantity of seed tubers
About 2 lb/1 kg of tubers is needed for a row 20 ft/6 m long. Not all seedsmen stock tubers and it is easier to buy them from the greengrocer. There are no named varieties.

Time to emergence
20 - 30 days. They never fail.

Season of use
Autumn - spring. Tubers are left in the ground and dug as required.

Storage life in freezer
3 months. Only worth freezing in early spring to prolong the season by preserving the remains of the crop.

Crop for average family
1 row (2 - 3 lb/1 - 1.5 kg of seed tubers) yields 15 - 20 lb/ 7.5 - 10 kg and few families eat more.

Reliable varieties
No named varieties.

Caring for the crop
Little attention is needed apart from early weeding. Later, the crop outgrows most weeds. The tall stems are liable to wind damage and in an exposed position should be supported by a wire stretched between posts about 4 ft/1.2 m above the ground.

When the leaves fall the stems are cut to within a few inches of the ground and left to mark the site of the tubers. Digging them is awkward in severe weather and if spare cloches are available they should be placed over the row.

For culinary applications see page 117

ONIONS / GROWING FROM SEED

Characteristics
Hardy, and some soils may be sown in autumn to get an early start in spring, though few gardeners now do this. Requires a completely open site with full sun to ripen the bulbs.
Best soil
Best results are obtained from soil well cultivated and manured over a period. It should be firm with a good tilth for sowing. Dig early in winter to allow time for it to settle and the surface to weather. Don't use organic manure unless very well rotted. Rake in 3 oz per sq yd/100 g per sq m of compound fertiliser before sowing.
When to sow
Early March if soil and weather permit. Tread the bed firm (but only if the surface is dry) and sow in very shallow drills 12 in/30 cm apart. The thread-like looped-over seed leaf is fragile and a fine soil is essential for good germination.
Quantity of seed
Average seedsman's packet sows 20 - 30 ft/7 - 9 m of row, according to thickness of sowing. Some gardeners sow thickly to have plenty of 'spring' onions, but this is bad practice and may reduce the eventual crop for storage.
Time to germination
21 days. Last year's seed will sometimes germinate normally but this is a gamble.
Season of use
July onwards from ground and store. Keeping time in winter depends upon ripening and correct storage (see Harvesting and Storing Crops pages 46/47).
Storage life in freezer
2 months. Usually only frozen chopped or sliced to have ready for use.
Crop for average family
Yields vary greatly with the season. A total row length of 60 ft/18 m can usually be relied upon for a crop of 30 lb/15 kg.
Reliable varieties
Globe-shaped   Bedfordshire Champion, James' Long Keeping, Red Globe.
Flat   Ailsa Craig, Giant Zittau (outstanding keeping qualities).

Caring for the crop
Thin to 4 - 6 in/10 - 15 cm, the wider spacing if you hope for large bulbs. Some thinnings are useful as spring onions, but don't keep crowded rows for the sake of the salad bowl. Thin the main crop and grow spring onions separately (see Salad Onions page 75). Thin when the soil is moist, firm up round the remaining plants and remove all thinnings from the bed. The scent entices the onion fly to lay its eggs.
Hand weed the rows and hoe carefully between them. This is really a job for the short-handled onion hoe, always useful in a restricted space close to small, delicate seedlings.

For culinary applications see page 117

ONIONS / GROWING FROM SETS

Characteristics
Sets are immature onion bulbs grown from seed the previous year under crowded conditions. When planted in spring they continue to develop and eventually make full-sized bulbs.
Best soil
Same as for seed-grown onions. A deep tilth is needed - 1 in/2.5 cm of friable topsoil - so that the set may be firmly planted.
When to plant
April. Sets are ready to harvest more quickly than onions and a very long growing season is unnecessary. Wait until the soil has warmed and rooting takes place quickly. Plant 4 - 6 in/10 - 15 cm apart in rows 12 in/30 cm apart. Take out a shallow drill, press the set into the soil at the bottom (making sure it is the right way up) and draw the soil back, leaving the neck of the set just showing.
Quantity of sets
Sets vary in size and 1 lb/500 g may contain from 120 to 200, planting a row length of 40 - 100 ft/12 - 29 m. Sets are now available in packs guaranteed to plant a specified length of row and this is the best way to buy.
Time to starting growth
14 - 21 days according to temperature.
Season of use
As for seed-grown. Onions from sets keep just as well if fully ripened.
Crop for average family
As suggested for seed-grown onions. As sets take less from the soil you might obtain a larger crop of medium-sized bulbs by slightly closer planting.
Reliable varieties
Stuttgarter (flat), Rijnsburger Wijbo (Giant Fen Globe), Sturon Autumn Gold (half-round).
Heat-treated sets give the best performance.

Caring for the crop
General cultivation is the same as for the seed-grown crop, the only differences being in the early stages. There is no thinning to do, but the sets must be watched after planting to ensure that they are not disturbed. They are sometimes pulled out of the ground before having a chance to root and although birds are always blamed, the trouble is often due to earthworms, which try to drag the top of the set into the ground. After a mild, damp night, sets may be found lying on the surface, sometimes in groups, and this is typical of earthworms. Before planting, trim off pieces of dried stem at the neck of the sets, plant very firmly, and leave only the tip protruding. As the set grows, scrape the soil away from round the top of the bulb.

For culinary applications see page 117

PARSNIPS

Characteristics
Very hardy. One of the earliest crops to be sown and usually left in the ground all winter and dug as required. An easy crop, but likes a long season of growth.

Best soil
Long varieties need a deep, open soil. Short ones succeed on shallow or heavy soil but it must have been well dug in winter. No manure or compost is used, but a light dressing of general fertiliser should be raked in before sowing.

When to sow
As early in March as soil and weather conditions permit. Get as good a tilth as possible and sow thinly in drills 1 in/2.5 cm deep and 15 in/37.5 cm apart. Hold the hand close to the ground when sowing in windy weather as the seed is very light and easily blown away.

Quantity of seed
Average seedsman's packet sows 20 - 30 ft/7 - 9 m of row. Don't save left-over seed, it rarely germinates well.

Season of use
October - April. Roots are left in the ground until early March but should be lifted and stored in a cool shed when the tops begin to grow as this make them inedible. Immature roots are not used in the summer, and freezer storage is generally regarded as a waste of space.

Crop for average family
One good row, yielding up to 4 lb per yd/2 kg per m is enough for most families.

Reliable varieties
On shallow or very heavy soils   Offenham, Avonresister.
Long-rooted for deep soils   The Student, Tender and True.

Caring for the crop
Parsnips need little care apart from thinning and weeding. Thin as early as possible to 4 - 6 in/10 - 15 cm apart and keep the hoe going close to the row.

The parsnip is not among the popular vegetables, which is a pity. Not only is it highly nutritious, its distinctive semi-sweet flavour brings variety to winter menus. If a few roots are left in the ground when growth recommences in spring the young leaves will be found to taste rather like celery and may be used in salads.

For culinary applications see page 118

POTATOES, EARLY

Characteristics
All potatoes are tender and both plant and tubers are damaged or destroyed by frost. The early crop is most at risk, being planted at the earliest possible date for digging when new potatoes are most expensive. In small gardens, only earlies are worth growing, in larger ones some space may be allotted to the less valuable maincrops.

Best soil
Potatoes grow in any soil, doing best in those rich in humus and worst in shallow chalky types. A soil well manured for the preceding crop but containing no fresh organic manure is suitable. Peat is a useful material to increase the humus content and improve the quantity and quality of tubers. Line the bottom of the planting trench with peat and cover each tuber with a double handful. Apply 2 oz per yd/66 g per m of general fertiliser along the trench after the potatoes are covered with peat and before filling in.

When to plant
Late March - mid-April according to likelihood of spring frosts in your district. Plant in trenches taken out with spade 5 in/12.5 cm deep. Space tubers 12 in/30 cm apart and rows 24 in/60 cm apart. Leave soil loose when filling in.

Quantity of seed tubers
5 lb/2.5 kg of tubers plants 30 ft/9 m of row if they are ideal hen's egg size. Order tubers early and stand upright in seed boxes in light, frost-free place to sprout.

Time to emergence
20 - 25 days. Where May frosts are possible nothing is gained by planting before mid-April.

Season of use
June - August. Tubers may be lifted and stored when tops die off.

Storage life in freezer
1 year, but much less if cooked. Only small, high quality new potatoes are worth freezing.

Crop for average family
A 30 ft/9 m row yields upwards of 15 lb/7.5 kg, depending on the season and how early you start digging. 2 rows should supply a family of 4 over the high-priced period.

Reliable varieties
Epicure, Arran Pilot (both recover well after frost), Home Guard, Foremost. The last takes full marks for yield and quality, though not among the earliest.

Caring for the crop
Cover the young shoots with soil if night frost seems likely. When about 6 in/15 cm tall earth them up, drawing soil up to the row, first along one side, then the other, to form a ridge. This gives the tubers more protection from light, which turns them green, and gives the plants added depth of soil for root and tuber formation. Hand weed and hoe until plants meet in the rows.

For culinary applications see page 118

POTATOES, MAINCROP

Characteristics
Chief differences between early and maincrop are that the latter crop more heavily, keep better through the winter and have a longer growing season.

Best soil
Soil requirements are the same as for earlies but the crop makes greater demands. Dig thoroughly in winter, applying well rotted manure or compost if available, but avoid fresh manure or nitrogenous organics such as dried poultry manure. Use peat and a general fertiliser at planting as advised for earlies. Potatoes are a fine crop for newly-dug grassland, the planting, earthing up and digging of the crop moving the soil repeatedly and cleaning the ground of weeds. Take precautions against wireworms on new ground (see Pests and Other Troubles, pages 42/43).

When to plant
April - early May. Don't risk frost damage by planting too early. Plant as advised for earlies, but spacing the tubers 15 in/ 37.5 cm apart and the rows 27 in/67.5 cm apart.

Quantity of seed tubers
Same as for earlies. Some tubers may be larger, giving fewer per lb but maincrop seed tubers may be cut in 2 if larger than average. At one end of the tuber - the 'rose end' is a cluster of shoots. Cut lengthwise so that each half retains a few of these shoots. Plant immediately after cutting, cut surface downwards, and ensure that the shoots are covered with peat to prevent breakage when filling in.

Time to emergence
21 days.

Season of use
August to following June.

Crop for average family
Upwards of 30 lb/15 kg may be expected from a 30 ft/9 m row, much more in a good season. Don't aim at self-sufficiency in potatoes at the expense of other and more valuable crops.

Reliable varieties
For top quality   King Edward, Majestic, Golden Wonder. The last is of exceptional flavour but moderate yield and needs more generous treatment than most.
For average quality and high yield   Pentland Crown, Pentland Dell, Desirée.

Caring for the crop
If growth is unsatisfactory in the early stages a light top dressing of general fertiliser can be applied before earthing up, but if the recommended dressing was used at planting this should not be neccessary.
    Earth up into a fuller ridge than for earlies, the larger tubers are ruined by greening if they poke through the soil.

For culinary applications see page 118

SHALLOTS

Characteristics
A very hardy, mild-flavoured member of the onion family. Planted as a bulb, the shallot differs from the onion set in that it does not increase in size when planted but divides into a cluster of small bulbs which then grow to the size of the parent.

Best soil
Because it is hardy and long-suffering, the shallot is often grown under poor conditions in the certainty of some sort of a crop. If planted on good soil, prepared as advised for onions, it makes better use of the space occupied and yields larger bulbs of better shape and quality.

When to plant
There is a saying to the effect that shallots should be planted on the shortest day and harvested on the longest. This is hardly practicable, but they may certainly be planted in February or March as soon as the ground is workable. Plant 8 in/20 cm apart in rows 18 in/45 cm apart, pushing the bulb in so that only the neck shows and making the soil firm around it. Inspect a week after planting to make sure that none has been disturbed by birds or earthworms.

Quantity of bulbs
A 2 lb or 1 kg pack should be ample for a 30 ft/9 m row. Choose large, round bulbs rather than small, angular ones.

Time to starting growth
14 days to rooting. Top growth begins to appear a week later.

Season of use
August - March.

Storage life in freezer
Shallots are not normally frozen. If properly ripened they store very well naturally and are of course widely used in pickles.

Crop for average family
This must depend on whether onions are also grown or whether they are not successful in the garden and shallots are grown as a substitute. The yield is about 10 times the weight of the bulbs planted.

Reliable varieties
Yellow Dutch, Red Dutch. Except in colour, there is little difference.

Caring for the crop
Shallots like a position in full sun. Keep them free of weeds and hoe frequently between rows and plants. Maintain a friable surface around the bulbs when they begin to split and form clumps so that there is no resistance to their expansion. A hard, compacted soil means small, badly-shaped shallots. Lift when the foliage dies down in late July, dry the clumps in the sun for a few days, separate the bulbs and trim off dead tops before storing as advised for onions.

For culinary applications see page 118

SWEDES

Characteristics
The swede is a larger and sweeter version of the turnip. It is hardy, but is usually sown later than the turnip because small, immature roots are not eaten during the summer. There is usually only 1 sowing and that is grown on to mature in the autumn.

Best soil
A well-dug soil manured for a previous crop but containing no fresh manure is suitable. If it is at all acid, dress with 6 oz per sq yd/200 g per sq m of garden lime after winter digging. Rake in general fertiliser at 3 oz per sq yd/100 g per sq m before sowing.

When to sow
Late April - early June. Earlier sowings are more likely to suffer from mildew in the summer. Sow in drills 1 in/2.5 cm deep and 18 in/45 cm apart. Soak the drills before sowing in dry weather.

Quantity of seed
Small packet sows 30 ft/9 m of row. Seed keeps several years.

Time to germination
5 - 10 days. Very quick in warm weather.

Season of use
October - April. A valuable winter crop.

Storage life in freezer
1 year. Storage without freezing is quite satisfactory for winter use, but a supply of frozen purée extends the season.

Crop for average family
One 30 ft/9 m row, yielding up to 25 lb/12.5 kg is usually ample.

Reliable varieties
Western Perfection, Best of All. Sow the first in May, the second in June.

Caring for the crop
Thin early to 9 in/22.5 cm apart. Keep weeded and hoed and water in dry weather. Garden varieties are not as large as those grown for fodder, but when well grown should be considerably larger than turnips. Good-sized roots in autumn are attained by rapid growth and are indicative of quality. Small, tough specimens result from overcrowding, competition with weeds and lack of water.

For culinary applications see page 119

TURNIPS

Characteristics
Hardy. Able to survive the winter if left in the ground and provide useful spring greens when growth starts again.

Best soil
Any good soil not deficient in lime. Heavy soils yield good crops after being manured for previous plantings but fresh manure should not be applied for turnips. For the main sowing rake in 3 oz per sq yd/100 g per sq m of compound fertiliser. No fertiliser needed for later crops following peas, beans or potatoes.

When to sow
March - April for early pulling. April - May for maincrops. June - July for small roots in autumn and turnip tops in spring. All in drills 1/2 - 3/4 in/2 cm deep and 12 in/30 cm apart, though the final sowing may be broadcast as described for carrots.

Quantity of seed
Average packet sows at least 30 ft/9 m of row. Left-over seed need not be wasted as it remains viable for several years.

Time to germination
5 - 14 days. Summer sowings germinate very quickly.

Season of use
June to late autumn from the ground. Throughout winter from store.

Storage life in freezer
1 year. Only young, mild-flavoured roots should be frozen.

Crop for average family
Yield of mature roots should be about 1 lb per ft/500 g per 30 cm of row after small roots have been used during thinning. 1 row sown in spring plus a late sowing is usually adequate.

Reliable varieties
For early sowing   Snowball, White Milan, Tokyo Cross. For maincrop and late sowing   Golden Ball, Purple Milan, Green Top Stone.
The yellow-fleshed Golden Ball is of outstanding quality. Green Top Stone is recommended for overwintering in the ground to provide 'turnip tops'.

Caring for the crop
Early and systematic thinning is essential. Crowded turnips run to leaf rather than root. Hoe and hand weed, especially in the early stages.

A strip sown broadcast as suggested for carrots not only provides small roots during a mild winter but is a useful insurance against a lack of green vegetables after a severe one. The insurance is more complete if the strip is cloched at the beginning of a hard spell.

For culinary applications see page 119

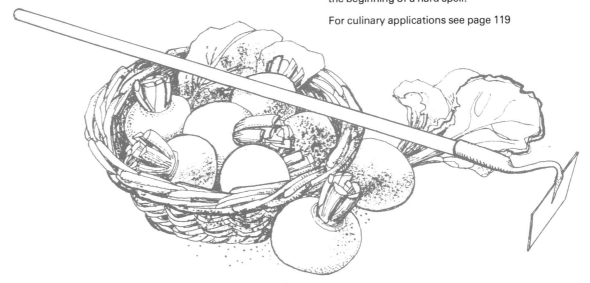

SALAD CROPS
They like: Conditions making for quick growth.
Organic manures rather than fertilisers.
An unfailing supply of moisture.

CELERY

Characteristics
There are two distinct types. Blanching or trenching celery is grown in a trench, earthed up and used in late autumn and winter. Self blanching varieties are grown on the flat, not earthed up and are used in late summer and autumn. The crop is not fully hardy and seedlings are raised under glass.

Best soil
Well-manured and moist. Wild celery is a ditch plant. For blanching celery take out a trench 1 spit deep and 15 in/37.5 cm wide. Dig manure or compost into the bottom well in advance of planting. Throw the excavated soil into a flat-topped ridge beside the trench and grow catch crops on it. Dig in manure for self blanching celery, and rake in a light pre-planting dressing of compound fertiliser for both this and blanching varieties.

When to sow
In the greenhouse in March if some warmth is available, prick out 2 in/5 cm apart as soon as the seedlings can be handled. Harden off in the frame or under cloches. If you have no glass, buy plants in June.

When to plant out
Late May - early July. Plant blanching varieties in a single row in the trench, 9 in/22.5 cm apart. Plant self blanching varieties 9 in/22.5 cm apart in short rows, also 9 in/22.5 cm apart, to form a block of plants sheltering each other. Keep soil round the roots and water the plants in.

Quantity of seed
Small packet. Viability of surplus seed, 2 - 3 years.

Time to germination
14 - 21 days. Don't be impatient.

Season of use
August - December for self blanching varieties, October - February for trench-grown. Self blanching celery will not stand hard frost.

Storage life in freezer
1 year. It cannot be frozen raw and used as a salad.

Crop for average family
24 plants of a self-blanching variety for use from August to November, and the same number of trench-grown to continue the crop until February.

Reliable varieties
Blanching or trenching varieties   White Ice, Giant White, Giant Pink.
Self blanching varieties   Avon Pearl, Greensnap, Golden Self Blanching.

Caring for the crop
Water freely throughout the summer. Give an occasional feed of liquid fertiliser. Begin earthing up trench-grown plants in mid-August. Gather the stems of each plant together and tie loosely just below the leaves. Draw in soil from the ridge, packing it carefully around the plants to halfway up the stems. Repeat this twice at monthly intervals until only a tuft of leaves is visible and the trench has become a ridge.

For culinary applications see page 119

CHICORY

Characteristics
The chicory plant is a native of Britain, growing wild on chalk soils. It is a biennial, establishing itself in the first season, dying down, and shooting up again the following year. In the cultivated form this new shoot is blanched by being grown in the dark and is used as a winter salad.

Best soil
Ordinary garden soil is all that is needed, provided it is thoroughly dug to permit good root development and is not short of lime.

When to sow
June. Earlier sowings result in a high proportion of bolters, which are useless. Sow in shallow drills 12 in/30 cm apart, watering before sowing in dry weather. Thin the seedlings to 9 in/22.5 cm.

Quantity of seed
Small packet. Viability of seed is doubtful, buy fresh each year.

Time to germination
10 - 12 days. The seedlings are bitter and rarely attacked by birds or slugs.

Season of use
The winter months. Most valuable in January and February when salad material is scarce.

Storage life in freezer
6 months. Cannot be used as a salad after freezing, but delicious as a cooked vegetable.

Crop for average family
Treat it as a sideline to fill any small area not required for a major crop from June onwards.

Reliable varieties
Witloof (White Loaf) is the almost universally grown Belgian varity. A recent introduction is the pink-tinted Red Verona.

Caring for the crop
The growing plants need little attention beyond routine weeding and watering. Lift the roots in November, avoiding damage. Trim off the tops *above* the crown and place them upright in a trench just covered with soil and a layer of peat or straw to keep the surface unfrozen.
Forcing   Lift a few roots at a time, stand them upright in a large pot and pack a mixture of soil, sand and peat round them so that their tops are just level with the surface. Cover with a light-tight box or another large pot and place in a cellar, cupboard or under the greenhouse stage. Keep moist and in a temperature of 50°F/10°C or a little higher. The heads or chicons of tightly packed leaves may not equal the imported product, but provided they are grown in complete darkness they will be very acceptable in midwinter.

For culinary applications see page 120

CUCUMBERS, GREENHOUSE

Characteristics
A tender plant, thriving in a temperature between 60° - 70°F/ 16° - 21°C and a humid atmosphere. This temperature level must be assured before seed is sown, so an early start is not practicable in the average amateur greenhouse. In summer, however, cucumbers grown and fruit very quickly.

Best soil
For each plant allow a large pailful of prepared soil. This may consist of 1/3 garden soil, 1/3 compost or rotted manure, and 1/3 peat. To each pailful add a good handful of John Innes Base and mix thoroughly. Alternatively, use John Innes Potting No 3. Arrange the soil in mounds on the border, 4 ft/ 1.2 m apart, or fill boxes or large pots with it and stand them that distance apart on the staging.

When to sow
In most cases it is not advisable to sow until May, but if considerable heat is available or the plants can be started in a heated propagator, sow in April. Use peat pots filled with seed compost and sow 2 or 3 seeds per pot, pushing them edgeways into the compost to a depth of ¾ in/2 cm. Keep moist and as warm as possible until germination.

When to plant out
Plant when 2 to 4 true leaves have developed and before the seedling is pot-bound or has a lot of roots showing through the sides of the peat pot. Plant 1 on each mound or in each box or pot. Water in and shade from direct sun for a few days. If you do not raise plants, order them from a nursery well in advance of the planting date. Only a limited number of greenhouse varieties are produced.

Quantity of seed
Small packet, but left-over seeds remain viable for several years.

Time to germination
5 - 7 days in warm conditions. Quick germination means robust seedlings.

Season of use
July - October.

Storage life in freezer
Cannot be frozen.

Crop for average family
2 or 3 plants is the maximum for a small greenhouse containing tomatoes or other crops. A properly trained cucumber occupies as much space as 3 tomato plants.

Reliable varieties
The best variety for the cold or cool house is Conqueror. The variety Femina produces practically all female flowers and the fruits are not spoiled by being fertilised, but it needs a slightly higher temperature than Conqueror.

Caring for the crop
Cucumbers dislike strong, direct sunlight but if the house contains tomatoes it should not be shaded. Plant the cucumbers where they will themselves be shaded by the tomatoes.

Provide each cucumber plant with a cane or wire from ground to roof and horizontal wires 12 in/30 cm apart. Train the main stem up the vertical support, stop it when it reaches the roof, and train the laterals along the wires. Stop each fruit-bearing shoot 2 leaves beyond the fruit. Remove all the male blooms you can to prevent fertilisation. The female blooms are distinguished by baby cucumbers just behind the flowers, male blooms have only stalks. The fruit develops without fertilisation, and if the bloom is fertilised the cucumber forms seeds and become club-shaped, 'bull-necked' and bitter. The trouble may be avoided by growing an all-female variety such as Femina, but it may not crop quite so well as other varieties in a cold house.

For culinary applications see page 120

CUCUMBERS, OUTDOOR

Characteristics
The outdoor or ridge cucumber (so called because it was traditionally grown on a raised bed of manure) is tender and cannot stand frost. It has been extensively hybridised and the fruits of some modern varieties are equal to those grown in the greenhouse.

Best soil
Prepare planting sites 3 ft/1 m apart if the plants are to grow on the ground, and half that distance if they are to be trained up a fence, trellis or other support. Dig deeply to ensure good drainage, mix a pailful of manure or compost with the soil at each site and make it into a low mound 12 in/30 cm across. Choose the sunniest and most sheltered positions available for the sites.

When to sow
Sow under glass in early May if a minimum temperature of 55° - 60°F/13° - 16°C can be maintained. Sow 2 or 3 seeds to a small peat pot and reduce to 1 seedling if more than 1 germinates. Alternatively, sow 3 seeds on each planting site in early June, scooping out a depression on the mound and filling it with seed compost to ensure a good start. Sow ¾ in/2 cm deep, cover the sowings with flower pots at night to conserve warmth, and reduce to a single seedling per mound on germination.

When to plant out
Plant glass-raised plants, home grown or bought, in the first half of June. In late districts mid-June is early enough, cucumbers make no progress until soil and air temperatures reach an acceptable level. Plant with care, avoiding damage to roots. Scatter slug pellets between plants immediately after planting or emergence of seedlings. Young plants are very vulnerable to attack by slugs.

Quantity of seed
Small packet provides more plants than usually required. Surplus seed is viable for several years.

Time to germination
7 - 10 days if temperature remains above 55°F/12°C.

Season of use
August - October.

Storage life in freezer
Cannot be frozen.

Crop for average family
2 - 6 plants, giving a yield of up to 10 fruits per plant, occupy as much space as the crop merits.

Reliable varieties
Ordinary varieties   Bedfordshire Ridge, Baton Vert.
Long Japanese varieties   Kaga, Kyoto.
Extra-digestible varieties   Burpless Early, Burpless Green King, Burpless Tasty Green.

Caring for the crop
Water freely in dry weather at a little distance from the stem. The object of planting on a mound is to ensure drainage and prevent over-wet conditions leading to stem rot. Stop the plant when it has 6 leaves and allow the subsequent laterals to grow on the ground or train them up supports. A lateral reaching 8 leaves without fruiting should also be stopped and a sub-lateral from it allowed to develop.

For culinary applications see page 120

ENDIVE

Characteristics
An autumn and early winter salad, bitter in its natural state but better than an indifferent lettuce when blanched. It is slowly becoming more popular, though still much less so than on the Continent. The amateur grower often encounters difficulties over blanching it in the autumn.

Best soil
Soil requirements are the same as for lettuce - plenty of organic matter to hold the moisture and a light dressing of compound fertiliser. Good drainage is important as wet soil conditions may lead to rotting of leaves during blanching.

When to sow
June or July. Sow in a drill ¾ in /2 cm deep, placing a few seeds at 12 in/30 cm intervals. Reduce each group of seedlings to one as they grow. Keep well watered in dry weather, especially in the early stages.

Quantity of seed
Seedsman's packet contains enough for a 30 ft/9 m row. Seed should remain viable for a second year.

Time to germination
10 days.

Season of use
November - February.

Storage life in freezer
Cannot be successfully frozen.

Crop for average family
Not more than 20 plants should be grown at the first attempt. When the technique of blanching has been mastered more may be attempted in subsequent years.

Reliable varieties
Moss-curled and Batavian or Broad-leaved. The former has curled, divided and very crisp leaves, but is less easy to grow than the Batavian.

Caring for the crop
General culture is the same as for lettuces, aimed at maintaining rapid growth by watering in dry weather and giving an occasional liquid feed if necessary.

Before blanching, clean the row of weeds, make sure that the plants are nowhere crowded together, and lightly hoe the soil between them. Cover them with light-tight boxes or large flower pots with the drainage holes plugged. If you have cloches to spare cover the row and exclude light by covering the cloches with black polythene sheet weighted down at the sides. The blanching method sometimes suggested, of gathering the leaves together and tying them, is likely to lead to the decay of the plant in a wet autumn. The foliage should be kept dry during blanching.

For culinary applications see page 120

LETTUCE

Characteristics
Some varieties are hardy enough to live through the winter with or without cloche protection and produce an early spring crop. Summer varieties are sown from March onwards to crop from June to October. Lettuces are also subdivided into **round or cabbage** types with soft leaves and solid hearts, **cos** lettuce with long, crisp leaves, **crinkled** varieties with crisp, curly leaves, and **loose-leaved**, which have no heart and can be used a few leaves at a time without cutting the whole plant.

Best soil
It must contain plenty of organic matter, more to hold moisture than for its manurial value. For summer lettuce dig in compost during the winter, rake to a fine tilth before sowing, incorporating 1 oz per sq yd/33 g per sq m of compound fertiliser. There would not be time for heavier doses of fertilisers to be taken up by summer lettuce and they would be wasted. Winter lettuce should succeed runner beans or potatoes without additional manuring.

When to sow
For an outdoor spring crop, sow in September. For a cloche spring crop sow in early October and cloche immediately. For crops from June to October, sow at 3 weekly intervals from late March to early July. Choose suitable varieties from those listed below.

Sow in drills about ½ in/1.25 cm deep and 12 in/30 cm apart. Bring the soil to a fine tilth, water the drills before sowing in dry weather and firm the surface after sowing. Space pelleted seeds 1 in/2.5 cm apart and sow non-pelleted seed very thinly. Protect uncloched sowings from birds.

Quantity of seed
Average packet sows a 20 - 30 ft/6 - 9 m row. Buy the smallest available packets of several varieties for successional sowing in spring and summer.

Time to germination
7 - 14 days.

Season of use
Autumn-sown, April - June. Spring and summer-sown, June - October. Season may be prolonged into December if last summer sowing is cloched.

Storage life in freezer
Lettuce cannot be frozen.

Crop for average family
30 ft/9 m row yields some 40 heads plus salading from thinnings. Lettuce run to seed if not used. Sow successive short rows in spring and summer.

Reliable varieties
For autumn sowing   Under cloches: May King, Attractive (cabbage), Little Gem (cos). In the open: Winter Density (cos), Artic King, Unrivalled (cabbage).
For early spring sowing   All The Year Round, Tom Thumb, Avon Defiance (cabbage), Lobjoit's Green (cos).
For late spring sowing   Continuity (cabbage), Webb's Wonderful (crinkled), Salad Bowl (loose-leaved).
For August sowing and November maturing under cloches Kwiek, Tom Thumb (cabbage).

Caring for the crop
Do not thin autumn-sown crops until spring. Thin all sowings to a final distance of 9 - 12 in/22.5 - 30 cm for most varieties, but to 6 - 8 in/15 - 20 cm for Little Gem and Tom Thumb. Thinning is much easier if pelleted seed is used and sown 1 in/2.5 cm apart. The final thinnings are usable in salads.

Keep the soil uniformly moist for summer lettuce, watering daily if necessary, and for May and June sowings rely on the variety Continuity, which stands for a long time without bolting.

For culinary applications see page 121

MUSTARD AND CRESS

Characteristics
The most quickly produced green salad, and probably the only crop consisting of nothing but seed leaves. Home grown mustard and cress is far superior to the bought product, which contains no cress and in which even the mustard is usually the coarser rape.

Best soil
Mustard and cress are grown indoors in shallow containers and the only really essential feature of the growing medium is that it should remain moist. However, better results are nearly always obtained from soil or soil-less compost than from soaked blotting paper or tissues.

When to sow
Any time. Fill a plastic pan or seed tray to within ¾ in/2 cm of the top with seed compost and make it firm and level. Moisten it before sowing. Sprinkle equal amounts of mustard and cress seed thickly over the surface pressing it down lightly but not covering it with compost. Cover the pan with a sheet of cardboard and keep in a warm place for 48 hours. If the seed has then germinated, remove the covering and leave in moderate light for 24 hours. Then move to a light window-sill for 1 - 2 days before cutting. Keep the compost moist at all times. Ignore the traditional advice to sow cress earlier than mustard, there is frequently no difference in germination times.

Quantity of seed
Buy both by the ounce. Seed remains good for 2 years.

Time to germination
24 - 36 hours.

Season of use
All the year round.

Crop for average family
An 8 in/20 cm diameter seed pan yields twice as much as the average retail carton. Allow 4 - 5 days from sowing to cutting.

Reliable varieties
No distinct varieties, but see that you buy genuine White Mustard.

Caring for the crop
A moderate temperature of between 60° - 70°F/16° - 21°C gives the best results. Average room temperatures are right for winter sowings but don't place the seed pan directly over a radiator or on top of a storage heater. Transfer to full light when the seed leaves have expanded and there is a fair length of stem.

For culinary applications see page 121

RADISHES

Characteristics
Radishes grow easily and quickly when sown in spring and early autumn. They like damp conditions and moderate temperatures, radishes grown under hot, dry conditions are themselves hot and dry.

Best soil
Any good garden soil, the only preparation required being the forking in of some peat or compost on sandy or chalky soils to retain moisture. Try to get a good fine tilth a few inches deep.

When to sow
March - September in the open, February - September under cloches. Sow in shallow drills 6 in/15 cm apart, very thinly and thinning the seedlings to 1 in/2.5 cm apart at the first opportunity.

Quantity of seed
It pays to buy seed by the ounce if you intend to make successional sowings. Seed remains viable for 3 - 4 years.

Time to germination
5 - 8 days.

Season of use
April - October from successional sowings made every few weeks.

Crop for average family
Sowings should be adjusted to demand. It is unwise to sow more than about 6 ft/2 m of row at any 1 time as roots soon become tough and hot if not used.

Reliable varieties
Sparkler, Saxa, Cherry Belle, French Breakfast. The first is perhaps the fastest growing, the last, a red and white oval variety is the best for quality and stands longest without deterioration.

Caring for the crop
Given a passable soil and plenty of moisture radishes should be the simplest of crops to grow. Failure is almost always the result of overcrowding, which produces more top than root. Keep every radish at least 1 in/2.5 cm from every other radish and they will all be usable.

For culinary applications see page 121

SALAD ONIONS

Characteristics
Thinnings from the main crop of bulb onions provide 'spring' or salad onions for a short time in early summer, but too much dependence on this source leads to the rows being left overcrowded. Where salad onions are popular it is better to make successional sowings of suitable varieties. The crop is not truly hardy but late sowings for early spring usually survive the winter under cloches and, on light soils, in the open.

Best soil
Any good garden soil if well cultivated. That manured for a previous crop gives the best results.

When to sow
In March, and at monthly intervals for a continuous supply. For early spring use sow in mid-August and if possible cloche in September. Sow fairly thickly in shallow drills 9 in/22.5 cm apart.

Quantity of seed
Buy ½ oz/16 g if offered in quantity and you intend to make several sowings. Seed more than a year old is unreliable. Surplus seed of bulb varieties may be sown for salad onions.

Time to germination
21 days.

Season of use
March - December with cloche protection. Otherwise, May - December with cloche protection. Otherwise, May - October.

Crop for average family
½ oz/16 g of seed sows 40 ft/12 m of row, yielding 30 - 50 retail bunches. A crop for odd corners as they become available rather than a continuous row.

Reliable varieties
White Lisbon or White Spanish. Plants of these varieties not used as salad may be grown on for use as bulb onions. They are mild flavoured, reach a good size, but will not keep.

Caring for the crop
Little work is entailed apart from routine weeding and watering when necessary. The overwintered crop is often affected by poor drainage or by mildew caused by continuously wet foliage. Cloches ensure drier conditions, but even protected winter crops should be sown rather more thinly than those maturing in summer and should be kept clear of weeds to allow free circulation of air.

For culinary applications see page 121

TOMATOES, GREENHOUSE

Characteristics
As described in Tomato, Outdoor except that specifically greenhouse varieties are slightly more tender and are bred more for weight of crop and quality of fruit than for resistance to adverse conditions.

Best soil
If the plants are to be grown in a border on the greenhouse floor this should be dug during the winter and a small quantity of compost or well rotted manure and a generous dressing of peat forked in. Before planting apply a light dressing of compound fertiliser. Plants should not be grown in the border for more than 3 years without a break as soil diseases build up. The alternatives are to grow in potting soil in 10 in pots, in tombags or in tompots.

Tombags are plastic containers of soil-less potting compost which are simply laid on the floor and planted up. Tompots are the bottomless containers filled with compost and placed on a bed of peat or clinker. This method is known as ring culture and has much to commend it when the borders have to be rested.

When to sow
See Tomato, Outdoor. To raise plants ready for cold house planting at the correct time seed must be sown in early March. Unless you have considerable heat available it is better to buy plants.

When to plant
In the cold house in late April - early May. Plant 18 in/45 cm apart. Conserve warmth by closing ventilators early.

Quantity of seed
See Tomato, Outdoor. F_1 hybrid packets contain comparatively few seeds in some cases, but always more than enough for the average amateur greenhouse.

Time to germination
10 days in suitable temperature. The necessary minimum is best maintained in a heated propagator, but the seedlings cannot stay in it long.

Season of use
July - November.

Storage life in freezer
See Tomato, Outdoor.

Crop for average family
Reckon on a yield of 6 - 8 lb/3 - 4 kg per plant, according to the height of the plants and the number of trusses. Periodic gluts are inevitable in spells of hot, sunny weather.

Reliable varieties
Moneymaker, Eurocross, Ailsa Craig. For exceptional quality, try Big Boy, a very large, sweet, solid Continental variety, or Carter's Fruit, of normal size and shape but also very solid and easily peeled. Bush varieties are not grown in the greenhouse, where the height of plants largely determines yields.

Caring for the crop
Stake with tall canes or stretch vertical strings from floor to roof and twist plants round them as they grow. Look for and remove side shoots regularly, ensuring that each plant has only one stem. Keep soil or compost always moist. Plants which must be left without watering all day will suffer in ordinary pots, grow them in the border or in tompots standing on material which retains enough moisture to support the plants.

For culinary applications see page 121

SOFT FRUIT They like: Soil with plenty of humus.
Moisture for their shallow roots.
Sun to ripen the fruits.

TOMATOES, OUTDOOR

Characteristics
Tender, destroyed by frost and intolerant of cold winds and
low night temperatures. Quantity of ripe fruit harvested varies
with the season. A sheltered situation is important and plants
grown in pots on a sunny patio are likely to do better than
those in an exposed position on open ground.

Best soil
Soil should be dug during the winter and should contain plenty
of compost and/or peat. A light pre-planting dose of
compound fertiliser may be raked in, but on a reasonably
fertile soil it is better to omit this and feed twice weekly with a
liquid high-potash fertiliser after the first truss of fruit has set.

When to sow
Early April under glass if temperature of 60°F/16°C can be
maintained until germination, and a minimum of 55°F/13°C
thereafter. Prick out seedlings, preferably into peat pots, just
before first true leaves develop. Grow on close to glass to get
sturdy plants. Harden off before planting out. Buy short-
jointed, deep green plants about 9 in/22.5 cm high if you
cannot grow from seed.

When to plant out
Mid-May under cloches, early June in the open. Delay planting
if weather is cold and windy. Plant tall varieties 18 in/45 cm
and bush varieties 24 in/60 cm apart. Stake and tie tall
varieties.

Quantity of seed
Small packet provides several dozen plants. Seed remains
viable 2 years.

Time to germination
10 days if suitable temperature is maintained.

Season of use
August - October. Last fruit is usually ripened indoors.

Storage life in freezer
1 year. Frozen fruit cannot be used in salads.

Crop for average family
A yield of 3 - 4 lb/1.5 - 2 kg of ripe fruit per plant is expected in
a good season. The main yield is usually concentrated in a
short period, and unless you are prepared to freeze a large
quantity 6 - 8 plants is enough.

Reliable varieties
Tall varieties   Outdoor Girl, Ailsa Craig, Ronaclave.
Dwarf or bush varieties   The Amateur, Sleaford Abundance,
French Cross.
Miniatures   (for growing outdoors in small containers) Tiny
Tim, Small Fry, Gardener's Delight.

Caring for the crop
Keep the soil uniformly moist. Alternate drying and wetting
leads to split fruit and blossom end rot.
　　Rub out side shoots from tall varieties before they get large.
When 3 trusses have set, or not later than mid-August, stop
the plants 2 leaves above the top truss.
　　The fruit of bush varieties must be kept from contact with
the soil. One way of doing this is to lay a strip of black
polythene on the planting site, make holes down the centre at
the required distances and plant a tomato in each. It also acts
as a mulch and weed suppressant.

For culinary applications see page 121

BLACKBERRIES

Characteristics
A vigorous hardy plant, native in its wild form. The cultivated
blackberry is a most useful fruit, coming as it does in late
summer and autumn. Fruit is borne on canes of the previous
year's growth, and the size and prickliness of the canes is the
plant's main disadvantage in the small garden.

Best soil
Heavy and slightly acid soils give the best results, but
blackberries grow well in most gardens with no special soil
preparation. Only on very dry, chalky land is it worth digging in
some peat or compost before planting. No fertiliser is needed.
The site should catch as much autumn sun as possible for the
late varieties. Blackberries do not flower until June and so are
a good choice for the garden with spring frost problems.

When to plant
Plant any time from October to March, November being the
best month. Remember when ordering plants that they need a
lot of space. In the small garden, start with a single plant and
propagate from it (see Propagation, below) if you find room
for more. Plant firmly, cut back to a few inches from the
ground and surround with a peat mulch in spring.

Time to first crop
21 months from an autumn planting.

Season of use
July - October according to variety.

Preservation
Blackberries may be bottled and frozen. Storage life in freezer,
1 year. In jam-making they are used alone or with apple, and in
the production of 'bramble' jelly.

Reliable varieties
Bedford Giant, Merton Thornless (July - August). Himalayan
Giant, John Innes (September - October). Merton Thornless is
the most manageable, Himalayan Giant the most vigorous.

Caring for the crop
Systematic annual pruning and training is essential (see
Loganberry page 78). Apart from a spring mulch and
protection of the fruit from birds little other attention is
needed.

Propagation
Blackberries and loganberries are easily propagated by tip
layering, which occurs spontaneously in the wild blackberry.
In late summer, select a young cane long enough to be bent
over and reach the ground at the tip without breaking. Make a
hole 4 in/10 cm deep at one end and sloping towards the plant
at the other, and lay the end of the cane in it with the tip at the
deep end. Hold the cane in position with a brick or a peg. Fill in
the hole with soil mixed with sand and peat. In the spring the
tip will have rooted and young shoots will appear. Sever the
cane from the parent plant and move the new one to
permanent quarters in the autumn.

For culinary applications see page 122

BLACKCURRANTS

Characteristics
Hardy, fairly long-lived if pruned regularly. Fruits on young wood growing up from the base. Crop is affected by spring frosts or cold winds which keep away pollinating insects. Fruit is nutritionally very valuable and increasingly hard to buy fresh.

Best soil
Does well on heavy land if it contains plenty of organic matter. Surface rooting and therefore appreciates an annual mulch of manure or peat. Prepare the site by digging in well rotted manure or garden compost some time in advance of planting. When planting, scatter a good handful of bone meal in the hole. Top dress the bushes every spring with 3 oz per sq yd/ 100 g per sq m of compound fertiliser, forking it in very lightly.

When to plant
October - March, when the soil is in suitable condition. Autumn planting is best. Order 2-year-old bushes in the summer, and if soil conditions make planting impossible on delivery heel them in immediately. Plant rather more deeply than the bushes had been growing, so that a few buds on the stems are buried. This encourages more basal shoots.

Time to first crop
18 months from an autumn planting.

Season of use
July - September.

Preservation
Keeps 1 year in freezer. Valuable for jamming and bottling.

Reliable varieties
There are many varieties. The following suit most soils and situations and bear high quality fruit.
Early to mid-season varieties Boskoop Giant, Tor Cross, Wellington XXX.
Late varieties Westwick Choice, Daniel's September, Amos Black.

Caring for the crop
Cut down bushes to a few inches from the ground immediately after planting. Water freely in dry weather during the first spring and summer to promote growth of new stems for fruiting the following year. Apply an annual mulch in late spring. Control weeds without digging near bushes by hoeing, hand weeding or the use of a contact herbicide.

Propagation
Take cuttings of new but ripened wood, 6 - 8 in/15 - 20 cm long in October. Leave all buds on the cuttings but trim off any unripened wood at the tips. Open a cleft in the ground with the spade deep enough to cover all but 2 buds on the cuttings. Insert the cuttings 6 in/15 cm apart, with only 2 buds above ground, sprinkle in some coarse sand and fill in with soil, making it quite firm. By the following autumn the cuttings will have rooted, stems will have grown up from the buried buds and the young bushes may be moved to their permanent site.

For culinary applications see page 122

GOOSEBERRIES

Characteristics
Hardy everywhere in the British Isles, though crops are affected by spring frosts. Appreciates a sheltered position and succeeds in partial shade. One of the earliest fruits to mature outdoors and one of all-round usefulness.

Best soil
Not fussy, but the soil must not be deficient in potash. Dig in manure or compost and any available bonfire ashes before planting. Beginning the first spring, hoe in an annual dressing of 1 oz per sq yd/33 g per sq m of sulphate of potash or 3 oz per sq yd/100 g per sq m of compound fertiliser.

When to plant
Autumn planting is best. Order 3-year-old bushes in the summer and plant or heel in immediately on arrival. Gooseberries are grown on a short stem or leg and are planted at the same depth as grown in the nursery.

Time to first crop
18 months from autumn planting. 3-year-old bushes should yield a substantial crop 2-3 years after planting.

Season of use
Late May - late July.

Preservation
May be frozen whole and uncooked or as purée. Storage life in freezer, 1 year. Suitable for bottling and jamming. Gooseberries preserved in any way retain their flavour well.

Reliable varieties
Keepsake, Whinham's Industry, Careless (cooking varieties). Leveller (dessert). Lancer (cooking, ripening to dessert).

Caring for the crop
Allow 8 or 9 main branches to develop from the stem but keep the lower part of the stem clear of all growth. Remove suckers coming from the ground. In late June, pinch back the laterals on the main branches to 5 leaves and in winter cut them back an inch or so. Do the same with cordons and also shorten the leading shoot of the main stem by one-third in the winter pruning. Prune branches regularly, shortening the leaders and drooping varieties so that branches do not drag on the ground.

Propagation
Cuttings may be taken in the autumn, all but the top few buds being removed. But it has been found that they root better if all the buds are left on and the shoots to which they give rise are mostly removed later. The cutting is left to grow after rooting and is dug up the following winter. All but the top 4 shoots are cut cleanly away and it is replanted with the proper leg or length of bare stem.

For culinary applications see page 122

LOGANBERRIES

Characteristics
Supposedly a blackberry - raspberry cross, the loganberry bears large, deep red, raspberry-shaped fruit on long prickly canes. Virus diseases at one time affected the yield of loganberries so badly that they almost ceased to be grown, but a virus-free strain is now available.

Best soil
Soil requirements are the same as for the blackberry. A good mulch, preferably of compost or rotted manure, applied in spring, improves the quality and quantity of the crop, for the loganberry makes a shallow root system like the raspberry and suffers in dry weather.

When to plant
Plant any time from October to March when soil conditions are right. Not more than 2 plants should be ordered for the average garden. Plant firmly and fairly deeply. Cut back the canes to just above a bud about 6 in/15 cm above the ground. Water freely if dry weather sets in during the first spring.

Time to first crop
About 20 months from an autumn planting.

Season of use
July - August.

Preservation
Excellent for freezing, jamming and bottling. Storage life in freezer, 1 year. The slightly sub-acid flavour of the fruit makes for a particularly delicious jam.

Reliable varieties
The most certainly virus-free variety at the moment is LY59, and this should be grown. In addition to the loganberry, several other hybrid berries of similar habit are worth growing. One of the best is the boysenberry, which appears to tolerate the drier soils.

Caring for the crop
Encourage as much growth as possible during the first summer by watering and mulching. Provide support for the young canes and tie them in as they grow. A south-facing fence is a good position, but if this is not available erect stout posts with 4 strands of galvanised wire 12 in/30 cm apart. Old canes are cut out annually after fruiting and young ones tied in. Both picking and pruning are facilitated if the 2 are kept separate, 1 year's growth being trained on wires to the right of the plant, leaving the wires to the left free to support the young canes as they grow. After fruiting, the old canes are cut out, leaving the wires vacant for new canes the following year. The same method is advised for blackberries.

Propagation
Propagate by tip-layering, like blackberries.

For culinary applications see page 123

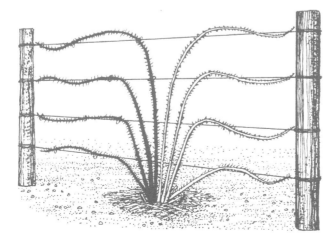

RASPBERRIES

Characteristics
Hardy, flowering late enough to escape spring frosts and succeeding in districts with cool, damp summers. The fruit is borne on canes of the previous year's growth. Thornless, easy to pick and a good fruit for the small garden if protected from birds.

Best soil
The raspberry is surface rooting and likes plenty of moisture in the topsoil. Dig in manure or compost before planting and mulch with some organic material every spring before the ground begins to dry out.

When to plant
October - March. Autumn planting is best if the soil is in workable condition. Order canes in advance and specify approximate time delivery is required. Plant firmly with the roots well spread out. Cut back the canes to a few inches above ground level immediately after planting. Inspect newly-planted canes after hard frost and tread back any that have been lifted; it is possible for the roots to be left so exposed that they dry out and the plant dies.

Time to first crop
Summer-fruiting varieties planted in autumn, 18-20 months. Autumn-fruiting varieties planted in autumn, 1 year.

Season of use
Summer-fruiting varieties, June - August. Autumn-fruiting varieties, September - November.

Preservation
Suitable for freezing and jamming. Storage life in freezer, 1 year. Raspberries retain their natural flavour when frozen better than almost any other fruit.

Reliable varieties
Summer-fruiters   Norfolk Giant, Malling Promise, Malling Jewel. The last is the most popular variety in Northern England and Scotland, but may be less vigorous than other varieties in the South.
Autumn-fruiters   September, Zeva. The latter is a new introduction, cropping into November in a favourable season.

Caring for the crop
Canes are cut back after planting so that energy may be concentrated on producing strong canes for future fruiting. If this is not done the canes will bear no worthwhile crop the first summer and the following year's crop will be jeopardised. Erect posts and 3 horizontal strands of wire, tying the new canes to them as they grow. Control weeds by hoeing, hand weeding or the use of a contact herbicide, never dig deeply close to the canes. Cut out old canes of established plants immediately after fruiting and reduce new canes in each clump to the 6 strongest.

Propagation
Propagate from the suckers which arise some distance from the row. These are normally hoed up, but if new canes are required, allow the strongest to grow through the summer, dig up, sever from the parent plant in autumn and replant on a new site.

For culinary applications see page 123

RHUBARB

Characteristics
The edible stems of rhubarb are not, of course, fruit. The plant is treated like a permanent vegetable crop and the reason for its inclusion among soft fruits is the similarity of its culinary uses. It is a hardy plant, starting into growth early in the year if given protection and providing the first fresh 'fruit' from the garden.

Best soil
The earliest crops are produced on light soils, but rhubarb is more at home on heavier land which does not dry out in summer. Dig thoroughly before planting to ensure a good run for the large roots, eliminate perennial weeds, and incorporate some manure or compost. An annual dressing of manure should be applied in winter and the plants should be well watered in dry weather when in full growth.

When to plant
Best planting times are autumn as soon as the tops die down or February - March before growth starts. The plants are bought as crowns with large roots and several buds, or as sets each consisting of a short piece of root with a single main bud. In any plant at least 1 good, fat bud is essential. Plant 24 in/ 60 cm apart, just deep enough for the topmost bud to be covered. Make very firm but take care not to break the brittle roots.

Time to first crop
From an autumn planting, 16 months. From a spring planting, 1 year. No stems should be pulled in the first season.

Season of use
March onwards if protected, April onwards without protection.

Preservation
Young, pink stems may be frozen or bottled. Storage life in freezer, 1 year. Older sticks are used in jam-making.

Reliable varieties
Victoria, Timperley Early. The following may be raised from seed sown outdoors in April, thinned to 6 in/15 cm apart, and planted out in the autumn: Glaskin's Perpetual, Holstein Bloodred.

Caring for the crop
Because rhubarb fits into any odd corner of the kitchen garden it is too often neglected. It should be mulched with manure in the winter and given occasional feeds of liquid fertiliser in summer. This applies especially to newly-planted roots which have to build up their strength to crop well the following year. Remove all flower stems as soon as they are noticed. Pull the sticks gently with a twisting movement, leaving as many stems on the plant as you remove. Protect the early crop by covering with wooden boxes, pails or oil drums with one end cut out. The covering should be completely light-tight to produce tender, pink sticks.

Propagation
Dig away the soil from one side of a plant in the autumn and slice through the crown with a sharp spade, removing part of the root with one or more buds. Replant immediately.

For culinary applications see page 123

STRAWBERRIES

Characteristics
There are 3 distinct types of strawberry. Summer-fruiting varieties crop from May to July and provide the main supply of the fruit. Perpetual varieties fruit from August to October and Alpine strawberries fruit intermittently through the summer. Strawberries give a quicker return than any other fruit and may be grown in open ground, under glass, in window boxes and troughs, or in holes cut in the sides of barrels or containers of similar form called Towerpots.

Best soil
Plenty of organic matter- compost, peat or rotted manure - should be dug in before planting. A slightly acid soil is preferred. The site for perpetuals should catch all the autumn sunlight possible, but summer-fruiters tolerate some shade and merely ripen more slowly.

When to plant
Plant summer-fruiters in August or September, the earlier the better. Plant perpetuals in Autumn or spring, removing all flowers until July. Plant Alpines in spring or sow seeds February-March, planting out in May. Plant all strawberries with a trowel, spreading the roots, making very firm but not covering the terminal bud in the centre. Water in if the weather is dry. Inspect new plantings in winter and press back any frost-lifted plants.

Time to first crop
Summer-fruiters from August planting, 9 months if cloched, 10 months in the open. Perpetuals from March planting, 5 months. Alpines from February sowing under glass, 6 months.

Season of use
The season for summer-fruiters can be extended from late May to mid-July by growing early and late varieties and using cloches. The main crop of perpetuals is picked in August and September, but by the use of cloches may be prolonged into November in some seasons.

Preservation
Suitable for freezing and jamming. Storage life in freezer, 1 year, but the fruit does not retain its natural flavour when frozen.

Reliable varieties
Summer-fruiters   Early varieties, Royal Sovereign, Cambridge Vigour (first year), Grandee. Mid-season to late varieties, Cambridge Favourite, Cambridge Vigour (second year), Talisman.
Perpetuals   Sans Rivale, St Claude, Hampshire Maid.

Caring for the crop
Hand weed and remove unwanted runners. Place straw, mats, black polythene or other material under ripening fruits or prop up the trusses on pieces of wire or forked twigs. Protect from birds with netting if not under cloches or in a fruit cage.

Propagation
A few runners from fruiting plants may be allowed to root for planting elsewhere in August. A better plan is to plant a few of the original stock away from the fruiting rows, spacing them well apart, removing all flowers, and keeping them solely to produce runners. Never take runners from plants showing discoloured or deformed foliage or stunted growth. These should be dug up and burned.

For culinary applications see page 124

TOP FRUIT They like: Soil not too rich.
Good drainage and dry feet in winter. Shelter in spring.
A gardener who knows when to prune and when not to.

APPLES

Characteristics
The apple is the most widely grown of top fruits. It is valuable for immediate use and for natural storage. It is available in many forms and on different rootstocks, so that trees may be found suitable for the smallest garden. For almost any part of the British Isles there is a dessert or culinary variety that will grow and fruit successfully, but although it is easy to make general recommendations on the choice of varieties the best advice on the choice for your garden will come from a local nurseryman. Remember that the variety which is perfect for Kent may be all wrong for Cumbria.

Best soil
Apples do not need rich soils and generally give satisfactory results on an average well cultivated garden soil without the use of nitrogenous manures or fertilisers. Excessive growth is not wanted, and on naturally fertile soils very dwarfing rootstocks such as M9 should be used. Improve drainage by breaking up the subsoil when planting and fork a few handfuls of bone meal into the topsoil of the site.

When to plant
Plant from November to early March. Autumn planting usually gives the best results but any time in the winter when conditions are reasonable is satisfactory. Stake and tie bush trees when planting and provide temporary stakes for trained trees for which permanent supports are not yet ready.

Time to first crop
A few fruits may be picked from 3-year-old trees on dwarfing stocks in the second year after planting. When in full bearing a single-stem cordon could be expected to average 5 lb/2.5 kg of fruit and a bush tree on M9 (probably the smallest mature tree in that form) should average 25 lb/12.5 kg. Of course, yields vary greatly with the season.

Season of use
August - April, according to varieties grown.

Preservation
Natural storage of keeping varieties is the most important way of preserving. Firm-fleshed varieties may be frozen for use in pies and the frothy culinary varieties frozen as purée. Storage life, 1 year.

Reliable varieties
The list is very large and only a few all-rounders are given here. Consult the catalogues for details of pollination, harvesting dates, and keeping period, before deciding.
Dessert varieties   Ellison's Orange, Laxton's Superb, Discovery, George Cave, Spartan, Fortune, James Grieve.
Culinary varieties   Bramley's Seedling, Lane's Prince Albert, Howgate Wonder, Crawley Beauty, Annie Elizabeth.

Caring for the crop
Young trees should not be allowed to carry too heavy a crop. Thin the fruit if branches are still crowded after the 'June drop', leaving the fruit well spaced and, in culinary varieties, only one apple per cluster of bloom. If this is done it reduces the tendency of some varieties to bear over-large crops one year and virtually nothing the following year.

For culinary applications see page 124

APRICOTS

Characteristics
The apricot succeeds in the milder parts of the British Isles if grown on a sunny wall. The tree itself is fairly hardy and has been grown here for more than 400 years. Unfortunately, it flowers very early, like the peach, and the blossom may appear on leafless branches in February. Some kind of protection from spring frosts is therefore essential. It is worth pointing out that the apricot, fig and peach might often have a better chance of fruiting in town gardens, where average night temperatures are slightly higher, than in rural areas.

Best soil
Apricots do not need a very fertile soil. Dig the planting site thoroughly and break up the subsoil to improve drainage. Work in a good double handful of bone meal and a light dressing of sulphate of potash. Allow a wall space for the mature tree of 6 - 7 ft/2 m high and 12 - 15 ft/4 - 5 m wide. The apricot, like the fig and peach is self-fertile and a single tree crops satisfactorily.

When to plant
The 2 - 3-year-old fan-trained tree should be planted in October or November. Plant firmly, and if the branches do not reach the wall for tieing in they should be secured to bamboo canes on either side until long enough.

Time to first crop
Apricot trees start to bear when 4 years old, but should not be expected to crop in the first year after planting. The first fruits may, with luck, be picked within 2 years.

Season of use
August - September.

Preservation
Apricots may be frozen as halves, slices or purée according to the degree of ripeness. Storage life in freezer, 1 year. They may also be bottled and made into jam.

Reliable varieties
Heemskirk and Moorpark, ripening early and late August respectively, are old favourites and still as good as any for vigour and heavy cropping.

Caring for the crop
Water freely the first year and in dry weather in subsequent seasons, remembering that wall trees often suffer more from lack of water than those growing in open ground. Like the plum, the apricot should not be pruned in winter and not over-pruned at any time. When the main branches have covered the available wall space the lateral shoots should be pinched back to about 3 in/7.5 cm in June if not bearing fruit, and later growth should be cut back or thinned out after fruiting but before the end of September.

For culinary applications see page 124

CHERRIES

Characteristics
The sweet cherry is not a tree for the small garden. There is no dwarfing stock for cherries and they make large trees. The sweet varieties are self-sterile and will not fruit unless pollinated by another variety of a compatible group or by the acid Morello variety. The Morello is self-fertile, is valuable from the culinary point of view, and may be grown as a fan-trained tree on a north wall. It is perhaps the only fruit tree to succeed in such a position. It should be added that trained sweet cherries may be grown on south or west walls, but they react badly to the intensive pruning involved and you cannot plant a single tree, as you can a Morello, because of the pollination difficulty.

Best soil
Cherries respond to a well drained, fertile soil. Like all stone fruit, they need lime, but they do not grow as well as plums on the poorer chalk soils. Dig the site deeply, breaking up the subsoil, and incorporate as much compost, rotted manure or hop manure as you can spare. Fork in a double handful of bone meal when planting.

When to plant
The cherry starts into growth fairly early, and autumn planting is safer than late winter or spring planting. If planted, as recommended, against a north wall, the tree should be mulched after planting with a thick layer of peat to prevent the penetration of frost. In a position not reached by winter sunlight frost may extend lower in the soil than where intermittent thaws occur during a hard spell. This would not affect an established tree but can delay effective rooting of transplants. Order 2 - 3-year-old trees, the younger the tree the easier it is to move.

Time to first crop
Probably 4 years to anything worth calling a crop. Yields may eventually be substantial but depend on plenty of wall space for extension and on systematic pruning.

Season of use
July - September.

Preservation
The Morello freezes well; storage life, 1 year. It is famous as the source of delicious preserves.

Reliable varieties
Although only the Morello is suggested here as suitable for the smaller garden, fan-trained sweet cherries may be grown where there is room for at least 2 trees. Consult the nurseryman about compatible varieties, which are essential for pollination. You should not plant standard or half-standard trees, even if you have plenty of room. You would wait 10 years for a crop and find protection from birds an insoluble problem.

Caring for the crop
Keep the base of the tree free of weeds, lightly fork in the remains of the mulch in autumn and put down a fresh mulch in spring. Keep the soil moist throughout the growing season, nothing is worse for cherries than alternations of wet and dry. Acid cherries fruit on growth made the previous season and are pruned in the same way as peaches and nectarines (see The Care of Growing Crops/Fruit pages 36/37). Do not allow the tree to become a mass of old and young shoots.

For culinary applications see page 125

FIGS

Characteristics
The fig can only be relied upon to crop in the south of England if it is to be grown in the open, and even in mild districts it requires the shelter of a south-facing wall. It must also be protected from winter frost by having the branches tied together and wrapped in protective material or by covering the entire tree with sacking kept dry by polythene sheeting. The fig tree is rarely killed outright by severe weather, but soft wood is cut back and immature fruits, which must survive the winter to provide the next year's crop, may be destroyed. The best situation is the back wall of a lean-to greenhouse.

Best soil
Poor soil and a limited root run are necessary. If given generous treatment the fig makes a lot of soft growth which is unripened at the end of the growing season and very susceptible to frost. Take out a hole 2 spits deep and about 3 ft / 1 m square and line the bottom and sides with bricks or tiles. The surrounding soil should be well dug to ensure good drainage between the bricks. Fill the hole with ordinary garden soil mixed with a pailful of gravel or coarse sand. In choosing a wall site, remember that the fig may reach a height of 7 ft / 2 m and a spread of twice that under favourable conditions.

When to plant
Order a pot-grown tree for delivery in April. If possible, have it delivered in the pot and give it a good soaking before knocking it out. Loosen the outside of the soil ball but do not break it up. If you have not prepared a brick-lined planting site, leave the tree in the pot, enlarge the drainage hole for the roots to escape, burying the pot rim 3 in / 7.5 cm deep to allow more roots to spread from the top. This restrains the growth of the tree for several years.

Time to first crop
1 ½ - 2 ½ years from a spring planting. Ultimate yields vary greatly with climatic conditions but in terms of space occupied the fig must be reckoned a luxury crop.

Season of use
Late summer and autumn. Fruit must ripen on the tree and be soft to the touch and on the point of shrivelling when picked.

Preservation
Ripe figs may be frozen or made into jam. Storage life in freezer, 1 year.

Reliable varieties
For hardiness and reliability choose either Brown Turkey or Brunswick.

Caring for the crop
Water frequently after planting, especially if the tree was planted in the pot. In subsequent years little watering is needed even in dry seasons. Cut out overcrowded and frost-damaged branches in spring or summer. Remove fruit from near the tips of branches before covering the tree for winter, those near the base of the branch have a better chance of survival and maturity. The traditional method of winter protection is to untie the branches from the wall, gather them in bundles, and wrap them in straw held in place by sacking. The use of polythene renders any form of covering more effective by keeping it dry.

For culinary applications see page 125

GRAPES

Characteristics

The grape vine is hardy and has been grown in Britain since Roman times. Outdoors, it stands the hardest winter frosts so long as it is grown in full sun to ripen and harden the growth. Sun is, of course, equally necessary to ripen the fruit. The vine benefits from a marked contrast between summer and winter temperatures, and even when grown under glass, winter temperatures should be low enough to keep it completely dormant for several months. For this reason, and also because it must be trained under the greenhouse roof and so reduce the light available to other plants in summer, the vine tends to monopolise the small greenhouse and is not a suitable indoor crop for the ordinary gardener. Here we deal only with outdoor vines, in which there is now much interest and of which new varieties are being introduced.

Best soil

Like the fig, the grape does best in poorish soil. It must not be encouraged to make lush growth as this is susceptible to frost. An established vine has a widespread root system and rarely suffers from drought. The roots like to run under paving stones, which act as a permanent mulch, and the vine is thus an excellent choice for a sunny courtyard. Break up the subsoil at the bottom of the planting hole and if it is of heavy clay mix some gravel or broken mortar rubble with it. Mix a little well rotted manure or compost and a double handful of bone meal with the topsoil before planting.

When to plant

Order 2-year-old vines, pot-grown, for planting between October and February. Plant against a south- or west-facing wall if available, otherwise in the sunniest and most sheltered spot you can find. Break up the soil ball very carefully, spreading the roots in the planting hole.

Time to first crop

First bunch may be picked in 2 years from an autumn planting.

Season of use

September - October.

Preservation

Apart from wine-making, which is of increasing interest, surplus grapes may be frozen in syrup. Storage life in freezer, 1 year. An entire bunch of grapes may be frozen for a few weeks and served for dessert straight from the freezer. Alternatively, bunches of ripe grapes will keep for weeks if the stalks are inserted in bottles of water in a cool, dark place.

Reliable varieties

The following have a reasonable chance of succeeding in a sheltered position in the open and are also suitable for cold greenhouse culture. New Continental varieties are continually being tried out and more than one nursery should be consulted. Black Hamburg, Buckland Sweetwater, Miller's Burgundy, Royal Muscadine.

Caring for the crop

Newly-planted vines are cut back to 3 or 4 buds in February. They must not be cut earlier or the wood may be damaged by frost, nor later, or the vine will bleed. From the remaining buds will grow the future fruiting stems of the vine and these should be carefully tied to wall nails or trellis as they grow. Old vine wood is tough, but the new growth is tender and brittle and must be secured against damage. Keep vines well-watered and mulched with peat for the first few months of growth.

For culinary applications see page 125

PEACHES

Characteristics

Although hardy, the peach flowers very early and the crop may be lost through spring frosts. In favoured parts of southern England it may be grown in bush form in open ground but in most areas only a fan-tailed tree on a south- or west-facing wall is likely to crop regularly.

Best soil

A good average soil is required, not too rich in nitrogen as you do not want excessive growth. It should be consistently moist in summer and this involves mulching and occasionally watering wall trees. Equally important, it must be well drained in winter. When planting in heavy clay, remove some of the subsoil from the bottom of the hole, put in a layer of brick rubble, cover it with some chopped turf and topsoil before planting.

When to plant

The tree should have 2 or 3 pairs of branches. Peaches do not like being moved and small trees transplant better than larger ones. Plant in autumn if possible, soon after leaf-fall, and do not allow trees to remain out of the ground a day longer than necessary.

Time to first crop

Probably at leat 3 years. The crop then increases with the size of the tree and may reach 100 ripe fruit in a good season.

Season of use

July - September.

Preservation

Peaches are best frozen in syrup, storage life, 1 year.

Reliable varieties

Hales Early, Peregrine, Duke of York. Hales Early is recommended for freezing.

Caring for the crop

Prune and tie in fan-trained trees regularly, they will not fruit well if allowed to become a thicket of shoots. Protect flowers with sacking or other material on frosty nights. If a large proportion of the flowers set, the fruits must be thinned. Begin by thinning to 4 in/10 cm apart in early June when the fruits are the size of hazel nuts, taking those that are pressed closely together or squeezed between branch and wall. A month later, when they are the size of walnuts, thin to 8 in/20 cm. These distances are, of course, only a guide. The aim is to have well-spaced fruits spread evenly along the branches.

For culinary applications see page 126

PEARS

Characteristics
Pears bloom earlier than apples and are more susceptible to spring frosts. The best dessert pears are grown in the warmer parts of the country and in many places trained trees on south- or west-facing walls give the best results. Several single-stem cordons take up very little space on a wall, and if of different varieties to ensure pollination offer the best chance of a regular crop.

Best soil
Pears prefer a medium soil, neither a heavy clay nor a dry chalk. Dig in some compost or well rotted manure when preparing the site and fork in a double handful of bone meal per tree at planting time. Give each tree an annual dressing of about 3 oz/100 g of compound fertiliser in the spring, forking it in lightly. Water wall trees in dry weather.

When to plant
Plant in autumn if possible, ordering trees in good time in the summer. Heel them in if planting is delayed by bad weather. Plant wall cordons with the stem 9 in/22.5 cm from the footings of the wall and slanting at an angle of 45°. Tie it temporarily to a cane if it is not long enough to reach the wall for permanent fastening. Stake bush trees when planting and check stakes and ties at intervals.

Time to first crop
Some fruit should be picked in the second year after planting a 3 - 4-year-old tree. A mature 1-stem cordon should average 5 lb/2.5 kg with double that in a good year. A mature bush tree could yield 40 lb/18 kg.

Season of use
August - February according to variety.

Preservation
A winter supply of pears is best assured by natural storage of keeping varieties. They loose quality in freezing, but a surplus of non-keeping varieties may be successfully frozen in syrup. Storage life, 1 year.

Reliable varieties
1 variety only, Conference. Several varieties for cross-pollination, Conference, Williams' Bon Chrétien, Packham's Triumph, Improved Fertility. For long-keeping, Winter Nelis, Josephine de Malines. The last two are less reliable croppers than the others.

Caring for the crop
Encourage the formation of fruiting spurs by regular summer and winter pruning. Protect blossom on wall trees when frost threatens by covering with fabric, though this is usually impossible with free-standing trees.

For culinary applications see page 126

PLUMS

Characteristics
This includes gages and damsons. They are hardy and grow in most parts of the United Kingdom, early-flowering and liable to be affected by spring frosts and wet, windy conditions which limit the flight of pollinating insects. A sheltered position should be chosen if possible. Plums may be grown as trained wall trees but dislike the amount of pruning this involves. The bush tree, once established, has the advantage of requiring almost no pruning and is the best form for the amateur grower.

Best soil
Any average garden soil suits plums provided it is not short of lime. They do better on chalk soils than some other fruits, though on poor and shallow soils they should receive an annual spring dressing of compound fertiliser, and fruit size will be improved by mulching and by thorough soakings of water in dry periods.

When to plant
The usual provisions apply. If planting has to be delayed until spring it should be done in the first week of March at the latest as the plum starts into growth fairly early. Work a double handful of bone meal into the planting site. Late-planted trees should be watered in dry spring weather and the young foliage sprayed.

Time to first crop
2-3 years from a 3-year-old tree. A prolific variety like Victoria may reach an average of 40 lb/18 kg over the next 10 years and thereafter increase to 100 lb/45 kg or more according to season. Gages are slow coming into bearing and yield about half these quantities.

Season of use
Late July - October according to variety. Consult the nurseryman about a succession if you intend planting several trees.

Preservation
All varieties of plum are excellent for bottling and jamming and reasonably good for freezing. Storage life in freezer, 1 year.

Reliable varieties
The following are all self-fertile and a single tree of any of them may be grown with fair prospects of a crop, though better results are achieved by growing more than 1 variety. Do not grow gages in districts of very high summer rainfall which may cause cracking of the fruit and the loss of much of the crop.
Dessert varieties   Victoria, Severn Cross, Oullins Golden Gage.
Culinary varities   Czar, Victoria, Marjorie's Seedling, Merryweather Damson.

Caring for the crop
Plums require little attention, but care should be taken to control silver leaf disease and aphid infestation, both of which are common and affect the crop very seriously. Do any necessary pruning in summer whenever possible.

For culinary applications see page 126

Gardening, like other crafts, has its own terms and expressions, which are added to as techniques change. You may not be familiar with the exact meaning of all those met with in this book and other gardening literature, so here is a selection.

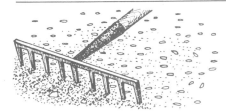

Acid
Description of a soil deficient in lime. One containing a lot of lime or chalk is described as *alkaline.* Many vegetables and fruits prefer a neutral soil, not strongly acid or alkaline. A soil that has become too acid is described as *sour*, crops are stunted and prone to disease and lime must be used to restore the balance.

Activator
Anything used in a compost heap to hasten the conversion of vegetable waste into usable compost. It may be a proprietary compound, or sulphate of ammonia, or small quantities of animal manure placed between layers of other material.

Blanch
Exclusion of light from certain crops to turn them white, because when green they are uneatable. This may be done, as with trench celery, by earthing up, or, as with chicory, by growing in a dark place.

Bolt
To run to seed. This may happen prematurely in the case of roots like beet and carrots, sometimes owing to seedlings being exposed to cold weather or left unthinned and overcrowded. Or it may happen naturally to crops like lettuce because too many have been sown at one time for all to be harvested in usable condition. Here the remedy is to sow little and often.

Brassicas
Vegetables related to the cabbage, including Brussels sprouts, cauliflowers and broccoli. All like good soil, firm and not lacking in lime. They should not be grown continuously on the same ground as all are susceptible to the soil-borne disease, club root, which does not affect other vegetables.

Broadcast
To sow by scattering seed thinly over a prepared site and raking it in, instead of sowing in a drill. Not generally recommended owing to the difficulty of removing weeds from the crop, but when used for a late sowing of turnips or carrots can produce a large yield of small roots from a limited area.

Cap
Soil is said to be capped when heavy rain or watering causes the surface to run together and form a hard crust when dry, a condition seriously affecting seedlings and germinating seeds. The cap should be broken up as close to the row as possible by very careful hoeing. If the seedlings have not actually emerged, the surface must be kept moist by further watering until they do.

Catch crop
Crop sown on temporarily vacant ground intended for another. The catch crop must be quick-maturing and may overlap the main crop by a few weeks if necessary. Thus, lettuce may be sown on ground prepared for Brussels sprouts and the latter planted between the lettuce if they are still being harvested. The catch crop must be cleared away as the main crop demands more space.

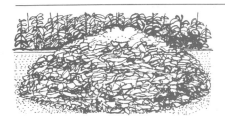

Compost
Waste vegetable matter decomposed in heaps or containers to a point at which the plant foods in it become available when dug into the soil. Ideally, all vegetable waste from garden and household, except diseased plants, perennial weeds and woody prunings, should be composted and returned to the soil.

Composts, seed, and potting
An entirely different meaning of the word, referring to the special soils for sowing seeds and growing plants in pots and other containers. Composts are now more usually bought than home-made. They are of two main types, the John Innes range, based on sterilised loam, and the soil-less composts based on peat. The latter are coming to be regarded as more consistent in results.

Curd
The white head of the cauliflower. The curd of the winter cauliflower is protected from frost by a close ring of leaves. Curds of summer cauliflowers should be sheltered from the sun by bending outer leaves over them.

Dormant
Literally, 'sleeping'. The time when a plant is not in active growth. Particularly the time from autumn to spring when fruit bushes and trees may be safely transplanted.

Drill
Small trench in which seeds are sown. Drills are usually made with a draw hoe and vary in depth and width with the size of the seed and the season of the year.

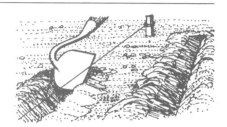

Earthing up
Drawing soil up to the stems of crop to form a ridge. It may be done to blanch the stems in the case of celery, or to prevent greening of the tubers by light in the case of potatoes.

F₁ hybrid
A variety produced by the crossing of 2 distinct parent strains. These hybrids are noted for their vigour and productivity. An F_1 hybrid cannot be reproduced from its own seed.

Fertiliser
Inorganic plant food. A straight fertiliser contains only 1 of the 3 principal elements essential to the plant, a compound, general or balanced fertiliser contains all 3.

Frost hollow
A low-lying area subject to spring frosts. In any garden laid out on a slope it should be remembered that fruit blossom will be less liable to damage on the higher part as cold air flows downwards and collects at the lowest point.

Good heart
Vague but often-used expression denoting soil fertility. It implies that the soil has been well manured in the past, is well cultivated and not weed-infested.

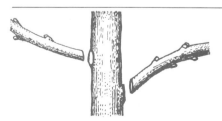

Growing on
Stage in the production of a plant

under glass following pricking out. A tomato plant, for instance, is pricked out into a small pot and grown on until the first flower truss is forming before planting in final quarters.

Hardening off
Getting a tender plant accustomed to outdoor conditions before planting in the open. It applies to subjects such as marrows and sweet corn, and is done by standing the plants in the open and bringing them in or covering with cloches at night for a week or so, or by putting them in a frame and leaving the lights off for increasing periods.

Hardy
Generally taken to mean a plant which can be exposed to frost, but there are many degrees of hardiness. Crops such as carrots and beetroot, for instance, are technically hardy and may be sown fairly early in spring, but if exposed to much frost they are severely checked and are more likely to bolt. Potatoes and runner beans are among the definitely tender crops and their planting dates are based on the need to escape late frosts.

Haulm
The stems and vines of certain crops such as potatoes, peas and runner beans.

Humus
The organic content of soil, formed by the breakdown of organic matter and essential to fertility. The physical structure of soil depends mainly upon adequate humus and the supply of plant foods.

Lateral
A side shoot or branch, springing from a main stem or larger branch. The cutting back of laterals is an important part of fruit tree pruning, and in the growing of tall varieties of tomatoes no laterals are allowed to develop, being rubbed out as soon as they are seen.

Leader
The main shoot of a stem or branch, with the growing point at its tip.

Legume
A pod-bearing plant, such as the pea or bean. Leguminous plants are important in crop rotation, leaving the soil richer in nitrogen if their roots are left to decay. This is because the roots carry nodules containing colonies of bacteria which fix atmospheric nitrogen. The ability of peas and beans to supply their own nitrogen is one reason for the seeds being so rich in protein.

Mulch
Layer of material spread on the soil to reduce loss of moisture by evaporation. Usually peat, rotted manure or compost, but black polythene is a possible alternative and effective in suppressing annual weeds. *Soil mulch* is a layer of loose soil produced by regular hoeing in dry weather. This prevents soil moisture being drawn to the surface by capillary action and so lost by evaporation.

Open
An open soil is one naturally loose and friable, like a sandy loam or a heavier soil generously manured; such soils permit good root development. *Open weather* refers to any period in winter when there is hard frost or heavy rain.

Organic
Anything that is, or has been, living matter. In *organic gardening* only such materials, compost, animal manures or such products as fish meal and bone meal, are used as plant foods.

Pollination
Fertilisation of a flower by the transference of pollen to produce seed or fruit. Some varieties of fruit are *self-sterile* and cannot be fertilised by their own pollen, so requiring a tree of another variety, blooming at the same time, to act as a pollinator.

Pot-bound
Condition in which a plant's root system has outgrown the pot in which it is planted, shown by the soil ball being enclosed in a dense mass of root. Plants such as tomatoes and marrows, intended for outdoor planting, should not be allowed to become pot-bound, as

they are liable to be starved and badly checked. It is unwise to start such crops too early under glass if they cannot be planted out for fear of frost.

Pricking out
Transferring seedlings from seed tray to pots or other containers where they have more room. It should be done as early as possible, preferably before the seedlings get their first true leaves. The longer it is left, the more entangled they become, the greater the damage done to their roots, and the longer they take to recover.

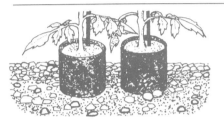

Ring culture
Method of growing tomatoes under glass. The tomato is planted in potting compost in a cylindrical pot open at both ends ('tompot') standing on a bed of shingle or clinker. This is kept watered and the tomato roots into it, liquid feeds being applied only to the compost. The method reduces the frequency of watering compared to ordinary pot culture and is very useful in a greenhouse which has to be left unattended during the day.

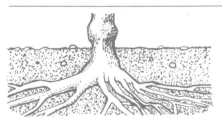

Rootstock
The root on to which a fruit tree is grafted. It is the main influence in deciding the size of the tree at maturity and the quickness with which it comes into bearing.

Rotation
The practice of growing groups of similar vegetables on a different part of the plot over a period of years. A plan of rotation cannot be followed exactly, but continuously growing the same crops on the same ground is a sure recipe for trouble.

Seed-leaf
The first leaf to appear from the seed on germination, usually different in form from those that follow, known as *true leaves.* If the seed-leaf is damaged, as by attacks of flea beetle, the seedling is crippled and may not survive.

Set
State of a flower which will form fruit after successful pollination.

The number of blossoms which set depends upon many factors - weather, presence of insects to carry pollen and of a suitable pollinator variety among them.

Soft fruit
Fruit produced on bushes, canes or plants, as opposed to *top fruit,* produced on trees. Soft fruit gives the quicker return on investment and the best opportunities for fruit production in the small garden. The term is not to be taken too literally - green gooseberries are very hard but are nevertheless classified as soft fruit.

Soil ball
Compact mass of potting compost and roots of a pot-grown plant. The soil ball should be disturbed as little as possible when planting out cucumbers and marrows.

Spur
Short lateral growth on a fruit tree, described as a *fruiting spur* if it bears one or more fruit buds. The main aim in pruning mature trees is to encourage the production of fruiting spurs.

Stop
To pinch out the growing point of a main stem or lateral. Thus, the main stem of a tomato is stopped when enough trusses have set, and the laterals of a cucumber are stopped when bearing 1 or 2 fruits apiece.

Subsoil
Soil layer immediately below the normal depth of digging. It may be of clay, gravel or chalk and determines the nature of the *topsoil* above it. Because no organic matter has accumulated in the subsoil, it is relatively infertile except as a source of minerals, and must be kept separate from the fertile layer above it. The physical structure of the subsoil is important and when composed of clay or a mixture of clay and chalk it may need to be broken up occasionally to facilitate drainage.

Successional sowing
Sowing of a quick-maturing crop to make use of ground previously occupied by a main crop, such as stump-rooted carrots following

early potatoes and being pulled in October. Also, frequent small sowings of crops such as lettuce and radish which deteriorate quickly and of which a continuous supply is needed.

Sucker
Growth from the base of a plant which forms its own roots. Globe artichokes are progagated by planting sucker growths in spring and raspberries by planting suckers in autumn.

Tilth
Topmost layer of soil in the right condition for sowing. Small seeds require a fine tilth, larger ones like beans tolerate a slightly more lumpy seed bed. On heavy soils the best tilth is obtained by leaving the soil in clods exposed to winter frosts. If this opportunity is missed, it is rarely possible to 'force a tilth' by any amount of mechanical action such as raking.

Vegetative reproduction
Treating part of a plant in such a way that it becomes a separate plant. Top fruits are propagated by *grafting,* a stem of the variety being united to a special rootstock. Currants and gooseberries are propagated by *cuttings,* strawberries by *runners* and blackberries and loganberries by *tip-layering,* in which the tip of a cane is buried and develops roots. These methods make it important to control virus diseases in soft fruit, because they are passed on much more easily than when a new plant is grown from seed.

Variety
Plant produced by selective breeding and hybridisation and having characteristics which distinguish it from other varieties of the same species. Varieties are named by those who introduce them and different names are sometimes given to what is essentially the same variety.

Waterlogging
A waterlogged soil is not merely wet, it is full of water unable to drain away. Normally, air is sucked into the soil as the water drains out, but this is impossible in water-logged conditions and plant roots die for lack of oxygen.

Crop (page number in brackets)	Date when sown or planted	Date when first harvested	Comments
Brussels sprouts (48)			
Cabbages (48/49)			
Calabrese (49)			
Cauliflowers (50)			
Kale (51)			
Sprouting broccoli (51)			
Chives (52)			
Majoram (52)			
Mint (53)			
Parsley (53)			
Rosemary (54)			
Sage (54)			
Thyme (55)			
Asparagus (55)			
Aubergines (56)			
Globe artichokes (56)			
Leeks (57)			
Marrows (57)			
Mushrooms (58)			
Peppers (58)			
Seakale beet (59)			
Spinach (59/60)			
Sprouted seeds (60)			
Squashes (61)			
Sweet corn (61)			

CROP RECORD

Crop (page number in brackets)	Date when sown or planted	Date when first harvested	Comments
Beans for drying (62)			
Broad beans (62)			
Dwarf or French beans (63)			
Garden peas (63)			
Runner beans (64)			
Sugar peas (64)			
Beetroot (65)			
Carrots (65)			
Celeriac (66)			
Jerusalem artichokes (66)			
Onions (67)			
Parsnips (68)			
Potatoes (68/69)			
Shallots (69)			
Swedes (70)			
Turnips (70)			
Celery (71)			
Chicory (71)			
Cucumbers (72)			
Endive (73)			
Lettuce (73)			
Mustard and Cress (74)			
Radishes (74)			
Salad onions (75)			
Tomatoes (75/76)			

Winter

DECEMBER

Vegetables

Dig and manure ground as it is cleared of spent crops. Early and thorough digging guarantees a good seed bed in spring.

Complete lifting of late-sown beetroot, carrots and swedes. Inspect root crops in store and remove any showing signs of decay. Make this a regular job throughout the winter.

Protect globe artichokes with straw or, better still, with dry peat and cloches. Protect the exposed tops of celery with straw.

Crops to be harvested Winter cabbage, late autumn cauliflowers and calabrese. Lift parsnips and Jerusalem artichokes as required. Use the last of cloched lettuce Kwiek and Tom Thumb before severe frost occurs.

Fruit

Continue the planting of all fruits if soil conditions are right. Heel in newly delivered trees if planting is impossible, making sure that the roots are completely covered.

Begin the winter pruning of apples and pears. Begin spraying with tar oil wash against pests and if possible complete the spraying of stone fruit this month. Apples and pears may be left until January.

Tie the branches of fig trees into bundles thickly wrapped in straw as protection against frost.

JANUARY

Vegetables

Plan crops for the year ahead. Order seeds, remembering to include those for successional sowings later in the year. Order seed potatoes, also asparagus plants if you want to plant them at the end of March.

Carry on with the digging whenever possible. Clear away remains of spent crops. Barrow manure or compost on to ground when it is frozen hard and leave in convenient heaps for digging in. Apply garden lime to newly-dug ground if it is at all acid.

Crops to be harvested Brussels sprouts, kale, winter cabbage. Lift parsnips, Jerusalem artichokes, leeks and celery as required.

Fruit

Plant trees, bushes and canes when conditions are favourable. Inspect recently planted canes, bushes and strawberry plants after hard frost and press back into the soil any that have been lifted by it.

Continue with pruning of established trees except in severe frost. Collect and burn prunings.

Spray trees with tar oil wash, if not done in December, to kill overwintering aphids and other pests. Choose a calm day and protect nearby grass or crops with polythene sheeting.

Inspect stored fruit. Remove immediately any showing signs of decay and keep a particularly close watch on pears, which ripen suddenly and are in perfect condition for only a few days.

FEBRUARY

Vegetables

Complete winter digging, manuring and liming early in the month. Later, if the surface is dry, dress with compound fertiliser and rake down to a tilth the area chosen for early sowing. Place cloches in position for a week or so before sowing to warm the soil.

Set up seed potatoes to sprout in a light, frostproof place.

Crops to be harvested Same as in January. Also perpetual spinach under cloches and sprouting broccoli in early districts. Dig and store parsnips still in the ground before they start to grow.

Crops to sow and plant Longpod broad beans, shallots, Jerusalem artichokes. **Under cloches,** early peas, summer spinach, radishes. **In the greenhouse,** early summer cabbage, early cauliflower.

Fruit

Try to complete planting of trees and bushes during the month. On light land where a potash deficiency is suspected apply sulphate of potash to all fruits at 1 oz per sq yd / 33 g per sq m and lightly fork it in.

Mulch young trees, bushes and canes with peat, compost or rotted manure. If the supply is limited reserve it for raspberries and blackcurrants. Cover summer fruiting strawberries with cloches at the end of the month, remembering that they may soon need watering if there is a spell of sunny weather.

Cover rhubarb with light-tight boxes or pails to forward growth.

MARCH

Vegetables

Continue to prepare ground for sowing in drying weather, leaving it severely alone as long as the surface is wet.

Thin autumn-sown lettuce in the open and under cloches.

Top dress spring cabbages with nitrogenous fertiliser to stimulate growth.

Crops to be harvested Sprouting broccoli, spring greens, turnip tops, Hungry Gap kale, perpetual spinach.

Crops to sow and plant Sow broad beans, early peas, Brussels sprouts and summer cabbage in a seed bed, early carrots, parsnips, onions, lettuce, radishes, summer spinach. **Under cloches,** beetroot, early carrots in cold districts, dwarf beans at the end of month in mild districts. Plant asparagus and early potatoes at end of month.

Fruit

Protect blossom on wall-trained trees such as peaches from frost by hanging fabric (old curtains etc) in front of them on cold nights.

Finish all planting and pruning before the middle of the month. Inspect stakes and ties of newly-planted trees and ensure that none has been loosened by wind.

Plant perpetual varieties of strawberries to fruit from July onwards. Pick off all blossoms that appear on them until the end of June.

APRIL

Vegetables

Clear away and burn Brussels sprout stems and remains of other winter brassicas which harbour aphids.

Prepare celery trenches and sites for marrows, squashes and outdoor cucumbers.

Crops to be harvested Asparagus, spring cabbage, autumn-sown cloched lettuce, later winter cauliflowers.

Crops to sow and plant Make further sowings of crops already sown in March. Sow maincrop peas, Windsor broad beans, beetroot, dwarf beans at end of the month, seed bed sowings of autumn and winter cabbage and cauliflower. **Under cloches,** sweet corn, beetroot in cold districts. **In the greenhouse,** sweet corn, tomatoes, celery. Plant early potatoes in late districts and maincrop varieties generally after mid-month. Plant onion sets, summer cabbage and cauliflower plants.

Fruit

Protect bushes and small trees in bloom by covering wherever possible on frosty nights.

Ventilate cloched strawberries on warm sunny days by opening ½ in/1.25 cm gaps between cloches

Inspect trees recently planted against walls and water thoroughly if soil at the roots is dry, as is sometimes the case even in spring.

MAY

Vegetables

Begin to build the new season's compost heap.

Hoe between rows of young crops in dry weather. Hand weed in rows and thin seedlings before tops become tall and entangled.

Draw soil over emerging potato tops if night frost threatens.

Crops to be harvested Cloched peas and carrots, early cauliflowers, autumn-sown broad beans. All at the end of the month.

Crops to sow and plant Last sowings of maincrop peas. Dwarf and runner beans, marrows, sweet corn and outdoor cucumbers at the end of the month, calabrese, sprouting broccoli and kale. Further sowings of lettuce, radishes, summer spinach and beetroot. **In the greenhouse,** marrows, squashes, pumpkins, cucumbers and melons in the first week. Plant maincrop potatoes, autumn and winter greens raised in the seed bed, sweet corn, tomatoes and other tender subjects in mild districts at the very end of the month.

Fruit

Arrange for the protection of strawberries and other soft fruit from birds by the temporary erection of nylon netting where there is no permanent fruit cage.

Control weeds round canes and bushes by hoeing or the use of a contact herbicide. Don't cultivate deeply near roots.

Fruit to be harvested Green gooseberries, strawberries under cloches. Both late in the month.

JUNE

Vegetables

Keep on top of weeds by hoeing, hand weeding and the use of a contact herbicide. This is the month of most rapid growth, and crucial in controlling weeds for the rest of the growing season.

Water freely when necessary and mulch following watering. Top dress or feed with liquid fertiliser, crops showing poor growth.

Stake runner beans and stop the leading shoots of those not being staked. Support the trusses of dwarf beans with twigs as the pods form. Pinch out the growing points of broad beans to hasten pod development and discourage blackfly.

Crops to be harvested Early potatoes, broad beans, peas, spinach, cauliflowers, carrots, turnips, cloche-sown beetroot. Stop cutting asparagus in the third week.

Crops to sow and plant Make further sowings of runner and dwarf beans. Sow an early variety of pea to pick in September. Sow, either on fresh ground or in succession to spent crops, turnips, shorthorn carrots, beetroot, garden swedes, summer and perpetual spinach, lettuce, radish and chicory for winter forcing. Plant out autumn and winter brassicas and all tender crops, choosing a warm, settled spell for the latter.

Fruit

Water newly-planted trees and spray the foliage with water in the evenings during hot weather.

Provide wires for the support and training of raspberries, blackberries, loganberries and hybrid berries planted in the autumn and winter. The canes should now be growing rapidly and care must be taken not to damage them.

Fruits to be harvested Strawberries, raspberries, red currants, cherries, mostly late in the month.

JULY

Vegetables

Tie up tall tomatoes and remove side-shoots. Reduce the number of branches on bush or dwarf varieties to 4.

Hand pollinate marrow and courgette female flowers if fruit is failing to set.

Give runner beans plenty of water and spray the flowers in the evenings to encourage the pods to set.

Crops to be harvested Runner beans, courgettes, marrows, earliest sweet corn, cos and crinkly lettuce, herbs for drying, all summer root and green crops.

Crops to sow and plant Make final sowings of carrots, turnips, beetroot, swedes, perpetual spinach and kale early in the month. Be sure to water the drills and to continue watering if necessary until the seedlings appear, especially when using pelleted seed. Plant out late-sown winter and spring greens, again watering freely to get them established quickly.

Fruit

Prop up heavily laden branches of plum trees. Broken branches are a point of entry for silver leaf disease and if a branch breaks it should be cut back cleanly and the cut surface covered with white lead or bituminous paint.

Stop disbudding perpetual strawberries. Clean up summer fruiting varieties when cropping finishes, removing and burning straw and dead leaves. If the plants are healthy some runners may be left to root for future planting.

Fruits to be harvested Strawberries, raspberries, all types of currants, peaches, early plums at end of the month.

AUGUST

Vegetables

Bend down onion tops when they show signs of dying off to complete ripening of the bulbs.

Stop tall tomatoes when 4 trusses have set or by mid-month at the latest. Stop the laterals on trailing marrows, outdoor cucumbers and melons when carrying 1 or 2 fruits.

Give plenty of water to runner beans, celery, celeriac, lettuce and late-sown peas.

Crops to be harvested Most summer vegetables and salads. Keep a daily watch on sweet corn cobs and harvest when the content of the kernels is the consistency of thin cream. Dig remaining early potatoes if the tops are dead and the skins set, storing in a cool, dark place.

Crops to sow and plant Sow spring cabbage in a seed bed for planting in autumn. Early in the month sow lettuce Tom Thumb to mature in the open, and at the end of the month Tom Thumb or Kwiek to mature under cloches.

Fruit

Cut out old canes of raspberries, loganberries and blackberries as soon as fruiting finishes and tie in the new ones.

Carry out any essential pruning of plums, gages and damsons after crops have been picked, covering large wounds with protective paint.

Send for nurserymens' catalogues if you intend to plant fruit in the autumn, inspecting different varieties in production if possible and ordering early.

Prepare vacant ground for future planting, digging deeply, working in rotted manure or compost and getting rid of all perennial weeds.

Fruits to be harvested Early (non-keeping) apples and pears, plums, peaches, apricots, blackberries, loganberries, perpetual strawberries.

Fruits to be planted Summer fruiting strawberries should be planted in August to ensure a crop the following June.

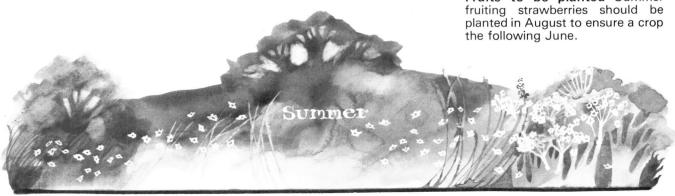
Summer

SEPTEMBER

Vegetables

Clear spent crops and place their remains on the compost heap, watering it well as each layer is completed to accelerate rotting down while the weather is still warm.

Make enquiries as to possible source of bulky organic manures in readiness for autumn and winter digging.

Crops to be harvested Lift onions and dry thoroughly before storing. Pull up tomato plants still bearing green fruits and hang up indoors before the end of the month. Cut marrows and winter squashes for storage when the skin hardens.

Crops to sow and plant Sow radishes and prickly-seeded spinach early in the month. Sow winter lettuce to stand without protection and mature in spring. **In the greenhouse,** sow lettuce in the border to cut in early winter.

Fruit

Cover perpetual strawberries now fruiting with cloches towards the end of the month.

Prune blackcurrants, cutting out completely a proportion of old branches. Young, well-ripened growth may be used for cuttings if the bushes are healthy.

Prune wall-trained peaches and nectarines and complete tying in of new shoots as fruiting finishes.

Fruits to be harvested Mid-season apples and pears, late plums and damsons, figs, grapes, autumn-fruiting raspberries.

OCTOBER

Vegetables

Earth up celery and leeks for the second time. First earthing is normally in August or September.

Apply sodium chlorate or a selective herbicide to uncultivated, weed-infested land required for planting in spring. 6 months of winter weather is required to make it safe for planting.

Begin winter digging and manuring as land becomes vacant. Break up the subsoil in areas where waterlogging occurred the previous winter.

Crops to to harvested Brussels sprouts, autumn cabbage and cauliflowers, parsnips and Jerusalem artichokes lifted as required. Lift for storage potatoes, carrots, beetroot, turnips and swedes, though the last may be better left until later. Lift all root crops, especially potatoes, very carefully to avoid damage which impairs keeping quality.

Crops to sow and plant Sow lettuce of the May King type in the first week and cover with cloches at the end of the month for use in spring. Sow round-seeded peas late in the month and cloche on emergence. Plant spring cabbage.

Fruit

Prune red and white currants and gooseberries when the leaves fall. Take cuttings of all varieties of currants and gooseberries.

Treat with dalapon, soft fruit which has become infested with twitch or couch grass, following the makers' instructions exactly.

Fruits to be harvested Apples and pears for storing. Test for ripeness when picking and store only undamaged fruit.

Fruits to be planted Trees, bushes and canes of top and soft fruit may be available for planting by the end of the month, depending on when the leaves fall and soil conditions for lifting. Have ready supplies of dry soil, bone meal, stakes and ties.

NOVEMBER

Vegetables

Carry on with digging and manuring when conditions are favourable.

Remove yellow and decaying leaves from stems of Brussels sprouts and other brassicas.

Cloche perpetual spinach and cover endive with flower pots to blanch it.

Cover the completed compost heap with polythene sheeting or other waterproof material.

Cut down dead asparagus 'fern' and cover the bed or rows with compost or rotted manure.

Crops to be harvested Most autumn and winter greens are now available. Use first those most likely to suffer from severe frost, such as cauliflowers. Complete the harvesting of root crops, drying them and rubbing off soil before storing.

Crops to sow and plant Sow Claudia Aquadulce broad bean early in the month. Complete the planting of spring cabbage.

Fruit

Hand weed strawberries and remove unwanted runners. Take care to get rid of young perennial weeds which become progressively more of a menace.

Begin winter pruning of apples and pears as soon as possible after leaf-fall.

Fruits to be harvested Finish picking late apples and pears before they blow down in gales and are spoiled.

Fruits to be planted All top and soft fruits are planted from now until early spring. This is the ideal month because the ground is still warm, but it is better to postpone planting than to attempt it in very unfavourable conditions.

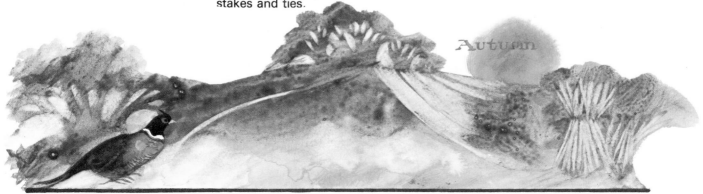

Autumn

There is no greater gift to the cook than a constant supply of top quality home-grown produce, but too often fresh fruit and vegetables are taken for granted and not treated with the respect they deserve. In my childhood home, we were always excited when the first early produce was ready. We had to make a wish with our first mouthful of peas, our first lettuce or bowl of strawberries. We loved those 'earlies' so much that they were often served as a complete meal - just new peas or beans, with new potatoes, all swimming in butter and sprinkled with fresh herbs. Another favourite accompaniment was a piece of boiled bacon, or a few crisp rashers which seemed to bring out the flavour of the vegetables. Perhaps as a family of devoted gardeners and cooks, we went too far, but in these days of processed and packaged foods, it might be nice to return to the days of seasonal treasures from the garden.

It is a great help if the kitchen can influence the garden at planning time, so that nobody gets bored with cabbages or carrots while longing for salads, exotic asparagus and artichokes, or even a plentiful supply of onions and herbs. Try to think beyond the routine family meals to the possibilities of home-made jams, jellies and pickles, and the requirements of the freezer. This may mean less emphasis of greenstuff and root vegetables, but more space for soft fruit or tomatoes perhaps. With this forward planning, there need never be any wastage of home-grown produce.

When the garden is in full swing, be sure to harvest both fruit and vegetables regularly. Early in the day, take in what is needed for main meals, and if there is surplus, freeze or process it at once. Never wait until there are glut quantities to tackle.

Aim at plenty of variety in planning meals and preserving, and don't stick to a rigid routine of stewed fruit and vast quantities of green tomato chutney or plum jam. It is far better to process 2 or 3 pounds of fruit each time, varying recipes, and the family will

There are two cardinal sins often committed in the kitchen - over-elaboration and the use of water. Vegetables and fruit in particular suffer from over-cooking and elaborate dressing, after being drowned in gallons of water. Avoid boiling anything and try serving your home-grown produce braised, steamed, stuffed, and even raw.

Fruit and vegetables should be eaten fresh and young. Nothing can restore the flavour of old stale produce. The aim of cooking is to produce vegetables which are just tender, not soft and pulpy, and they should always be served immediately after cooking. Properly-cooked fruit should be tender without total disintegration, and with just enough juice to make the dish look attractive rather than the traditional bath of sweetened water.

VEGETABLES

Prepare only as many vegetables as you need for the meal, unless you have plans for a cooked salad in the immediate future. Cook them in enough water just to cover, lightly salted, but avoid bicarbonate of soda. Cook until tender (green vegetables are nicer when slightly crisp). Drain well and serve at once with a knob of butter.

Braising is a good way of conserving flavour, and it saves fuel when vegetables can be cooked in the oven along with the main dish and pudding. Put the vegetables into a tightly-lidded ovenware dish, and just cover with water or stock, seasoned with salt and pepper. Allow 20-25 minutes in a moderate oven. The vegetables can be served in the juices, or you can reduce these juices by fast boiling in a clean saucepan until you have a glaze. Add a knob of butter and pour over the vegetables.

Stuffing need not be confined to the traditional marrow. Try filling a cabbage, courgettes, cucumbers, aubergines or tomatoes with a meat, cheese or breadcrumb stuffing, with plenty of seasoning and herbs, and perhaps a home-made tomato or mushroom sauce. A complete meal can be cooked in the oven if accompanying potatoes are baked in their jackets, and a pudding is put on the bottom shelf.

Roasting and Frying are particularly good for root vegetables. Boil potatoes, parsnips, Jerusalem artichokes, turnips or swedes for 5 minutes, then drain them well and put them round a joint, basting occasionally with the hot fat. When frying chips, cook them in hot clean fat until soft but pale. Remove from the fat for a few seconds to allow its temperature to rise, then plunge them back into the

welcome different delicacies instead of groaning at yet another jar of the same old stuff.

The same method goes for freezing, when fruit may be prepared in 2 or 3 different ways, as well as in the form of favourite puddings and pies. It is good too to be a little unconventional with your own fresh produce. Fruit doesn't automatically have to be served stewed after the main course of lunch or dinner. What's wrong with a bowl of fresh sugared raspberries or strawberries for breakfast or a late-night snack? And why not a bowl of plums or raw carrots for the children to nibble on between meals whenever they feel like it?

In the same way, don't be tied by the traditional serving of potatoes and one vegetable (usually boiled) with the main meal meat or poultry. What is wrong with serving 3 or 4 vegetables and no potatoes, or trying hot cooked beetroot or celeriac as an accompaniment rather than as a salad? Likewise, freshly grated carrot or cabbage is good with grilled meat, fish, or poultry. In these days of rising prices, there is a lot to be said as well for serving a single well-prepared vegetable as a first course, or for making vegetable flans for light meals.

Growing your own vegetables is a marvellous way of saving money, and it's important that the economy should be carried over into the kitchen. Even a few vegetables or a handful of fruit can be turned into a special dish, or used as part of a pickle or jam recipe, or frozen ready for the leaner days of winter. Never let the oddments linger in a basket or bowl until they have to be thrown out, but plan to use them up quickly. The same applies to leftover cooked vegetables or fruit which should never be left to clutter up the refrigerator. Try cooked vegetables in salads, or adding them to pies or flans, or making them into soup, and use cooked fruit as a flan filling, or convert it into a mousse or fool. That way you'll enjoy some wonderful meals and save a few pennies.

very hot fat to become golden and crisp.

SALADS
A salad is much more than a lettuce leaf and a piece of tomato. All kinds of vegetables can be eaten raw, and many cooked vegetables are delicious eaten cold with a dressing or sauce.

Salad Vegetables such as lettuce, radishes, cucumber and tomatoes are at their best prepared individually. If they are mixed in a bowl, the wetter vegetables quickly look limp and unattractive and leak juices over the rest. Prepare each item separately and serve in a bowl with its own dressing or garnish e.g. tomatoes in French dressing with a topping of basil; cucumber in vinegar with a seasoning of salt, pepper, sugar and parsley. Each person can assemble his choice of vegetables and the salads remain fresh and attractive.

Other Vegetables which are good eaten raw are carrots, celeriac, cabbage, celery, peppers and cauliflower florets. They are best cut in small pieces or in rings and can be served with nothing but some coarse sea salt, mayonnaise, or lemon juice. Carrots, celeriac and cabbage can be finely grated too.

Cooked Vegetables are excellent in salads. Broad beans, peas and cauliflower are delicious dressed with French Dressing or with mayonnaise while slightly warm. They can be mixed with cubed potatoes and carrots to make a more substantial salad. Cooked young leeks, asparagus and globe artichokes can also be dressed with oil and vinegar while slightly warm and served as a first course or as a salad.

FRUIT
Most fresh fruit is so delicious that it seems to be a pity to cook it at all but for many centuries raw fruit was considered unwholesome and this tradition dies hard in the kitchen. The result is too often a mass of pale apples or rhubarb floating in sweet water. It is much better not to add water at all when cooking fruits which contain plenty of natural juices. Simply cook the prepared fruit in enough sugar to sweeten, with a knob of butter, in a thick saucepan on top of the stove, or in a casserole in the oven. Instead of sugar, you can use honey, syrup or an appropriate jam. For pies, puddings and crumbles follow the same principle, avoid adding water, but do add sugar and a little butter. To finish a fruit dish, try adding a little spice (cinnamon with raspberries or plums for instance, or cloves with apples) or a touch of an appropriate liqueur.

Freezing is the best way of preserving most fruit and vegetables because it retains their flavour, colour, texture and nutritive value better than any other method. It is important to choose only young tender vegetables and fresh, ripe fruit and they should all be processed immediately after harvesting. The home gardener should harvest regularly each day and freeze the produce at once, rather than waiting until a large batch is ready, by which time some vegetables will be tough and stringy, and some fruit will certainly be over-ripe.

A freezer can easily be overloaded with fresh produce. Generally, it is recommended that no more than 3 lb/1.5 kg of fresh food should be frozen for each cu. ft. of freezer space at any one time. It takes about 6 hours to completely freeze garden produce, so it is quite possible to deal with two batches during one day.

VEGETABLES
Prepare vegetables just before freezing. Make plenty of extra ice and store it in the freezer during the peak freezing season, as a lot will be used during preparation. Switch to fast-freeze 2-3 hours before freezing. Wash all vegetables thoroughly in cold water, grade by size or cut as necessary. It is possible to freeze unblanched vegetables for storage for up to 3 months, but they will quickly lose colour, flavour and nutritive value after that and it is a pity to risk spoiling top-quality produce by neglecting correct preparation.

Blanching
You will need a blanching basket or wire salad basket, a lidded saucepan which will hold at least 8 pints/4.5 l of water, a large bowl, a colander, a stop watch or minute timer and a bucketful of ice. Blanching must be timed accurately, over-blanching results in flabby, colourless vegetables, and under-blanching means a colour change and loss of nutritive value.

Put 8 pints/4.5 l of water into the saucepan with the wire basket. Bring to the boil and add the vegetables (blanch not more than 1 lb/400 g vegetables at a time), put on the lid, and bring the water quickly back to the boil. Start timing as soon as it boils, and when the time is up, lift out the wire basket. Tip the vegetables into the colander in a bowl of water chilled with ice cubes; running water from a tap is simply not cold enough. The vegetables should be chilled for the same length of time as they were blanched. Drain thoroughly and open-freeze or pack at once. Put bags in single layers in the fast-freeze compartment, or in an older freezer, see that each bag touches a side or the base of the cabinet.

Open-freezing
Many vegetables can usefully be open-frozen before packing so that they remain separate and will pour freely. Use a baking sheet, or tray, a polythene box lid, or a special fast freeze tray with a foil lining. Simply spread the vegetables out in a single layer and freeze till hard. Pack in bags or rigid containers.

Packaging
A variety of freezer packaging is available to suit different types of produce. Polythene bags in a range of sizes are extremely useful, but these must be made of heavy-gauge material to withstand very low temperatures. They are most easily sealed with a twist-tie. Rigid containers are best for delicate produce which could be broken or damaged during storage, such as asparagus or broccoli, these are made of aluminium foil or a rigid plastic. All packages should be labelled with the date of freezing and the weight of produce, and a record kept to ensure a regular turnover of stocks. It is important to exclude air from packages in the freezer. It can be pushed out with the hands, extracted with a drinking straw or with a special pump. When a rigid container is used, allow ½ in/1.25 cm free space above the contents to allow for their expansion which can push off a lid.

Cooking
Vegetables are partly cooked by blanching, and need only a little additional cooking before serving. Broccoli and spinach are better partly thawed before cooking and corn-on-the-cob must be completely thawed to allow the heat to penetrate. Use the minimum of water for cooking vegetables, steam them or cook them without water in a casserole in the oven with a knob of butter.

Storage times
Most vegetables will keep well for 12 months in the freezer, but 9 months or so is about the maximum time before fresh produce is in season again. It is good freezer practice to use your stock regularly, storage space costs money and frozen vegetables such as peas or beans, can be served with a fresh cabbage or root straight from the garden. Vegetable purée and fried vegetables from the freezer are best used within 3 months.

Non-freezables
Salad vegetables which contain a lot of water, e.g. lettuce and radishes, are not suitable for freezing. Some crops such as celery, chicory and tomatoes can be frozen, but are only useful for cooking and cannot be eaten raw after thawing. If space is short, freeze luxury produce such as asparagus, artichokes, peas, beans and courgettes. Most greenstuff will stand well in the ground for some time as will roots, or these can be stored dry. Onions and shallots do not need freezing, but a few frozen ones are useful for quick meals. Marrows and pumpkins will store well for some time in a cool, dry place.

FRUIT
Fruit does not change its character appreciably during freezing, and it will taste freshly picked, unlike that which is bottled or canned. Freeze only top-quality fruit (which is completely ripe but not over-ripe) immediately after picking and work with small quantities which can be prepared quickly. Wash fruit in ice-chilled water to firm it before processing so that no juice is lost and remove all stems and stones carefully. Fruit can be packed in a variety of ways:

Unsweetened dry pack
Dry the fruit after washing it and pack in bags or rigid containers. If preferred, open-freeze before packing. Light-coloured fruits which discolour badly should be

packed with sugar, as this helps to retard the action of the enzymes which cause darkening.

Sweetened dry pack
Mix the sugar with the fruit before packing, or arrange alternate layers of sugar and fruit in a rigid pack, starting with a layer of fruit and ending with a layer of sugar.

Syrup pack
Syrup for freezing fruit should be made with white sugar dissolved in boiling water and cooled completely before use. A little lemon juice, citric or ascorbic acid should be added to the syrup for apples, peaches and pears which discolour easily. Syrups can be prepared in any of 3 strengths:
Light syrup - 8 oz/200 g sugar to 1 pint/500 ml water.
Medium syrup - 12 oz/300 g sugar to 1 pint/500 ml water.
Heavy syrup - 1 lb/400 g sugar to 1 pint/500 ml water.
Fruit should be packed in rigid containers and covered with syrup, allowing 1/2 in/1.25 cm headspace for expansion. For light-coloured fruit, this space should be filled with crumpled foil or freezer paper to prevent the fruit rising above the syrup and discolouring on contact with the air.

Purée
Fruit purée can be either raw or cooked, and should be sweetened to taste before freezing.

Storage times
Fruit will keep well for 12 months in the freezer, but fruit purée may lose some quality after 4 months. Use frozen fruit regularly and clear out stocks early so that you appreciate the new season's produce.

Thawing and cooking
Thaw fruit only in usable quantities as it quickly loses quality and flavour once thawed. If possible, thaw in the refrigerator allowing 6 hours for 1 lb/400 g fruit. It is best served when just thawed and still frosty. Unsweetened packs take longer to thaw than sweetened ones, and dry sugar packs thaw most quickly. Partly thawed fruit can be used in pies or puddings, or can be cooked in hot syrup. If frozen unsweetened fruit is to be used for jam, allow 10% more fruit than listed in a standard recipe, as there is a slight pectin loss in the freezer.

PREPARATION OF CROPS FOR FREEZING

Asparagus	Wash well and remove woody stems and small scales. Cut asparagus into 6 in/15 cm lengths, and grade according to thickness. Do not tie in bundles, but blanch each size separately. Allow 2 minutes (thin stems), 3 minutes (medium stems), 4 minutes (thick stems). Cool and drain thoroughly and pack according to size in rigid containers, alternating the heads.
Aubergines	Use tender, mature, medium-sized aubergines. Do not peel but cut into 1 in/2.5 cm slices. Blanch for 4 minutes, cool, drain and pack in rigid containers in layers separated by clingfilm or freezer paper.
Beetroot	Use small young beet no more than 3 in/7.5 cm diameter. Cook completely, cool quickly and rub off the skins. Pack either whole, sliced or diced.
Broad beans	Use small young beans with tender skins. Remove them from the pods and blanch for 1 1/2 minutes. Open-freeze and pack in bags.
Broccoli and Calabrese	Use compact heads with tender stalks not more than 1 in/2.5 cm thick. Trim off woody stems and outer leaves. Wash well in salted water for 30 minutes, and rinse in clean water. Blanch for 3 minutes (thin stems), 4 minutes (medium stems), or 5 minutes (thick stems). Cool and pack in rigid containers, alternating the heads.
Brussels sprouts	Use small compact sprouts and remove discoloured leaves. Grade for size and blanch for 3 minutes (small), 4 minutes (medium). Cool, open-freeze and pack in bags.
Cabbage	Shred finely and blanch for 1 1/2 minutes. Pack in rigid containers.
Carrots	Use young carrots, remove tops, wash and scrape well. Leave the small ones whole, but slice the larger ones. Blanch for 3 minutes (whole) or 2 minutes (sliced), cool, drain and pack in bags.
Cauliflower	Use firm heads with close white curds. Freeze very small heads whole, or break into sprigs. Wash thoroughly. Add the juice of 1 lemon to the water and blanch for 3 minutes.
Celeriac	Cut into slices, add the juice of 1 lemon to the water and blanch for 3 minutes. Cool and pack in bags. Celeriac can be cooked in a little water and frozen as a purée. It cannot be used in salads after freezing.
Celery	Use crisp stalks and remove strings. Wash well, cut into 1 in/2.5 cm lengths and blanch for 3 minutes. Cool, drain and pack dry in bags. Pack some of the blanching liquid to use for cooking later. Leave 1/2 in/1.25 cm headspace in rigid containers. Celery cannot be eaten raw after freezing, but is useful to serve as a vegetable, or to add to stews and soups.

Chicory	Use compact heads with yellow tips. Trim stalks and remove any bruised outside leaves. Add the juice of 1 lemon to the water, and blanch for 2 minutes. Cool and drain thoroughly before packing in rigid containers. Chicory cannot be used for salads after freezing.
Dwarf beans	Use young tender beans about the thickness of a bootlace. Top and tail. Freeze small beans whole, or cut into 1 in/2.5 cm pieces. Blanch for 3 minutes (whole) or 2 minutes (cut). Cool and pack in bags.
Globe artichokes	Trim outer leaves and stalks and wash thoroughly removing hairy 'chokes'. Blanch for 7 minutes with 1 tablespoon/15 ml lemon juice in the water. Cool, drain well and pack in rigid containers. Alternatively, remove all the leaves and blanch the hearts for 5 minutes. Pack in bags or rigid containers.
Herbs	Pick soft-leaved herbs (basil, chervil, chives, mint, parsley, tarragon) when young. Wash the sprigs and pack them in bags. Alternatively chop the herbs finely and put them into ice-cube trays with a spoonful of water. Freeze and transfer the frozen cubes to bags for storage. This method is particularly useful for mint and parsley. Frozen herbs become limp when thawed and are not then suitable for garnishing.
Jerusalem artichokes	Peel and cut into pieces. Soften slightly in hot butter and cook in chicken stock. Sieve and freeze as purée in rigid containers.
Kale	Use young, tender, tightly curled kale, and discard any discoloured or tough leaves. Wash well and separate leaves from stems. Blanch for 1 minute and drain thoroughly after cooling. Leaves can be chopped for easier packing in bags, but do this after blanching.
Leeks	Use young even-sized leeks, remove coarse outer leaves and trim off green tops. Wash in cold running water. Cut larger leeks into ½ in/ 1.25 cm thick rings, but leave the small ones whole. Blanch for 3 minutes (whole), 2 minutes (sliced). Cool, drain and pack in rigid containers or in bags, but overwrap bags as leeks smell strongly.
Marrows and Courgettes	Large older marrows are best cooked and frozen as purée. Cut tender young courgettes, or very small marrows into ¼ in/5 mm slices without peeling. Blanch for 1 minute, or toss in hot butter until tender. Open-freeze blanched slices and pack in bags, pack the fried slices in rigid containers.
Mushrooms	Grade mushrooms for size, wipe but do not peel them. Pack in bags. Small button mushrooms can be cooked in butter (3 oz/75 g butter to 1 lb/ 400 g mushrooms) for 5 minutes and then packed in rigid containers for freezing.
Onions	Peel small onions and leave them whole, but peel and chop larger ones. Blanch for 3 minutes (whole), 2 minutes (chopped). Cool, drain and pack in rigid containers or in bags, but overwrap bags as onions smell strongly.
Parsnips	Old parsnips are best cooked and frozen as purée. Young parsnips should be peeled and cut into thin strips or small dice. Blanch for 2 minutes. Cool, drain and pack in bags.
Peas	Use young, tender sweet peas. Blanch for 1 minute. Cool, drain and pack in bags. Peas may be open-frozen before packing. Sugar peas (mangetout) should be frozen while the pods are still flat. Top, tail and string them and blanch for 2 minutes. Cool drain and pack in bags.
Peppers	Use firm, plump, glossy peppers. Wash and dry them, cut off the stems, and remove the seeds and membranes. Cut into halves, slices or dice. Blanch for 3 minutes (halves), 2 minutes (slices or dice). Cool, drain and pack in bags.
Potatoes	Do not freeze potatoes blanched in water, or plainly boiled old potatoes. Cooked jacket potatoes, roast, creamed, duchesse and potato croquettes can all be frozen. Chips must not be frozen raw nor boiled in water, but fried in clean fat until soft (not coloured). Drain, cool and pack in bags. New potatoes should be scraped, graded for size, and slightly undercooked. Drain, toss them in butter and pack in boil-in-bags (for serving, put the whole bag in boiling water, remove from heat and leave 10 minutes).
Runner beans	Use young beans, no longer than 7 in/17.5 cm. Do not shred finely, but string the beans and slice them thickly. Blanch for 2 minutes, cool and pack in bags.

Spinach	Use young tender leaves without heavy ribs. Strip leaves from stems, and remove any that are bruised or discoloured. Wash well and blanch for 2 minutes, shaking the wire basket occasionally so the leaves do not mat together. Cool quickly and press out excess moisture. Pack in bags or rigid containers. Do not add any water during reheating.
Squashes and Pumpkins	Cook the flesh of squashes and pumpkins in very little water until soft. Mash well and freeze as purée in rigid containers.
Tomatoes	Tomatoes cannot be used for salads after freezing but they are very useful for cooking. Wipe whole tomatoes, grade them for size and freeze in bags (the skins will drop off when thawed). Alternatively cut tomatoes into halves and open-freeze before packing (these halves are useful for grilling or frying). Tomatoes may also be skinned and simmered in their own juice before sieving and freezing as purée.
Turnips and Swedes	Peel, dice and blanch for 2½ minutes. Cool, drain and pack in bags. Or these roots can be cooked completely, sieved and frozen as purée, a form in which they are so often eaten.
Apples	Peel, core and drop into cold water. Cut into slices and pack in bags or rigid containers. Use sweetened dry pack (8 oz/200 g sugar to 2 lb/1 kg fruit) or a medium syrup. 'Fluffy' cooking apples are better cooked, sweetened and frozen as purée.
Apricots	Wash firm ripe fruit, cut into halves and take out stones. Drop into boiling water for 30 seconds and chill in cold water. Pack at once in rigid containers. Use sweetened dry pack (8 oz/200 g sugar to 2 lb/1 kg fruit) or a medium syrup containing ¼ teaspoon/1 g ascorbic acid.
Blackberries	Use fully-ripe, dark glossy berries. Open-freeze and pack unsweetened in bags. If preferred, use sweetened dry pack (8 oz/200 g sugar to 2 lb/1 kg fruit), a heavy syrup, or pack as sweetened purée.
Blackcurrants	Strip stems from currants and wash the fruit in ice-cold water. Dry well and pack in bags or rigid containers. Use unsweetened dry pack, sweetened dry pack (1 lb/400 g sugar to 2 lb/1 kg fruit) or a medium syrup. Blackcurrants may also be cooked, sweetened and packed as purée.
Cherries	Use sweet or sour varieties and leave in ice-cold water for 1 hour before freezing. Dry the cherries and remove the stones. Pack in rigid containers. Use sweetened dry pack (8 oz/200 g sugar to 2 lb/1 kg fruit), a medium syrup (for sweet fruit) or a heavy syrup (for sour fruit).
Figs	Wash in ice-cold water and remove stems without bruising. Pack, peeled or unpeeled, in unsweetened dry pack, or in a light syrup.
Gooseberries	Wash in ice-cold water and dry. Pack in bags or rigid containers. Use unsweetened dry pack, a medium syrup or freeze as sweetened purée.
Grapes	Peel, halve and remove seeds. Pack in a light syrup in rigid containers.
Peaches	Peel, halve, remove stones, and brush the fruit with lemon juice; work quickly because it tends to discolour. Pack in halves (or slices) in a medium syrup containing ¼ teaspoon/1 g ascorbic acid.
Pears	Use strongly-flavoured ripe pears. Peel and quarter the fruit and remove cores. Dip pieces in lemon juice and poach in a light syrup for 1½ minutes. Drain, cool, and pack in the cold syrup in rigid containers.
Plums	Wash in ice-cold water, dry well and remove stones. Whole raw plums may be packed unsweetened in bags. Use a sweetened dry pack for halved plums (8 oz/200 g sugar to 2 lb/1 kg fruit) or a medium syrup.
Raspberries and Loganberries	Wash in ice-cold water and drain well. Open-freeze and pack unsweetened in bags or use sweetened dry pack (8 oz/200 g sugar to 2 lb/1 kg fruit) or a light syrup. Fresh berries may be sieved, sweetened and frozen as purée.
Rhubarb	Use young pink sticks, and freeze either raw or cooked. Wash, trim and cut into lengths. Pack in aluminium foil or polythene bags, unsweetened. Alternatively, pack in a medium syrup in rigid containers, or cook, sweeten and pack as purée.
Strawberries	Remove hulls, wash in ice-cold water and dry well. Open-freeze and pack unsweetened in polythene bags, in a medium syrup, or as raw unsweetened purée.

JAMS AND JELLIES

It is not difficult to make fruit jams and jellies, and this is a very good way of preserving small quantities of fruit. No special equipment is necessary, and most items will be found in every kitchen.

Equipment
A large saucepan which should not be made of zinc or iron. Enamel is suitable if it is not chipped. Copper will keep green fruits (such as gooseberries) green, but can spoil the colour of red fruits. Aluminium is ideal. The pan should be a thick one, and wide enough to allow rapid evaporation of liquid to speed up setting. It may be worth buying a special preserving pan because it can be useful for many other kitchen tasks. Also needed are a set of scales, a large jug and a long-handled wooden spoon. A sugar thermometer is not essential, but it can help the amateur cook to achieve certain success. If jellies are to be made, a jelly bag is worth buying, to suspend from four hooks or from the legs of an upturned chair.

It is important to pack jam properly so that it will not be spoiled by moulds, or attacks from insects or mice. Save jam jars from year to year, or use screwtop honey, pickle or preserving jars. Sets of waxed paper discs, transparent covers and labels can all be bought in packets, and should be used to give the jam a neat appearance and help to keep it clean and airproof. Plastic covers can also be bought, which are particularly useful if there is likely to be any mouse damage.

Ingredients
Jams and jellies can be made from single fruits or from a mixture of two or more. Use fresh sound fruit which is not mushy nor over-ripe. The setting property of jam depends on its pectin content, which is particularly high in apples, blackcurrants, damsons, plums, gooseberries and redcurrants. The addition of these fruits, or their extracted juices, to fruit such as cherries and strawberries which are low in pectin content, will ensure a firm set. A similar result can be achieved with acid in the form of lemon juice, citric or tartaric acid, which help to extract pectin, retain colour and prevent crystallisation. For 4 lb/2 kg low-pectin fruit or vegetables for jam, allow 2 tablespoons/30 ml lemon juice *or* ½ teaspoon/3 g citric or tartaric acid *or* ¼ pint/125 ml redcurrant or gooseberry juice. Special preserving sugar is available, but is more expensive than other types. It has the advantage of dissolving quickly, but lump or granulated sugar can be used instead.

Making jam
Pick over the fruit and discard damaged or bruised pieces, together with leaves and stems. Just before cooking, wash it gently in a colander with cold water, then stone or peel as necessary with a stainless steel or silver knife. Weigh the ingredients accurately, it is important to get the right balance between fruit and sugar, according to pectin content. The fruit has to be cooked slowly to extract pectin, soften skins, and keep a good colour. The sugar should then be stirred in carefully until it has dissolved (if the sugar is warmed slightly in the oven first, it will dissolve more quickly). Once the sugar has melted into the fruit, the mixture must be brought to the boil and cooked quickly to setting point.

It is advisable to test jam for setting after as little as 5 minutes' boiling, because some fruits actually lose their setting qualities if boiled for too long. Jam sets at 220°F/110°C but it can be tested without a thermometer by dropping a little onto a saucer, and leaving it to cool. If the jam forms a skin and wrinkles when pushed with a finger, it is ready. Remove the pan from the heat as soon as the jam has reached the setting point.

Making jelly
The fruit should be prepared as for jam, and cooked until very tender. It should then be strained through a jelly bag or a clean piece of muslin or a tea-towel. The juice should drip slowly into a bowl, the bag must not be squeezed, stirred or shaken, or the jelly will be cloudy. After measuring the juice, add the sugar specified by the recipe and stir until dissolved, before boiling and testing as for jam.

Packing and storing
Finished jams or jellies should be skimmed with a perforated spoon. Whole-fruit jam should be left in the pan for 10 minutes, then stirred gently and put into clean, dry, warm jars. Jelly need not stand, but should be poured into jars carefully to prevent air-bubbles from forming. Fill all jars right to the top and cover at once with waxed discs. Moisten transparent covers on one side only, fit over the jars and secure with elastic bands. Label with the variety and date of making, and leave the jars until cold before moving, wipe and polish them with a clean cloth, and store in a cool, dark, dry place.

Surplus fruit and vegetables can be turned into delicious pickles and chutneys which are a great asset to the winter store-cupboard. Make small quantities so you have plenty of variety to eat with cold meats or cheeses.

Equipment
Use only unchipped enamel or aluminium saucepans and avoid any kind of equipment which can impart a metallic flavour. For this same reason, use nylon or hair sieves, stainless steel knives and wooden spoons. Clean, dry, warm bottles must be used and it is important to use plastic or metal lids lined with a ceresin disc. Uncovered metal will rust and taint the pickles and paper covers will allow evaporation. It is a good idea to save proprietary pickle or sauce bottles because these have the correct tops.

Pickles
A variety of vegetables can be preserved in spiced vinegar. They should be young and very fresh. Clean them, skin or chop according to type and soak them in brine or dry salt, before rinsing, draining, packing and covering with vinegar. Use cooking salt (sold in blocks or bags), not table salt.

Cold vinegar gives a crisp pickle, while boiling vinegar gives a soft pickle. To make a good spiced vinegar, put 1 pint/500 ml vinegar into a bowl with ¼ oz/6 g each of cinnamon stick, whole cloves, whole mace and whole allspice, and 6 peppercorns. Cover with a plate, and stand the bowl in a saucepan of cold water. Bring to the boil slowly, then remove from heat. Leave to stand for 3 hours and strain before use.

Brine for pickling is made by dissolving 4 oz/100 g cooking salt in 2 pints/1 l water.

Prepare onions by soaking unpeeled in brine for 12 hours, peel and soak in fresh brine for 24 hours. Rinse and drain, pack into jars and cover with cold spiced vinegar. Store for 3 months before use.

Red cabbage should be shredded and arranged in layers with salt in a basin, finishing with salt. Leave for 24 hours, drain, rinse, pack in jars and cover with cold spiced vinegar. This can be used after 1 week, it loses its crispness after about 3 months'.

Gherkins should be soaked in brine for 3 days, then drained, packed and covered with hot spiced vinegar. Cover and leave for 24 hours in a warm place. Pour off the vinegar, boil it and cover the gherkins with it again for 24 hours. Repeat the process until the gherkins are a good green colour, then finally cover and store.

Sweet Pickles
Fruit such as pears, peaches, apricots and blackberries are very good preserved in spiced vinegar to which sugar has been added and reduced to a syrupy consistency. To 4 lb/2 kg fruit, allow 1 pint/500 ml vinegar, 1 teaspoon/5 ml lemon juice and 2 lb/1 kg sugar. Prepare the fruit and cut into halves or quarters. Dissolve the sugar in the vinegar with the lemon juice and simmer the fruit until just tender. Drain and pack the fruit and keep it hot. Boil the liquid until thick and syrupy and pour over the fruit. Cover and store for 3 months before use.

Piccalilli
A good mustard pickle can be made with a mixture of vegetables, and this is a useful way of dealing with a few late items from the garden. For a good mixture, collect 3 lb/1.5 kg vegetables, including cauliflowers, beans, small onions, green tomatoes, marrow or cucumber. Dice them and leave in brine for 24 hours, covered with a plate (sprigs of cauliflower, small tomatoes and onions can be left whole). Rinse and drain the vegetables and put into a pan with 1¼ pints/625 ml vinegar, 6 oz/150 g sugar, ¾ oz/18 g dry mustard, ¼ oz/6 g each of ground ginger and ground cardamon. Simmer for 20 minutes, drain and pack into hot jars. Mix ¾ oz/18 g plain flour and ¼ oz/6 g turmeric with ¼ pint/125 ml vinegar. Add the mixture to the hot vinegar and boil for 2 minutes. Pour over the vegetables and seal tightly.

Chutney
Good chutney needs time to mature and is best stored for 6 months before use, so start making early batches with gooseberries and rhubarb, and continue later with apples and green or ripe tomatoes, so that there is a year-round supply in the cupboard. Chutney is made from a mixture of fruit and/or vegetables with vinegar, brown sugar, and spices. Dried fruit and onions are other favourite additions.

Chop or mince the fruit or vegetables and put them into half the amount of vinegar in the recipe, together with the spices, and cook for 45 minutes. Add the sugar and dried fruit, and the remaining vinegar, and then simmer very slowly until the chutney is richly brown and there is no trace of unabsorbed liquid. Fill hot dry jars completely to the brim, cover, and store in a cool, dark place.

BOTTLING

There are 2 principle methods of bottling fruit 1/by sterilisation in a water-bath 2/by heating in a moderate oven. The old method of heating in a slow oven is not suitable for other than dark-coloured fruit and gooseberries, so it is better to use the moderate oven method which is equally suitable for all types of fruit as well as tomatoes. It is not advisable to bottle vegetables unless you are used to using a pressure cooker very accurately.

Packing the fruit

Pack soft fruit as tightly as possible without bruising, and add syrup or water every 4 layers as packing progresses. Pack hard fruit tightly, and fill with syrup or water after packing, giving the bottle a sharp tap to remove any air bubbles.

For tomatoes use a brine made from 1/2 oz/15 g salt to 1 3/4 pints/1 l water.

For apples use a syrup made from 8 oz/200 g sugar to 1 pint/500 ml water.

For soft fruit, peaches, pears and apricots use a heavier syrup using 12 oz/300 g sugar to 1 pint/500 ml water.

To make a syrup, dissolve the sugar in half the water, boil for 2 minutes, then add the remaining water and stir.

Water bath method

For processing, screwband bottles are needed, either with glass lids and rubber rings, or with the more modern closing of a metal lid fitted with a rubber ring and a screwband. If the older type of jar is used, new rings must always be fitted to ensure a perfect seal. A large container is needed for heating the water; a preserving pan, a ham or fish kettle are all very suitable. The container must be deep enough to hold sufficient water to cover the bottles completely. A wire rack (a cake rack or grill rack will do), a wooden rack or a thick pad of newspaper must be used as a false bottom to the pan to insulate the bottles from direct contact with the heat; a thermometer is essential.

Pack the fruit into the bottles using a long-handled wooden spoon and cover with cold syrup (or brine for tomatoes), put on the lids securely and loosen the screwbands one quarter of a turn. The bottles should then be completely submerged in cold water, and the pan itself covered with a lid or board. Heat the water slowly allowing 1 hour for it to rise to 130°F/55°C. The water temperature should then be raised to the required level, according to the fruit, in 30 minutes. Process for the length of time shown on the chart, remove the bottles from the water and tighten the screwbands immediately.

Oven method

Preheat the oven to 300°F/150°C/Gas Mark 2. Pack the fruit into the bottles and fill with boiling syrup (or brine for tomatoes) leaving 1 in/2.5 cm headspace. Put on the lids (but not the screwbands), and place the bottles onto a baking tray thickly lined with newspaper - do not let the bottles touch. Position the tray in the centre of the oven, process for the length of time shown on the chart, remove from the oven and secure the screwbands.

Testing the seal

When the screwbands have been tightened after processing, the jars should be left for 24 hours. Then take off the bands and lift the bottles carefully by the lids. If they are secure, the seal is complete. If the seal is not complete, the fruit can be re-processed but may become rather soft, or it can be used at once.

Water bath method	Oven method
165°F/74°C maintained for 10 minutes	300°F/150°C/Gas Mark 2 maintained for 40 minutes

Apples
Blackberries
Gooseberries
Raspberries
Rhubarb
Strawberries

Water bath method	Oven method
180°F/83°C maintained for 15 minutes	300°F/150°C/Gas Mark 2 maintained for 50 minutes

Apricots
Cherries
Currants
Damsons
Greengages
Peaches
Plums

Water bath method	Oven method
190°F/88°C maintained for 30 minutes	300°F/150°C/Gas Mark 2 maintained for 70 minutes

Pears
Tomatoes in brine

This is the oldest method of food preservation. It needs no special equipment but can take from a few hours to several days because it is important not to scorch or to cook the produce that is being dried.

Peas and beans, onions and leeks, mushrooms, apples, pears, plums and grapes can all be successfully treated. They can either be dried in a very low oven, on the slatted shelves of an airing cupboard, or on a shelf over a solid fuel cooker. In a cupboard or over a cooker, the food must be spread out on a wire rack and covered with muslin to prevent dust contamination. There should be a constant gentle heat with a current of air to carry off the moisture, so that the cupboard or oven door must be left slightly open. The ideal heat for drying is between 120°F - 150°F/50°C - 65°C/Gas Mark ¼.

Peas and beans

Leave marrowfat peas and haricot beans on the plants until dry and withered. Pull up the plants and hang in an airy shed. Shell the peas and beans and spread them on a tray in a warm place, as above. When they are completely hard and dry, store in an airtight container in a cool dark place. Young sweet peas need slightly different treatment - shell the peas, tie in muslin and blanch in boiling water for 5 minutes. Chill in cold water, drain and pat dry with kitchen paper. Spread on trays and dry as above.

Onions and leeks

Onions can of course be hung up in strings for storage, but if they show any signs of being damp, it is better to dry them. Peel medium-sized onions and cut them into slices about ¼ in/5 mm thick. Separate the slices into rings, and use the small inner rings for immediate cooking, as they are too small for drying. Put the larger rings into fast boiling water for 30 seconds, pour into a colander, then chill in cold water. Drain and dry the rings on kitchen paper. Spread onto a rack and dry in the oven as above. The rings may discolour slightly. Allow to cook and store in jars or boxes. Leeks should be well cleaned and cut into strips before blanching for 15 seconds and drying.

Mushrooms

Use fresh, open mushrooms for drying and remove the stems (these can be used for immediate cooking). Clean the mushrooms with a damp cloth, and thread them onto a fine string with knots between each to prevent them touching. Hang in an oven from the rack, or in a warm airy place and dry as for other vegetables. The mushrooms will be like dry chamois leather. Store in jars.

Fruit

Apple rings. Use firm, juicy, crisp apples which are not over-ripe. Peel and core them, and cut into ¼ in/5 mm thick rings. Place the rings in a solution of 1 oz/25 g salt to 4 pints/2.25 l water for 10 minutes. Drain, thread onto thin sticks and rest the sticks across oven racks so that the apple rings do not touch each other. Dry until the apples are like dry chamois leather but pliable. Cool thoroughly and pack in jars.

Pears should be firm but ripe, and after peeling should be cut into halves and the cores removed. Put into salt water as for apple rings for 5 minutes only. Drain and arrange on a wire cake rack covered with muslin. Dry as for apples until the pears are rubbery but not coloured, and store.

Purple plums should be dried whole or in halves with the stones removed. Spread onto a rack as for pears, with the cut side uppermost to prevent the juice running out. The temperature for drying plums should be low so that the pulp dries without the skins hardening off too quickly. The fruit is ready when it can be squeezed without any moisture coming out. Cool thoroughly before packing.

Grapes, fresh and fully ripe, can be dried whole in a single layer on a rack. When they are dried, no moisture will appear if the fruit is squeezed.

Herbs

The most suitable herbs for drying are sage, thyme, marjoram, tarragon, mint and bay. Gather the herbs just before they come into flower, early in the day when the dew has dried. Tie them loosely in small bunches and cover lightly with muslin or thin paper. Hang in a dry place where the air can circulate. When completely dry, leave bay leaves whole, but crush the other herbs with a rolling pin and pack them in air-tight tins or jars. Parsley needs different treatment because it must be dried quickly if it is to keep its colour. Wash it in cold water, shake well, and remove leaves from the main stems. Spread onto a wire rack and dry at 375°F/190°C/Gas Mark 5 for 4 minutes. Cool, crush the leaves and store in an air-tight tin or jar.

Storage and use

All dried foods must be completely cold before being packed. They should be stored in a dry, airy place, dark if possible because light causes colour changes. Any sign of mould developing indicates that the food was not properly dried, or that the storage place is warm or damp. Do not use dried foods if they are musty or sour-smelling. Herbs should not be left in paper bags or exposed to the air, as they will quickly lose their scent and flavour.

Herbs can be added directly to recipes. Mushrooms can be added directly to casseroles and soups, but should be soaked for a few minutes in cold water and dried before frying or grilling. Onions and leeks are both best soaked for 30 minutes before adding to dishes. Dried fruit should be soaked in cold water for an hour, and may then be cooked in the same water, with added sugar and flavouring. Peas and beans are best soaked in cold water overnight before cooking very gently.

Don't be frightened of making simple country wines with surplus fruit and vegetables from your garden. The equipment is simple and there is no need to invest in large quantities of ingredients. Major chemists stock yeast and the few ingredients which will ensure clarity and purity in your wine, they can also supply fermentation jars, air-locks, bottles and corks.

Utensils
The first mixture of ingredients has to be made in a large container. Traditionally, this was an old glazed bread-crock, but today it is possible to buy a large lidded bucket or small polythene dustbin for the purpose. Buy a colourless bin because some colourants are toxic. For the second stage of fermentation, one-gallon jars made of thick glass with 'ear' handles are used. These can be specially bought, but are often sold containing cider, vinegar or fruit squash, and can be used again. Half-gallon jars are well worth keeping as they can be used for later bottling of wine. Wine needs to be stored in wine bottles which can be corked, not in old squash, sauce or spirit bottles. The only essential purchase is a fermentation- or air-lock which costs a few pence at the chemist. New corks should always be used as old ones may be infected. A polythene funnel, a nylon sieve, jellybag and siphoning tubes are very useful, but may already be available in the kitchen.

Ingredients
Apart from the basic raw fruit or vegetable, and water, it is necessary to add sugar and yeast to the wine mixture.

Sugar may be white or brown, but brown sugar adds colour and flavour which may not be suitable for delicate wines. 3 lb/1.5kg of sugar to 1 gallon/4.5l wine gives a medium wine. Adding 8 oz/200g more sugar will produce a sweet wine, while 8 oz/200g less will make a dry one. It is unwise to use less than the stated amount, or the wine may not be strong enough to keep.

Yeast may be baker's yeast or dried yeast, but a wide variety of wine yeasts is now available. These specially prepared yeasts allow the wine to ferment further and become stronger. Wine yeast helps to make a firmer sediment, makes it easier to siphon off clear liquid, and does not give 'off' flavours to the wine. They may be obtained as Port yeast, Sherry yeast, Tokay, Burgundy, Sauternes and many more. They give different nuances of flavour to the wines, but a Port yeast will not yield Port - it will give a port-like wine if all the ingredients are suitable.

Yeast nutrient helps to give a vigorous ferment which is a great help in preparing strong dry wines.

Pectic enzyme helps to replace pectin in the crushed fruit.

Campden tablets are used to inhibit unwanted wild yeasts.

Winemaking procedure
Basically, the flavour of the chosen fruit or vegetable has to be extracted in water. Sugar, yeast and yeast nutrient are then added to cause fermentation. This is best carried out in a stoppered jar with an air-lock which prevents liquid foaming over. A temperature of about 70°F/21°C is necessary for good fermentation, and the jar is best left standing in a warm kitchen but not on a stove or where it can be overheated and the yeast killed. After about 5 days at this temperature, the jar should be moved to a slightly cooler place to continue fermentation. When bubbles no longer move through the air-lock, the wine should be siphoned into a clean jar, left to mature, and then finally bottled and corked. It is most important that great cleanliness should be observed at all stages of wine-making, only sterilised equipment should ever be used. It is also important to give the wine plenty of time to work, mature and lie in store - some 12 months will be necessary from the initial preparation to first sampling.

Apple Wine

6 lb/3kg apples
3 lb/1.5kg sugar
8 oz/200g raisins
1 lemon
1 gallon/4.5l water
Yeast and nutrient

Windfall apples may be used if bruises are cut away, and any mixture of apples is suitable. A Sauternes wine yeast is good for this fruit. Wash the apples and cut them up without peeling. Put them into the water and simmer for 15 minutes. Strain the liquid onto the sugar, and add the thinly peeled rind of the lemon. Stir very well, and when the liquid is lukewarm, add the juice of the lemon with the yeast and yeast nutrient. Cover and leave for 24 hours in a warm place. Pour the liquid into a fermentation jar and fit an air-lock. Leave in a warm place for 4 weeks to ferment. Siphon into a clean dry storage jar, add the raisins chopped into small pieces, fit an air-lock and leave for 6 months to mature. Bottle and cork. Leave for 6 months before drinking.

Parsnip Wine

7 lb/3.25kg parsnips
2 lemons
2½ gallons/11l water
Sugar
Yeast and nutrient

Scrub and wash the parsnips thoroughly and scrape them. Cut into slices and boil in the water until tender but not mushy. Strain through a jelly bag and do not try to hurry the process or the wine will be cloudy. Measure the liquid and add 3 lb/1.5kg sugar to each gallon/4.5l liquid. Add the juice of the lemons. Bring to the boil, simmer for 45 minutes, and put into a bowl. When the liquid has cooled to 70°F/21°C, add the yeast and nutrient. Cover well and leave in a warm place for 10 days, stirring well each day. Strain into a fermentation jar and fit an air-lock. Leave in a cool place for 6 months until the wine starts to clear. Bottle and cork. Leave for 6 months before drinking.

Plum Wine

6 lb/3kg ripe plums
3½ lb/1.75kg sugar
1 gallon/4.5l water
Yeast and nutrient
Pectic enzyme

Victoria plums give the best flavour and the most 'body'. Bordeaux, Tokay or Sauternes wine yeasts are all suitable for this fruit. Cut the plums into halves, and remove the stones. Crush the pulp with the hands or a wooden spoon. Bring half the water to the boil and pour it onto the fruit. Leave for 5 hours and add the remaining cold water and the pectic enzyme. Leave for 48 hours, strain off the clear juice. Bring the juice to the boil and pour it over the sugar, stirring until it has dissolved. Leave the liquid to cool to 70°F/21°C and add the yeast. Pour into a fermentation jar and fit an air-lock. When the wine begins to clear, siphon off into a clean jar with an air-lock. When fermentation has finished completely, bottle and cork. To give greater 'body' to this wine, 1 lb/400g wheat or barley grain may be added to the plums and liquid.

Gooseberry Wine

6 lb/3kg ripe green
  gooseberries
2½ lb/1.25kg sugar
6½ pints/3.5l water
Yeast and nutrient
Pectic enzyme

Top and tail the gooseberries and wash them. Put them into a large bowl and squeeze with the hands or a wooden spoon until they are pulpy. Add the pectic enzyme and water, cover and leave to stand for 3 days, stirring occasionally. Strain through a jellybag or 2 thicknesses of muslin and add the sugar. Stir until the sugar has dissolved completely, add the yeast and yeast nutrient. Put into a fermentation jar and fit an air-lock, leave until the bubbles stop rising. Siphon off into a clean storage jar fit an air-lock and leave for 6 months to mature. Bottle and cork. Leave for 6 months before drinking.

Rhubarb Wine

6 lb/3kg rhubarb
3½ lb/1.75kg sugar
2 lemons
1 gallon/4.5l water
Yeast and nutrient
1 Campden tablet
1 oz/25g precipated
  chalk

The precipated chalk in this recipe removes any excess of oxalic acid in the rhubarb. It is obtainable from chemists. Wipe the rhubarb and cut it into short lengths. Put into a bowl and crush with a wooden spoon. Pour on the cold water and add a crushed Campden tablet. Cover well and leave for 3 days, stirring 2 or 3 times each day. Strain and squeeze the fruit pulp as dry as possible. Add the precipated chalk, the sugar, yeast, nutrient and juice of the lemons. Put into a fermentation jar and fit an air-lock. Keep about ½ pint/250ml water in a separate bottle plugged with cotton wool. When the fermentation becomes quiet, top up with the spare liquid. Leave until the wine begins to clear and the yeast to settle. Siphon off into a clean storage jar, fit air-lock and leave for 6 months to mature. Bottle and cork. Sauternes, Tokay or Sherry yeasts are good for rhubarb wine.

Every cook needs a few basic recipes to use almost automatically and speed up work in the kitchen without spoiling the quality of good raw ingredients. Here are some easy-to-prepare and foolproof methods for making pastry, sauces and soup garnishes. With these

Shortcrust Pastry

8 oz/200g plain flour
½ teaspoon/3g salt
2 oz/50g margarine
2 oz/50g lard
2-3 tablespoons/30-45ml cold
    water
Sift the flour and salt into a bowl. Cut the fat into pieces and rub into the flour until the mixture is like fine breadcrumbs. Add the water and mix to a stiff dough. Turn out on to a floured board and knead lightly until smooth. Roll out to required thickness. Bake shortcrust pastry at 425°F/220°C/Gas Mark 7 for 20 - 25 minutes. This is a useful basic pastry for all kinds of pies and tarts. For a savoury pastry, add 4 oz/100g finely grated hard cheese and a little pepper, and mix the pastry with 1 egg yolk and 2 teaspoons/10ml cold water.

Sweet Shortcrust Pastry

6 oz/150g plain flour
¼ teaspoon/1g salt
3 oz/75g butter
1 oz/25g castor sugar
1 egg yolk
1 tablespoon/15ml cold water
Sift the flour and salt into a bowl. Rub in the butter until the mixture is like fine breadcrumbs. Stir in the sugar. Mix the egg yolk and water together, add to the flour mixture, and work to a firm dough. Knead lightly and roll out to required thickness. Bake sweet shortcrust pastry at 400°F/200°C/Gas Mark 6 for 20 - 25 minutes. This is a good pastry for fruit pies and flans.

Rough Puff Pastry

8 oz/200g plain flour
½ teaspoon/3g salt
3 oz/75g lard
3 oz/75g hard margarine
6 - 8 tablespoons/90 - 120ml cold
    water
Sift the flour and salt into a basin. Cut the fat into small cubes, add to the flour and mix to a soft dough with the water. Roll out on a floured board to an oblong 6 × 12 in/15 × 30cm and fold the bottom third upwards and the top third downwards over it. Turn the dough so that the folded edge is on the left-hand side, and seal the edges. Roll out, and then fold and seal edges again. Roll, then fold and seal once more, always keeping the folded edge to the left. If the pastry becomes very soft, chill between rollings. Roll out to required thickness, usually about ¼ in/5mm. Glaze rough puff pastry with egg or milk before baking, and bake at 425°F/220°C/Gas Mark 7 for 25 minutes. This is a quickly made puff pastry which can be used with both savoury and sweet fillings, and it is much easier to make than the traditional puff and flaky pastry.

Crumble Topping

6 oz/150g plain flour
3 oz/75g brown sugar
4 oz/100g butter or margarine
Sift the flour into a basin and stir in the sugar. Rub in the butter until the mixture is like breadcrumbs. Press on top of the chosen fruit and bake at 375°F/190°C/Gas Mark 5 for 1 hour. This amount of crumble topping is enough for 1 lb/400g fruit mixed with 3 oz/75g sugar. No water should be added to the fruit, and it should not be cooked before adding the crumble topping.

Custard

1 pint/500ml milk
3 oz/75g castor sugar
2 eggs
Flavourings
Put the milk into a saucepan and bring just to the boil. Stir in the sugar and cool slightly. Put the lightly beaten eggs into a bowl, pour on the milk and beat lightly. Strain into a clean bowl over hot water, or into a double saucepan. Cook gently over hot water until the mixture thickens but does not boil. Serve with all kinds of fruit and puddings. Custard may be flavoured with a bayleaf or vanilla pod heated with the milk. Alternatively a little vanilla or almond essence or a spoonful of liqueur may be added after cooking.

important aids to good cooking, home-grown vegetables and fruit can be turned into delicious dishes, without recourse to can, packet or frozen food cabinet of the supermarket.

Salad Cream for Keeping

4 oz / 100g margarine
3 oz / 75g plain flour
3 oz / 75g sugar
½ oz / 15g dry mustard
1½ pints / 750ml milk
¾ pint / 375ml vinegar
2 eggs

Melt the margarine and remove from the heat. Stir in the flour, sugar and mustard to make a smooth paste, and then work in a little of the milk. Return to the heat and gradually work in the remaining milk, stirring all the time to avoid sticking. When the mixture begins to thicken, remove from the heat and beat well. Leave to cool and then beat in the eggs. Slowly beat in the vinegar to desired thickness. Season to taste with salt and pepper. This salad cream will keep up to six weeks in a cool place, and is less rich than mayonnaise.

Whole Egg Mayonnaise

1 egg
1 tablespoon / 15ml vinegar or
    lemon juice
½ teaspoon / 3g salt
1 teaspoon / 5g sugar
¼ teaspoon / 1g dry mustard
¼ teaspoon / 1g pepper
½ pint / 250ml olive oil

Put the whole egg, vinegar or lemon juice and seasonings in a bowl and work them together with a spoon to a paste. Slowly beat in the oil, drop by drop, until the mixture is thick. This is an easy mayonnaise to make with a creamy texture. Salad oil can be substituted for olive oil. Mayonnaise can be made quickly in a blender by mixing all the ingredients except oil at low speed, then slowly pouring in the oil with the motor running until the mixture thickens.

White Sauce

1 pint / 500ml milk
1 small onion
Sprig of parsley
Sprig of thyme
1 bayleaf
6 peppercorns
Pinch of salt
1½ oz / 40g plain flour
1½ oz / 40g butter

Put the milk into a saucepan with the onion, herbs and seasoning. Heat gently for 10 minutes without boiling, and strain. Melt the butter in a heavy saucepan and work in the flour. Cook for a minute or two so that the flour loses its raw taste, but the mixture remains pale. Add the milk a little at a time, stirring all the time to keep the mixture smooth. When all the milk has been added over a low heat, keep stirring until it boils. Boil for a minute or two and check the seasoning, then simmer for up to 30 minutes until needed.

French Dressing (Vinaigrette)

3 parts olive or salad oil
1 part wine vinegar or lemon juice
Salt
Pinch of dry mustard

Put the vinegar into a bowl with the salt and mustard. Stir well and slowly add the oil, beating until mixed. The oil will float to the top if the dressing stands, but it can be beaten again just before serving. If this dressing is used frequently, it can be made up in a large quantity in a screwtop jar, and kept in a cold place. The jar can be shaken to mix the oil and vinegar. For a plain green salad, try adding a little pepper, a pinch of sugar, some made mustard, and some freshly chopped herbs. This dressing can be stirred together in the base of a salad bowl, then the salad vegetables added, and tossed just before serving. Basic French Dressing can be used for salad, and is also good served over just warm leeks, asparagus and artichokes.

Hollandaise Sauce

1½ tablespoons / 23ml lemon juice
1 tablespoon / 15ml cold water
1 egg yolk
Salt and white pepper
8 tablespoons / 120g soft butter

Put the lemon juice, water, egg yolk, salt and pepper, and 3 tablespoons / 45g butter into a bowl over hot water. Beat with an egg beater until the butter has melted. Gradually add the rest of the butter in small pieces, beating until the sauce thickens like mayonnaise. Keep the water hot, but not boiling, as it will spoil the sauce if it splashes into the mixture. This is a simple version of a sauce which is delicious with asparagus and artichokes.

Flavoured Butters

4 tablespoons / 60g butter
Flavourings

The butter should be soft but not melted. Cream it in a bowl with the flavouring until well incorporated. Good flavourings are; finely chopped mint, parsley, chives, crushed garlic or grated horseradish. Cool until the butter is firm, then shape into a cylinder and cut with a sharp knife into circular pats. Use with grilled meat or fish, or with individual portions of vegetables. The pats can be made up well in advance and kept in the refrigerator until needed.

Soup Garnishes

Most vegetables can be turned into delicious soups, either on their own or as part of a mixture. Rough-cut soups are very acceptable for family meals, smooth ones may be preferred for more formal meals. Cooked soup can be put through a sieve, or creamed in a blender, and then a garnish will look very attractive on the smooth soup.

Bacon Grill or fry lean bacon rashers until very crisp. Crumble into small pieces and sprinkle on soup. This is particularly good with pea or bean soups.
Cheese Use very hard dry cheese, and grate it finely. Parmesan is ideal, but really hard Cheddar is good too.
Cream Whip double cream into soft peaks and put a large spoonful on each bowl of soup just before serving. This is particularly good with tomato or beetroot soup. Commercial soured cream can also be used as a soup topping, it is thick enough without whipping.
Croûtons These small cubes of bread may be fried or toasted. For fried croûtons, cut bread in small cubes and fry in oil until golden. Drain well before putting onto soup. Alternatively, toast slices of bread and cut into small squares before serving.
Herbs Chop herbs finely and sprinkle on soup. Basil, mint, tarragon, chives and parsley are all ideal for vegetable soups.
Pasta Short lengths of macaroni or spaghetti, or spaghetti shapes, can be used as soup garnish, also adding a little bulk to a recipe. Cook the pasta first for 10 minutes in boiling water before draining and adding to the soup to finish cooking without breaking up. About 2 oz/50g pasta is enough for 4 servings of soup.

BRASSICAS

BROCCOLI AND CALABRESE

All types of broccoli are delicious cooked until just tender and served with plenty of butter. Slightly warm broccoli and calabrese make a good salad well seasoned with salt and pepper, and French dressing, accompanied by a bowl of sliced tomatoes. Broccoli may also be served with Hollandaise sauce.

Italian Broccoli

1 lb/400g broccoli
2 garlic cloves
2 fl oz/50ml olive oil
2 oz/50g cooked ham
Salt and pepper
1 oz/25g grated Parmesan cheese
Clean and wash the broccoli and cook in boiling water for 15 minutes. Drain well. Crush the garlic cloves and warm in the olive oil. Stir in the finely chopped ham and season well. Pour over the broccoli and sprinkle on the grated cheese.

Creamed Broccoli

1 lb/400g broccoli
8 fl oz/200ml soured cream
½ oz/15g plain flour
½ oz/15g grated horseradish
1 teaspoon/5ml wine vinegar
Salt and pepper
Clean and wash the broccoli and cook in boiling water for 15 minutes. Drain well. See that the soured cream is at room temperature, or it may curdle when heated. Mix the cream and flour together and put into a bowl over boiling water, or the top of a double saucepan. Cook until warm and smooth, stirring all the time. Add the remaining ingredients and pour over the hot broccoli. A few oven-browned almonds may be scattered on top of the sauce. Serve with ham, pork or veal.

For notes on cultivation see pages 49/51

BRUSSELS SPROUTS

Sprouts are best eaten when small and firm, and they should only be cooked until tender, but still crisp. Their flavour has an affinity with chestnuts, onions and celery, and they are good dressed with cream and with cheese, so that a good vegetable course can be prepared without meat. Sprouts quickly smell unpleasant if left in the refrigerator, but it is worth cooking some extra ones to be used later with potatoes in Bubble and Squeak to which they lend a special flavour.

Sprout Soup

2 lb/1kg Brussels sprouts
2½ pints/1.5l chicken stock
1 oz/25g butter
1 oz/25g plain flour
1 tablespoon/15ml lemon juice
Pinch of nutmeg
Salt and pepper
Grated cheese
Clean the sprouts and simmer them in stock for 10 minutes. Reserve 10 small sprouts, and put the rest through a sieve with the cooking liquid. Melt the butter and work in the flour. Add the sieved sprouts gradually and heat gently, stirring well until the mixture is creamy and smooth. Add the lemon juice, nutmeg, salt and pepper and simmer for 5 minutes. Serve very hot with a garnish of whole sprouts and some grated cheese (Parmesan is best for this).

Bubble and Squeak

Cooked Brussels sprouts
Cooked potatoes
Cut sprouts and potatoes into slices. Melt some dripping, lard or oil in a thick frying pan and cook vegetables until golden, turning them frequently. Season well and serve hot.

For notes on cultivation see page 48

CABBAGES

Cabbage is often despised, but with proper cooking it can be one of our most delicious vegetables. Cabbage should be cooked in boiling salted water only until tender, but still crisp. It must be drained thoroughly, and served hot with plenty of butter and seasoning. Firm-hearted cabbage is very good shredded and served raw with a dressing, while cooked cabbage may be dressed with a white sauce. Whole cabbage heads or large leaves are good stuffed with a meat and rice filling, and they may be finished with a white or tomato sauce.

Stuffed Cabbage

1 firm cabbage
2 oz/50g long grain rice
1 small onion
1 tablespoon/15g chopped parsley
1 lb/400g pork sausagemeat
Put the cabbage into a bowl and remove any discoloured or bruised leaves. Pour on boiling water and leave to stand for 15 minutes. Drain, cover with boiling water and leave again for 15 minutes. Drain thoroughly. Meanwhile, cook the rice in boiling water for 12 minutes and drain well. Mix the rice, chopped onion, parsley and sausagemeat together and season well. Cut the stalk out of the cabbage and put in some mixture. Fold over 2 or 3 leaves, cover with more mixture. Continue until each layer is stuffed. Tie in a cloth, put in a pan of beef or chicken stock and simmer for 1½ hours. Put cabbage in a dish and serve with butter. If liked, the cabbage may be cooked in a casserole in a moderate oven 350°F/180°C/Gas Mark 4.

For notes on cultivation see pages 48/49

CAULIFLOWERS

Small cauliflowers can be cooked whole, but it is better to break larger ones into sprigs. Cook sprigs for 10 minutes, but allow 15-20 minutes for whole heads in boiling water with a squeeze of lemon juice. Drain well and serve with butter and seasoning, or with white or cheese sauce. If a sauce is not suitable with the rest of the course, dress the cauliflower with a sprinkling of browned breadcrumbs, crumbled crisp bacon and grated cheese. Cooked cauliflower is particularly good for salads, and for second-day dishes such as soup and cauliflower cheese.

Cauliflower Cheese

1 medium cauliflower
½ pint/250ml white sauce
½ teaspoon/3g salt
1 teaspoon/5g made mustard
Pinch of nutmeg
4 oz/100g grated cheese
1 tablespoon/15g browned crumbs
Cook the cauliflower whole or in sprigs as preferred. Heat the white sauce, remove from the heat and stir in the seasonings and most of the cheese. Put the cauliflower in a dish, and cover with the sauce. Sprinkle on the remaining cheese and crumbs and brown under a hot grill. Serve very hot.

Cauliflower Salad

1 small cooked cauliflower
4 oz/100g cooked broad beans
4 oz/100g cooked peas
1 oz/25g capers
4 hard-boiled eggs
Mayonnaise
Mix together cauliflower sprigs, beans, peas, capers and eggs cut in quarters. Dress with mayonnaise thinned with a little lemon juice if liked.

For notes on cultivation see page 50

KALE

Kale must be cooked when young and tender. It can be used for any spinach recipe but needs slightly longer cooking to make it tender. If the vegetable is to be chopped, do this after cooking, not before. Kale is particularly good with all kinds of sausages, and with rabbit dishes, and it may be dressed with white or cheese sauce, or with chopped onion and crisply cooked bacon.

Creamed Kale

2 lb/1kg kale
1 large onion
2 tablespoons/30g bacon fat
1 tablespoon/15ml lemon juice
1/2 pint/250ml white sauce
3 oz/75g grated cheese
Wash the kale thoroughly, then cook in boiling water for 8 minutes. Drain and chop roughly. Chop the onion very finely and cook in the bacon fat until soft and golden. Add the lemon juice. Heat the white sauce, remove from the heat and stir in two-thirds of the cheese until melted. Add the onion mixture. Stir the sauce into the kale and put into a greased baking dish. Top with the remaining cheese and bake at 350°F/180°C/Gas Mark 4 for 25 minutes until hot and golden brown. Serve with sausages or boiled bacon.

Colcannon

1 lb/400g cooked kale
1lb/400g cooked potatoes
1 oz/25g butter
6 fl oz/150ml milk
Cut the cooked kale up finely and mix with the potatoes mashed with butter and milk. Season well with salt and pepper and serve with plenty of extra melted butter. A few chopped spring onions may be added if liked. Eat hot on its own or with bacon.

For notes on cultivation see page 51

HERBS

Many herbs can be gathered all the year round, but the tender-leaved varieties which die down in winter may be dried or frozen. Dried herbs are strongly flavoured, and only half quantities should be used when substituted for fresh ones in a recipe. Each herb has its special affinity with certain foods:

Chives. Light onion flavour for cream cheese, eggs, salads.
Marjoram. Good with lamb, pea dishes, potatoes, fish, marrows.
Mint. Refreshing flavour for tomatoes, lamb, peas, new potatoes, fresh fruit salad, lemonade.
Parsley. Good in sauces, soups and salads, and with bacon, broad beans.
Rosemary. Pungent flavour for beef stews, duck, lamb, pork, mushrooms.
Sage. Best with rich meats such as pork, duck, goose.
Thyme. Particularly good in stuffings for poultry.
The classic **bouquet garni** consists of thyme, parsley and a bayleaf, but occasionally marjoram is added. **Fines herbes,** used for salads and for egg dishes, consists of chopped parsley, chervil, chives and tarragon. When **mixed herbs** are specified, these consist of chopped sage, parsley and marjoram mixed with small leaves of thyme. It is useful to make up a supply of mixed herbs, which are so often needed in the kitchen. Herbs can be used to make flavoured vinegars which can be used for salad dressings and mayonnaise. A good handful of the herb should be put into a pint/500ml wine vinegar for 4 days to infuse, then the vinegar drained and bottled for use. Tarragon and fennel are the two herbs most often used. All kinds of herbs can be chopped and mixed with softened butter and a squeeze of lemon juice. This may be used to spread the bread for sandwiches, or chilled and used in small squares on grilled meat or fish. Cottage cheese and cream cheese are also good flavoured with chopped herbs, particularly chives, parsley and thyme, with some crushed garlic if liked.

ASPARAGUS

Use asparagus immediately after picking as it goes stale quickly, and grade it for size before cooking. Trim off woody portions and small scales, and tie into small bundles of even-sized spears. Cook in boiling water until just tender, keeping the tips at the top of the pan so that they only steam while the stems are cooking more thoroughly. If you have different sized spears, start cooking the thicker ones first and add the bundles of thinner ones at intervals. Mix the sizes together before serving with melted butter, French dressing or Hollandaise sauce. If you have a lot of trimmings, or any leftover cooked asparagus, make a purée to use as asparagus soup with chicken stock. A pinch of nutmeg helps to bring out the flavour. Cold asparagus can be served with French dressing and a sprinkling of sieved hard-boiled egg, or the tips may be dressed with mayonnaise or Hollandaise sauce. A few asparagus tips make a colourful and tasty garnish for chicken or fish, or they can be added to mixed salads. Thick tender asparagus is delicious served on buttered toast, or as an omelette filling.

Asparagus Flan

8 oz/200g shortcrust pastry
1 lb/400g asparagus
1/2 pint/250ml milk
3 eggs
3 oz/75g grated cheese
Salt and pepper
Line a tin with pastry, prick well, line with foil and baking beans and bake at 400°F/200°C/Gas Mark 6 for 10 minutes. Cook and drain the asparagus and cut in 2 in/5cm lengths. Mix milk, eggs, salt and pepper and cheese. Put the asparagus into the pastry case, pour on milk mixture and bake at 350°F/180°C/Gas Mark 4 for 30 minutes.

For notes on cultivation see page 55

For notes on cultivation see pages 52-55

AUBERGINES

Aubergines are most useful for adding a touch of glamour to all sorts of dishes. They go particularly well with lamb, and partner onions, peppers and tomatoes in a variety of unusual recipes. Before cooking aubergines, do not peel them, but split them lengthwise or cut across in slices. Sprinkle well with salt and leave to stand for an hour. Drain well before using. Aubergines are very good stuffed with meat, vegetables and rice, and a tomato sauce is delicious with them. Plain slices may be fried in oil, or battered and fried to serve as a vegetable, or they can be strung on skewers with onions, mushrooms and lamb to make kebabs. If you have a surplus of aubergines, cook them with onions, peppers and tomatoes in olive oil very gently to make Ratatouille which can be eaten hot or cold.

Aubergine Savoury

1 large aubergine
2 rashers bacon
1 medium onion
2 sticks celery
4 oz/100g tomatoes
1 egg
Salt and pepper
4 oz/100g fresh breadcrumbs
2 oz/50g grated cheese
Peel the aubergine and cut the flesh into cubes. Steam over boiling water for 5 minutes and put into a bowl. Cut the bacon in small pieces and fry without additional fat until crisp. Add the bacon and the fat that runs out of the aubergines. Add the finely chopped celery. Skin the tomatoes, remove the pips and cut the flesh in pieces. Add to the aubergine together with the beaten egg. Put into a greased ovenware dish and sprinkle with mixed breadcrumbs and cheese. Bake at 325°F/160°C/Gas Mark 3 for 30 minutes.

For notes on cultivation see page 56

GLOBE ARTICHOKES

Artichokes are usually served on their own as a first course, or as a light main dish when stuffed. They go stale very quickly and should be used immediately after cutting. Take off the outer leaves and trim the stalks and leave the artichokes to soak, tips downwards, in plenty of cold water, for an hour before cooking. Dig carefully into the artichokes and remove the hairy 'chokes', and trim the points from the leaves with sharp scissors. Put the artichokes into a large pan of lightly salted boiling water and boil gently for 40 minutes until a leaf pulls out easily. Drain very well and eat hot with melted butter or Hollandaise sauce, or cold with French dressing or mayonnaise. If you have a large number of artichokes, take off all the leaves, rub the hearts with lemon juice and cook for 15 minutes, and serve in a salad mixed with mushrooms or seafood, or hot in a cheese sauce.

Stuffed Artichokes

4 globe artichokes
4 oz/100g cooked ham
2 oz/50g mushrooms
1 small onion
1 garlic clove
1/2 pint/250ml stock or white wine
2 oz/50g butter
Salt and pepper
Prepare and cook the artichokes until just tender. Mince the ham and mix with finely chopped mushrooms and onion, and crushed garlic. Fill the artichokes and put them into an ovenware dish with the stock or wine. Cover and bake at 350°F/180°C/Gas Mark 4 for 25 minutes. Put artichokes on serving plates. Melt the butter in the cooking liquid, season well and serve as a sauce.

For notes on cultivation see page 56

LEEKS

Leeks are very much appreciated for their light onion flavour. They must always be very carefully cleaned as fine earth tends to get between the layers of skins. To prepare leeks, trim off most of the green tops, leaving about 1-2 in/2.5cm-5cm green, and wash in cold running water, slightly separating the edges of the skins so that loose earth is washed out. Thinly sliced leeks are good in a winter salad with chicory, celery and shredded cabbage with French dressing. Leeks may be braised in butter and beef or chicken stock to use as a vegetable with a dressing of butter or white sauce. Leeks are also good cooked and served cold with Hollandaise sauce or French dressing. As a garnish, thick circular slices of leeks can be fried in butter, and they are particularly good with grilled meat or fish. Leeks are very popular as a soup ingredient, and go particularly well with chicken stock and with potatoes - they are best cooked lightly in butter before adding to soups. Like many mild-flavoured vegetables, they make a good dish on their own served as a savoury flan.

Creamy Leek Pie

6 large leeks
1/2 pint/250ml milk
Salt and pepper
3 fl oz/75ml single cream
8 oz/200g shortcrust pastry
Clean the leeks, remove green tops, and cut white parts into 1 in/2.5cm pieces. Put into the milk with salt and pepper and simmer until the leeks are just tender. Put into a pie dish and stir in the cream. Cover with the pastry and bake at 400°F/200°C/Gas Mark 6 for 30 minutes. Serve on its own, or with meat.

For notes on cultivation see page 57

111

MARROWS AND COURGETTES

Large marrows and small courgettes are both popular in the kitchen, but they need careful cooking to retain their delicate flavour and texture. Marrows are delicious stuffed whole or in rings, but to serve them as a vegetable the flesh should be steamed (rather than boiled) before serving with plenty of melted butter, or with white or cheese sauce. Courgettes should be eaten when young and small, with tender skins which are also eaten. They may be split lengthwise and baked with a stuffing of meat or cheese, served with cheese or tomato sauce. As a vegetable, they are best cut in 1 in/2.5cm slices with the skins on, and lightly fried in oil until golden. Courgettes go very well with onions and tomatoes, and are good simmered in oil with these two vegetables and green peppers. Aubergines may also be added to the mixture.

Savoury Marrow

1 large marrow
1 lb/400g cold meat
2 oz/50g bacon
1 oz/25g plain flour
Salt and pepper
2 oz/50g fresh breadcrumbs
1 teaspoon/5g chopped parsley
2 tomatoes
1 oz/25g dripping
Peel the marrow and cut in half lengthwise. Scoop out seeds and pulp. Mince the meat and mix with the finely chopped bacon, flour, seasoning, breadcrumbs and parsley. Skin the tomatoes, take out the pips, and chop the flesh. Mix with the meat and fill the marrow. Put in a baking dish with the dripping and bake at 350°F/ 180°C/Gas Mark 4 for 1 hour, basting with pan juices. Serve with gravy.

MUNG BEANS

Sprouted Mung bean shoots are best eaten after four days' growth, and they quickly lose their nutritive value and their crispness if left longer. Before cooking or serving, bean sprouts should be rinsed quickly in cold water and drained thoroughly. It is not necessary to remove loose husks or little roots as these parts contain both vitamins and flavour. They are of course ideal in mixed salads, or served alone with French dressing. They can be stir-fried in a little oil and seasoned with soy sauce and a pinch of sugar, and should be served at once while still crisp. Bean sprouts are particularly delicious with chicken or pork, or with seafood.

A mixture of bean sprouts and cottage cheese makes a nourishing filling for an omelette. If you have plenty, try mixing them with other vegetables. Just toss the sprouts in melted butter and pour over cauliflower, new potatoes or dwarf beans.

Mung Bean Salad

1 breakfast cup bean sprouts
3 stalks celery
2 large carrots
2 oz/50g cashew nuts
1 tablespoon/15g sesame seeds
French dressing
Lettuce
Mix together the bean sprouts, finely chopped celery and grated carrots. Add chopped nuts and sesame seeds and toss lightly in French dressing. Serve on a bed of lettuce.

Mung Eggs

2 oz/50g butter
4 eggs
1 breakfast cup bean sprouts
Melt the butter and stir in the beaten eggs. Cook gently, stirring until eggs begin to set. Season and stir in bean sprouts.

For notes on cultivation see page 60

For notes on cultivation see page 57

MUSHROOMS

Mushrooms should be used when very fresh, and they should never be washed or peeled, just gently wiped to get rid of surface dirt. Only trim the ends of the stalks, because the stalk holds much of the mushroom's flavour - if a recipe uses only caps, save the stalks in the refrigerator to use for a sauce or soup. For a simple garnish, poach small button mushrooms in a little salted water with a squeeze of lemon juice and a cover on the pan so that they remain creamy white. When cooking in butter, add a little oil to prevent the butter browning, and a squeeze of lemon juice, and cook just enough to make the mushrooms tender. Mushrooms are delicious raw in a dressing of oil and lemon juice left for about 2 hours in the refrigerator to absorb the liquid. If you have a lot of mushrooms, they can be made into a concentrated paste or *duxelles* which will keep for weeks in the refrigerator or may be frozen. This consists of softening 2 shallots or a small mild onion in 2 oz/50g butter, then adding 1 lb/400g chopped mushrooms and another 3 oz/ 75g butter and simmering gently for an hour, stirring often, until the mixture is thick, then seasoning lightly. Mushrooms of course can be added to dozens of dishes, but they make a delicious meal on their own, served on toast or with grilled bacon.

Mushrooms in Cream

1 lb/400g mushrooms
3 oz/75g butter
1 oz/25g plain flour
8 fl oz/200ml single cream
Thyme and parsley
Wipe mushrooms and toss in butter until just soft. Sprinkle with flour and add a pinch of thyme, salt and pepper. Add cream and cook gently for 5 minutes. Sprinkle with chopped parsley.

For notes on cultivation see page 58

PEPPERS

Peppers are rapidly gaining in popularity now that so many people find they can be grown quite easily and need not cost a fortune at the greengrocer. This delicious vegetable goes with many others, particularly tomatoes and onions, can be used raw in salads, or cooked in dozens of dishes, and it makes excellent pickles. Peppers are also excellent stuffed and baked, particularly with rice in the stuffing, and a topping of fresh tomato sauce. Finely chopped peppers are very useful to give texture to sandwich fillings - try them with eggs, mashed sardines or salmon, or minced ham or corned beef. The peppers must be carefully prepared to avoid the fiery little seeds. Cut away the stem and central core with a sharp knife, and remove all the soft membrane and tiny white seeds. Use whole or in half for stuffing, or cut in strips or rings.

Roast Peppers

4 large peppers
4 garlic cloves
4 fl oz/100ml olive oil
1 teaspoon/5g salt
Wash the peppers and roast them at 350°F/180°C/Gas Mark 4 for 20 minutes until the skin blisters and blackens and may be pierced easily with a sharp knife. Crush the garlic and heat in the olive oil, adding the salt. Skin the peppers, remove membranes and seeds, and cut the flesh in 1 in/2.5cm strips. Put into a glass preserving jar, pour on the oil and seal. When cool, store in the refrigerator. These peppers are excellent in rice dishes, or to garnish dishes, or in salads, and are much nicer than raw peppers.

For notes on cultivation see page 58

SEAKALE BEET

The leaves of seakale beet may be used for spinach recipes, but the best part of the vegetable lies in the broad white thick midribs of the leaves. Over-cooking toughens these stalks, and they are best steamed for 25 minutes, or simmered very gently in stock. Try them served with melted butter or Hollandaise sauce, or with white or cheese sauce. The flavour is particularly good with chicken or veal. The stems may also be cooked and served on toast with plenty of melted butter as a separate course or light snack.

Seakale Beet in Butter Sauce

2 lb/1kg seakale beet
8 oz/200g butter
Lemon juice
4 tablespoons/60g chopped
    parsley
Salt and pepper
Remove leaves from stems (the leaves can be used for another dish), and steam the stems for 25 minutes. Meanwhile melt the butter without letting it colour. Add a good squeeze of lemon juice and the parsley chopped very finely. Serve the stems on individual plates, seasoned with salt and pepper. Serve the hot butter sauce separately. If the butter cannot be watched, melt it in a bowl over hot water, and leave the water to simmer until the butter is very hot.

Baked Seakale Beet

2 lb/1kg seakale beet
1 pint/500ml cheese sauce
1 oz/25g grated cheese
Strip the leaves from the stems and cook the leaves like spinach until tender. Steam the stems for 25 minutes. Arrange the leaves in an ovenware dish and put stems on top. Cover with sauce and grated cheese, and bake at 350°F/180°C/Gas Mark 4 for 25 minutes.

For notes on cultivation see page 59

SPINACH AND SPINACH BEET

Old cookery books recommend cooking spinach in huge quantities of water, but this is totally wrong. Spinach needs to be very well washed in two or three waters, then shaken dry and cooked in a covered pan with a knob of butter. The spinach needs frequent shaking or stirring so that it does not stick to the pan, and it will cook very quickly and reduce in bulk. To serve as a vegetable or as the basis of a main dish, use 2 lb/1kg spinach. It makes a good vegetable served on the leaf stems and dressed with butter, but the stems may be removed before cooking, and the spinach then finely chopped or made into purée. It may also be folded into white sauce to make a very creamy purée. Spinach soup and soufflé are excellent, and a favourite dish is a purée of spinach topped with poached eggs and cheese sauce (Oeufs Florentine). Spinach Beet is coarser-textured but abundant, and can be used for all spinach recipes.

Spinach Soup

2 lb/1kg spinach
1 medium onion
1 small green pepper
2 oz/50g butter
1 teaspoon/5g sugar
Salt and pepper
1 teaspoon/5g tarragon
4 fl oz/100ml single cream
Milk
2 rashers bacon
Strip the spinach stems from the leaves. Wash the leaves very well and drain. Chop the onion and pepper finely and soften in the butter for 5 minutes. Stir in the spinach, sugar, salt and pepper and tarragon. Cover tightly and cook until the spinach is tender. Put through a sieve, or purée in a blender. Add cream and enough milk to thin to the consistency of cream. Reheat gently and sprinkle with small pieces of crisply grilled bacon.

For notes on cultivation see pages 59/60

SQUASHES AND PUMPKINS

Squashes and pumpkins are full of flavour and both can be used for savoury and sweet dishes. To preserve their flavour, it is better to steam or fry, rather than cooking them in water. A delicious way to serve squash or pumpkin is to cut a small 'lid' on the top, scoop out a little flesh and put in a large piece of butter, salt and pepper, then bake at 325°F/160°C/Gas Mark 3 for an hour. This makes a lovely supper dish with additional butter. If preferred, sugar may be put into the vegetable instead of salt and pepper, and it can then be served with grated nutmeg and a little clear honey. Squash or pumpkin flesh may be steamed until tender, then mashed or blended with some chicken stock and milk to the consistency of cream, and reheated to serve as soup. Salt and pepper make the usual seasoning, but some people like the addition of a pinch of ginger and a little brown sugar.

Pumpkin Pie

8 oz/200g shortcrust pastry
12 oz/300g pumpkin purée
4 eggs
8 oz/200g sugar
½ teaspoon/3g ground cinnamon
¼ teaspoon/1g ground allspice
¼ teaspoon/1g ground ginger
½ oz/15g plain flour
3 tablespoons/45ml melted butter
¼ pint/125ml single cream
Line a flan ring or sandwich tin with the pastry. Line with foil and baking beans and bake at 400°F/200°C/Gas Mark 6 for 20 minutes. Remove the foil and beans. Mix the pumpkin with beaten egg yolks, sugar, spices, flour, butter and cream. Beat egg whites and a pinch of salt to soft peaks and fold into the mixture. Pour into the pastry case and bake at 325°F/160°C/Gas Mark 3 for 50 minutes.

For notes on cultivation see pages 57/61

SWEET CORN

It is most important that sweet corn should be prepared immediately for cooking after harvesting, because at room temperature the sugar in the corn quickly becomes starch and the calorific and carbohydrate values increase rapidly. This also happens as soon as the husks are removed, so do not take these off until ready to cook the corn-cobs. The perfect cob for cooking should have plump, tender kernals, full of milk, and surrounded by soft 'silk'. If you prefer to cook the kernals off the cob, scrape them off with a sharp-pointed knife. Cobs may be steamed over boiling water for 15 minutes, or cooked in boiling water for just 5 minutes with a pinch of sugar and a squeeze of lemon juice. They can also be left in their husks, with the 'silk' removed and a knob of butter inserted, and roasted in the oven at 350°F/180°C/Gas Mark 4 for 35 minutes. Corn should never be salted before cooking as this makes it tough. Corn mixes well with other vegetables, particularly tomatoes and is useful for soup, and for making fritters to serve with poultry or bacon.

Corn Chowder

4 bacon rashers
1 large onion
1 lb/400g potatoes
1½ pints/750ml milk
12 oz/300 g cooked corn kernals
Salt and pepper
Pinch of rosemary
1 teaspoon/5g sugar
Cut the bacon into thin strips and heat gently in a thick pan until the fat runs. Continue frying until the bacon is crisp. Drain off the fat and keep the bacon pieces on one side. Slice the onion thinly and cut the potatoes in cubes. Cook in the bacon fat, stirring gently for 3 minutes, then cover and cook until tender. Bring the milk to the boil, add the onions, potatoes and corn, and seasonings. Simmer for 5 minutes, then remove from heat and leave to stand for 1 hour. Just before serving, reheat and garnish with bacon pieces.

For notes on cultivation see page 61

BROAD BEANS

Broad beans are at their best served small and young, when their skins can be slipped off after cooking, before serving hot or cold. They are very good tossed in butter with a little crisply cooked crumbled bacon, or dressed with parsley sauce. Beans are particularly good served with boiled bacon which is also traditionally served with parsley sauce. Cooked broad beans make an unusual salad if covered with French dressing with plenty of pepper and finely-chopped parsley, chives or winter savory.

Broad Bean Soup

1½ lb/600g shelled broad beans
3 pints/1.75l water
2 rashers bacon
1 small onion
1 oz/25g butter
1 oz/25g plain flour
Salt and pepper
1 teaspoon/5g chopped parsley
Cook the beans in the water for 10 minutes, and then drain, reserving the liquid. Remove the skins from the beans. Chop the bacon and the onion and cook in the butter until golden. Work in the flour and add the cooking liquid. Stir over gentle heat until smooth, and then add the beans. Simmer for 10 minutes, and then put the mixture through a sieve, or into an electric blender. Season with salt and pepper, reheat and serve sprinkled with parsley. If liked, the soup can be garnished with a little extra bacon, cooked until crisp and then crumbled. An alternative garnish can be small cubes of fried or toasted bread.

For notes on cultivation see page 62

DRIED BEANS

Dried beans can be used as individual types or as mixtures in soups and stews. Traditionally, they were soaked overnight before using, but in fact three hours' soaking is enough. If you are really in a hurry to start cooking the beans, don't soak them, but bring them to the boil, remove from heat, leave for 40 minutes, then drain and use in a recipe. They can be cooked in the water in which they have been soaked, or in stock (bacon stock is particularly good). It is important not to salt bean dishes until the end of cooking, or the beans will harden. Cooked beans are useful when cold as they mix well in French dressing with plenty of seasoning to make an unusual salad. Dried beans go particularly well in lamb and pork dishes.

Pork and Bean Casserole

12 oz/300g dried beans
2 large onions
2 carrots
Salt and pepper
1 tablespoon/15ml oil
8 oz/200g lean pork
1 oz/25g black treacle
6 rashers bacon
6 pork sausages
8 oz/200g garlic sausage
¼ pint/125ml red wine
Soak the beans for 3 hours in enough water to cover. Do not drain but put into a large pan with the diced onions and carrots, cloves, salt and pepper, and 1¼ pints/625ml water. Cover and simmer for 1½ hours. Meanwhile, cut the pork in pieces and brown on all sides in the oil. Put the oil into the bottom of a large casserole and put on half the beans, then the pork and the remaining beans. Add the black treacle and top with bacon. Cover and bake at 300°F/150°C/Gas Mark 2 for 4 hours. Grill sausages, cut into pieces and stir in the beans, with the garlic sausage cut in chunks and the wine. Cover and continue cooking for 30 minutes.

For notes on cultivation see page 62

DWARF BEANS

Try to use dwarf beans while they are young and still pencil-thin, so that they can be cooked whole. Otherwise they must be cooked in chunks, but they should never be shredded. Dwarf beans may be dressed with butter and seasoning, or a little grated onion or crushed garlic can be added. This vegetable mixes well with others, and looks attractive served with a garnish of thinly-sliced mushrooms cooked in butter. Cold beans make a good salad mixed with sliced tomatoes in a French dressing.

Bean Salad

1 lb/400g dwarf beans
French dressing
3 oz/75g can anchovies
2 hard-boiled eggs
Cut the beans into chunks and cook until tender. Cool slightly, then toss in French dressing. Arrange in a serving dish and garnish with drained anchovies and finely chopped eggs.

Creamed Beans

1 lb/400g dwarf beans
1 small onion
1 small green pepper
2 rashers bacon
Salt and pepper
3 tablespoons/45ml single cream
Cut the beans in chunks and cook until tender. Meanwhile chop the onion, green pepper and bacon finely. Put the bacon into a pan and heat until the fat begins to run. Add the onion and pepper and cook gently for 5 minutes. Add the beans with ¼ pint/125ml cooking water and cover tightly. Simmer for 15 minutes, watching carefully so that the beans do not burn. Season well with salt and pepper. Remove from the heat and stir in the cream. These beans are good with poultry or with ham.

For notes on cultivation see page 63

PEAS

Eat peas while they are young, tender and sweet. Their flavour will be enhanced by a little mint and a pinch of sugar in the cooking water. Peas go very well with other vegetables, and can be served in a mixture with young carrots, small pieces of dwarf beans and sweet corn kernels. They are also good cold served as part of a salad. Sugar peas with edible pods should be eaten when the pods are just beginning to swell. They should be cooked only until just tender, and served with plenty of melted butter as a first course, or as a separate vegetable.

French Peas

1 oz/25g butter
12 spring onions
1 small lettuce
1 lb/400g peas (shelled)
Salt and pepper
Pinch of nutmeg
1 teaspoon/5ml honey
Tarragon, thyme and chervil
Melt the butter in a thick saucepan. Chop the onions and lettuce finely and put into the pan, topped with the peas. Season well with salt and pepper, nutmeg and honey. Chop the herbs and add about 1 tablespoon of them. Add 3 tablespoons/45ml water, cover tightly and cook very gently for 12 minutes. Serve very hot.

Green Pea Salad

1 lettuce
8 oz/200g cooked peas
1 small cucumber
4 spring onions
French dressing
Mint
Clean the lettuce and tear leaves in small pieces. Mix with the peas, thinly sliced cucumber and finely chopped onions (include some of the green tops). Toss in French dressing and arrange in a bowl. Garnish with chopped mint.

For notes on cultivation see pages 63/64

RUNNER BEANS

Traditionally, these beans are finely shredded before cooking, but this often means a mushy result and loss of flavour. It is better to cook young runner beans whole or to slit them in half lengthways, or to cut them coarsely. Season runner beans well when cooked and dress with butter. They go particularly well with chicken and with roast or grilled meats, but runner beans are not so versatile as the dwarf and broad varieties, and do not make such good dishes on their own.

Beans with Mushrooms

1 lb/400g runner beans
1 small onion
1 small green pepper
2 rashers bacon
9 oz/225g mushrooms
3 oz/75g butter
Pinch of nutmeg
2 fl oz/50ml single cream
Remove the tips from the beans and cut them in half if they are large. Chop the onion, pepper and bacon in small pieces. Put the bacon in a thick pan and heat gently until the fat runs. Add the onion and pepper and cook until soft and golden. Add the beans and ¼ pint/125ml water, cover tightly and cook gently for 15 minutes until the beans are tender. Meanwhile wipe the mushrooms and cook them in the butter for 5 minutes. Drain off liquid from the beans and mix them with the mushrooms. Season with nutmeg and stir in the cream. This is particularly good served with boiled bacon or roast chicken. If liked, some grated cheese may be sprinkled over the beans and mushrooms, and the dish cooked under the grill or in the oven until the top is golden brown and bubbling.

BEETROOT

Beetroot is usually served as a salad, cold and sliced into vinegar, but it also makes an excellent hot vegetable. Traditionally, beetroot is boiled until tender, and it is important not to break the skin or cut off the stems too close or the vegetable will 'bleed' into the water. Beetroot cooked in this way can be served hot in a white sauce, or the beetroot may be cooled and sliced into vinegar. It is very good mixed with celery, which provides a texture contrast. If beetroot is mixed with other vegetables in a salad, it tends to stain everything pink, so it is better served in a separate bowl. Cold boiled beetroot may be frozen or can be bottled in vinegar for winter use. If you really enjoy beetroot, try baking instead of boiling to save all the flavour. Choose small beetroot of even size, wash them well, and leave about 1 in. stems. Put into an ovenware dish without liquid, and bake at 350°F/180°C/Gas Mark 4 for 30 minutes, then at 325°F/160°C/Gas Mark 3 for 1 hour. When they are tender, peel the beetroot and serve with melted butter, salt and pepper.

Beetroot Soup

8 medium beetroot
1 small onion
¾ pint/375ml chicken stock
Salt and pepper
Juice of 1 lemon
1 tablespoon/15ml honey
Pinch of ground cloves
Wash the beetroot well and simmer until tender. Peel and sieve them with ½ pint/250ml cooking water (use an electric blender if you like). Mix with remaining ingredients and simmer for 5 minutes. Serve plain, or with a little sour cream and chopped chives.

For notes on cultivation see page 64

CARROTS

Carrots are at their best when young and tender, and they should be cooked in the minimum of water until tender before dressing with butter. They mix well with other vegetables such as peas, beans and sweet corn kernels, and are an important ingredient in stews. Raw carrots are delicious, coarsely grated and dressed with lemon juice.

Braised Lamb and Carrots

2¼ lb/1kg shoulder lamb
1 crushed garlic clove
1 large onion
1 green pepper
4 tablespoons/60ml olive oil
¼ pint/125ml tomato juice
½ pint/250ml stock
12 oz/300g young carrots
1 teaspoon marjoram
1 tablespoon/15g cornflour
6 tablespoons/90ml white wine
Cut the lamb into cubes. Dice the onion and green pepper. Heat the olive oil in a thick pan and put in the garlic, onion and green pepper. Stir and cook for 1 minute, then add the lamb and cook gently for 5 minutes, stirring well. Season to taste with salt and pepper and add the tomato juice and stock. Cover and simmer for 30 minutes. Scrub the carrots and cut into short lengths. Cook them in a little water for 2 minutes, drain and add to the lamb with the marjoram. Cover again and simmer for 45 minutes. Add the wine and the cornflour mixed with a little water. Cover and simmer for 15 minutes. This is a good dish to start on top of the stove, and then to transfer to the oven set at 325°F/160°C/Gas Mark 3 for complete cooking. Garnish with a little chopped parsley or more marjoram.

For notes on cultivation see page 65

CELERIAC

This vegetable has all the concentrated flavour of celery, and can be used to intensify flavour in celery soup, and in casseroles. It is however delicious in its own right, both raw and cooked. Coarsely grated celeriac in French dressing or mayonnaise makes an excellent salad. It may also be cooked in boiling water or stock until tender and served dressed with butter or white sauce. Celeriac also makes a good purée with cream and seasonings added, and it can also be mixed in equal quantities with potato purée.

Celeriac Casserole

1½ lb/600g celeriac
8 oz/200g onions
8 oz/200g tomatoes
1 carrot
3 oz/75g butter
1 crushed garlic clove
Salt and pepper
2 slices bread
Peel the celeriac and cut it into slices. Simmer in stock or water for 10 minutes. Peel and slice the onions. Peel the tomatoes, take out the pips, and cut the flesh into pieces. Peel and slice the carrot. Melt the butter and fry the onions, tomatoes and carrot lightly until the onion pieces are soft and golden. Add the drained celeriac pieces and the garlic. Season with salt and pepper, and add enough of the liquid used in cooking the celeriac to cover the vegetables. Cover and simmer until the vegetables are tender. Just before serving, cut the bread into triangles and fry in oil until golden. Use to garnish the casserole, which can be served on its own or with meat or fish.

For notes on cultivation see page 66

JERUSALEM ARTICHOKES

For those who love the flavour of artichokes in cooking, the Jerusalem artichoke is invaluable, as the life of the summer Globe artichoke is so limited. They may be peeled, or boiled first and skinned when hot, and used for recipes in which artichoke hearts are specified, or for potato recipes. Jerusalem artichokes are delicious baked around a joint of beef, or served as a creamy purée. A very good artichoke soup can be made by cooking the tubers in chicken stock, sieving and thinning the purée with milk.

Artichoke Pancakes

1 lb/400g Jerusalem artichokes
1 small onion
1 large egg
Salt and pepper
1 oz/25g plain flour
Peel the artichokes thinly, grate them, and drain off surplus juice. Grate the onion and mix with the artichokes, beaten egg, seasoning and flour. Do not leave the mixture to stand, or surplus liquid will run out. Fry spoonfuls of the mixture in hot oil until golden, and serve hot with grilled meat or fish, or with bacon.

Artichokes with Cheese

1½ lb/600g Jerusalem artichokes
½ pint/250ml white sauce
Salt and pepper
Pinch of nutmeg
3 oz/75g grated cheese
Peel the artichokes thinly and boil them in just enough water to cover for about 20 minutes until tender. Drain, but keep ¼ pint/125ml cooking liquid. Cut the artichokes in slices and arrange in a shallow ovenware dish. Mix the sauce with the cooking liquid, season well with salt, pepper and nutmeg, and pour over the vegetables. Sprinkle on the cheese and grill until golden-brown. Serve with roast meat, or with chicken.

For notes on cultivation see page 66

ONIONS

The onion is one of our most popular flavourings, essential to many savoury dishes. Use onions as a vegetable with grilled meat or sausages, cook them with cheese, or add them to brown or white sauces as the perfect accompaniment to beef and lamb. Herb and onion stuffings are the perfect accompaniments to rich fat meats like pork and duck. Mild onions are delicious sliced and served raw in salads, or mixed with orange slices, or with beetroot, tomatoes or potatoes in salad dressings. Onions make good supper dishes, cooked in their jackets in the oven like potatoes, or braised with dripping and beef stock, or made into a clear soup served with toasted bread and cheese. They are also excellent combined with pastry in savoury flans.

Herb and Onion Flan

8 oz/200g shortcrust pastry
3 medium onions
1 oz/25g butter
¼ pint/125ml creamy milk
1 egg
1 tablespoon/15g fresh sage
1 teaspoon/5g fresh parsley
4 oz/100g bacon
Salt and pepper
Line a flan ring or sandwich tin with the pastry. Chop the onions finely. Melt the butter and cook the onions until soft and golden. Mix the onions with the milk, beaten egg, chopped sage and parsley, chopped bacon, salt and pepper. Pour into the pastry case and bake at 400°F/200°C/Gas Mark 6 for 35 minutes. Serve hot with vegetables, or with a green salad. Some grated cheese may be sprinkled on top before baking if liked. If using a flan ring, remove the ring 5 minutes before the end of cooking to brown the pastry.

For notes on cultivation see page 67

PARSNIPS

This slightly sweet vegetable is not to everybody's taste, but the flavour is so good with meat and poultry, and mixed with other vegetables that it can be an asset in the kitchen. Parsnips are particularly good part-boiled, then roasted or fried, and they can be cooked around a joint like potatoes. Parsnips are also excellent mashed, either on their own, or mixed with carrots or potatoes. Always use plenty of butter with them or a sprinkling of grated cheese.

Parsnip Balls

1 lb/400g parsnips
4 oz/100g butter
1 tablespoon/15ml milk
Salt and pepper
1 egg
4 oz/100g breadcrumbs
Cook the parsnips, mash them and mix with the butter, milk and seasoning. Heat and stir until the mixture is thick. Cool and beat in a little of the egg to give a smooth mixture. Shape into balls and roll in the remaining egg, then dip into breadcrumbs. Fry in hot fat until golden, and serve hot.

Chicken and Parsnip Pie

1½ lb/600g cooked chicken
1 large onion
1 lb/400g parsnips
1 pint/500ml white sauce
3 tablespoons/45ml sherry
Pinch of nutmeg
12 oz/300g rough puff pastry
Dice the chicken. Cook the onion and parsnips in a little water until tender, and cut into dice. Arrange chicken and vegetables in a pie dish. Flavour the white sauce with sherry and nutmeg and season well, and mix with the chicken and vegetables. Cover with the pastry and bake at 425°F/200°C/Gas Mark 7 for 20 minutes, then at 375°F/190°C/Gas Mark 5 for 25 minutes.

For notes on cultivation see page 68

POTATOES

Potatoes are sadly mistreated in the kitchen when served plainly boiled or mashed. They deserve careful cooking to make a delicious vegetable on their own. New potatoes are good cooked with mint, then drained and tossed in butter. A garnish of dill or chopped parsley helps to give them a special flavour. When slightly cool, they can be tossed in French dressing or mayonnaise for potato salad. Older potatoes are good chipped or roasted (boil potatoes for 5 minutes before roasting for the best results), or baked in their jackets. Jacket potatoes may be served with nothing more than butter and seasoning, but they can also be filled with cream cheese, with grated Cheddar cheese, with creamed fish or chicken, or with crisply grilled bacon. Thinly sliced potatoes can be cooked in the oven in a covered casserole with plenty of butter, seasoning and a little milk until tender and golden to accompany whatever meat has also been cooked in the oven. Potatoes in soups and stews give bulk and help to thicken the liquid.

Champ

8 large potatoes
6 spring onions
¼ pint/125ml milk
Salt and pepper
Butter
Boil the potatoes in salted water. Drain well and dry off by putting a folded cloth on top and returning the pan to a gentle heat for a few minutes. Chop the spring onions very finely, including the green tops. Put into a bowl, pour on some boiling water, then drain them. Add to the milk and bring to the boil. Season well and pour on to the potatoes and mash them well until fluffy with salt and pepper. Put on individual plates, make a well in each pile of potatoes, and put in a large lump of butter.

For notes on cultivation see pages 68/69

SHALLOTS

Shallots have a mild onion flavour and are very useful for dishes where subtlety is important. In particular, they are used for classic French sauces. They can be used for pickling, but are seldom served as a vegetable.

Sauce Béarnaise

1 tablespoon/15g chopped shallot
½ teaspoon/3g chopped tarragon
5 tablespoons/75ml vinegar
3 tablespoons/45ml water
3 egg yolks
9 oz/225g butter
Pinch of chervil
Be sure to chop the shallot very finely, and put into a saucepan with the tarragon and vinegar. Cook gently until all the liquid disappears. Remove from the heat and add the cold water. Beat in the egg yolks, and put on a low heat, stirring until the mixture thickens. Melt the butter separately and add to the eggs gradually, drop by drop. Avoid using the bottom of the butter which will spoil the sauce. Stir constantly until all the butter is added and season with chervil, salt and pepper. Serve warm (not hot) with lamb.

Sauce Bordelaise

1 tablespoon/15g chopped shallot
5 fl oz/125ml dry red wine
1 teaspoon/5g crushed
    peppercorns
1 sprig of thyme
3 fl oz/75ml beef stock
2 tablespoons/30g butter
1 teaspoon/5g plain flour
Chop shallot very finely and cook in half the butter until golden. Add the wine and peppercorns and reduce liquid over heat to one-third. Add stock, thyme, butter and flour and cook until thick. Season with salt, put through a fine sieve, and serve with steak.

For notes on cultivation see page 69

SWEDES

Swedes have a slightly sweeter flavour than turnips, and are particularly good with poultry. They are at their best cooked and made into a purée with plenty of seasoning and butter or single cream. Swedes blend well with potatoes in a purée, and any leftover mixture can be formed into flat cakes and fried to serve at a later meal. Turnip recipes may be used for cooking swedes.

Swedes in Cider Sauce

12 oz/300g carrots
12 oz/300g swedes
1 oz/25g butter
1/4 pint/125ml creamy milk
1 tablespoon/15g cornflour
5 tablespoons/75ml cider
1 teaspoon/5g castor sugar
Salt and pepper
Scrape and slice the carrots. Peel the swede and cut into dice. Cook together in boiling salted water for 15 minutes until tender but unbroken. In a separate saucepan, melt the butter and add the milk. Blend the cornflour with half the cider and then add to the milk together with the remaining cider. Bring to the boil, stirring well. Add the sugar, salt and pepper, and simmer for 3 minutes. Drain the vegetables well and mix with the sauce. Serve hot with bacon or ham.

Oven-Baked Swedes

1 1/2 lb/600g swedes
2 oz/50g butter
1/2 pint/250ml chicken stock
Salt and pepper
1 tablespoon/15g sugar
Peel the swedes and cut into matchstick pieces. Heat butter, stock, salt, pepper and half the sugar until boiling, and pour over swedes. Cook for 10 minutes, then put into a casserole and sprinkle with sugar. Bake at 375°F/180°C/Gas Mark 5 for 45 minutes.

For notes on cultivation see page 70

TURNIPS

Only small young mild turnips are worth eating, lightly cooked in water, and dressed with butter and seasoning. Turnip purée is particularly good with rich fat meats like duck, pork, ham and sausages. Turnips are good mixed with small red onions to serve with roast meat, and they may be cooked in beef stock. Part-boiled turnips may be finished off around a roasting joint, basted with the meat juices occasionally.

Roast Duck with Turnips

4 1/2 lb/2kg duck
2 tablespoons/30ml honey
1 teaspoon/5g thyme
10 small turnips
10 button onions
1 oz/25g brown sugar
Salt and pepper
1/4 pint/125ml red wine
1/4 pint/125ml single cream
1 tablespoon/15g cornflour
Wipe the duck inside and out and brown it in a heavy pan in a little butter. Drain off any fat which runs out. Mix the honey and thyme and spread over the duck skin, and put the duck into a roasting tin. Peel the turnips and onions and brown them in some butter mixed with the brown sugar. Arrange around the duck, and season with salt and pepper. Add the red wine, cover and cook at 325°F/160°C/Gas Mark 3 for 1 1/2 hours. Put the duck and the vegetables on to a serving dish and keep them warm. Heat the pan juices to reduce them to 1/2 pint/250ml. Mix the cream and cornflour, and stir gently into the pan juices. Simmer until creamy and serve separately.

For notes on cultivation see page 70

CELERY

Celery is good raw and cooked, and its crispness provides a useful texture in many dishes. To prepare celery for eating raw with cheese, separate the stalks and wash them well, removing any blemishes. Leave a few of the young leaves on the stalks. Put the stalks into iced water containing a few ice cubes and leave in the refrigerator for two or three hours before serving. Drain well and serve very cold. Chopped raw celery is good in green salads, or mixed in seafood cocktails. Short lengths of celery can be stuffed with cream cheese and garnished with chopped chives as a cocktail snack. Short lengths of celery may be used in casseroles, while long stalks or whole hearts can be braised in butter and stock to serve as a vegetable. It is worth drying some celery leaves like herbs to give a hint of celery flavour to dishes, or to augment the vegetable's own flavour.

Celery Soup

1 large head celery
1 large onion
2 oz/50g butter
1 carrot
1 large potato
1 teaspoon/5g brown sugar
Salt and pepper
1/2 pint/250ml chicken stock
1 pint/500ml creamy milk
Clean the celery and cut into small pieces. Chop the onion. Melt the butter, add the celery and onion, and stir over gentle heat for 4 minutes. Add diced carrot and potato and cook for 2 minutes. Add sugar, salt and pepper, and 1/2 pint/250ml water and simmer until vegetables are tender. Put through a sieve, or liquidise. Add stock and milk and simmer for 10 minutes. Garnish with chopped herbs.

For notes on cultivation see page 71

CHICORY

Chicory is equally good raw or cooked, although some people dislike its slight bitterness. The heads should be used when the tips are pale yellow and white - when they begin to turn green, the vegetable is getting old. Allow one head of chicory for each person in a salad, but two heads as a cooked vegetable. To serve as a salad, remove outer leaves and rinse the heads in cold water. Use individual leaves, or cut across into circular slices. Use immediately after cutting, as chicory discolours quickly, and never leave to soak in water which increases the bitterness. Serve chicory in a French dressing, or add to a mixed salad, or mix with orange slices and black olives (very good with duck). Chicory should never be boiled to serve as a vegetable, but is best braised with a little lemon juice, salt and pepper, a large knob of butter and a few spoonfuls of chicken or beef stock. It will take about 30 minutes in a tightly-covered saucepan, or in a casserole in a moderate oven. White sauce and cheese sauce may be served with chicory.

Chicory and Ham Rolls

8 chicory heads
8 thin slices cooked ham
1 pint/500ml white sauce
2 oz/50g grated cheese
Salt and pepper
1 oz/25g fresh breadcrumbs
1 oz/25g butter
Cook the chicory in water with a squeeze of lemon juice for 15 minutes, and drain very thoroughly. Wrap each head in a slice of ham and put in a buttered shallow ovenware dish. Mix cheese with white sauce, season and pour over chicory. Sprinkle with breadcrumbs and dot with butter. Bake at 375°F/190°C/Gas Mark 5 for 30 minutes.

For notes on cultivation see page 71

CUCUMBERS

The cucumber is one of our most refreshing and attractive salad vegetables, but it may also be cooked, and makes excellent pickles. Cucumbers should not be peeled before slicing, as they are more digestible with the skin on, and the skin contains the main food value. Thick chunks of cucumber can be hollowed out and filled with seafood or cream cheese as cocktail snacks or light first courses. Thinly sliced cucumber makes refreshing sandwiches, dressed with a little lemon juice, between slices of white or brown bread. Cubed or sliced cucumber is an attractive addition to salads and to chilled summer soups, or may be dressed with sour cream to make a tempting salad. Small cucumbers may be cooked in the same way as courgettes, and are particularly good stuffed with a creamy ham and onion stuffing topped with cheese and baked until tender. Dill gives a special flavour to cucumber salad, and can be added to white sauce to serve with lightly poached cucumber cubes as a cooked vegetable. Outdoor cucumbers with rough skins are particularly useful for pickling.

Cucumber Pickle

8 large cucumbers
2 oz/50g cooking salt
10 oz/250g soft brown sugar
1 tablespoon/15g mustard seed
5 cloves
2 cinnamon sticks
1½ pints/750ml white vinegar
Peel the cucumbers and cut in ½ in/1.25cm slices. Remove the seeds, sprinkle with the salt and leave to stand for 24 hours. Drain in a sieve for 1 hour. Mix the remaining ingredients, and boil for 5 minutes. Add cucumber slices and simmer for 25 minutes. Put in hot preserving jars and seal.

For notes on cultivation see page 72

ENDIVE

The rather bitter, curly-crisp foliage of endive makes a refreshing salad with French dressing, or the leaves may be mixed with other greenstuff in a salad. It is a particularly useful salad during the winter when little else is available. The leaves only need rinsing well and chilling before use, and it is possible to use just a few leaves from a plant without using a whole head at a time. Endive combines well with a mixture of spring onions, diced cucumber and thinly sliced radishes. Endive may also be cooked, and can be prepared with spinach recipes as it goes particularly well with cheese, and it has a piquant faint bitterness.

Chicken Endive

1 large bunch endive
3 chicken joints
Salt and pepper
2 oz/50g butter
½ pint/250ml white sauce
2 oz/50g Cheddar cheese
Wash and drain the endive, shred and cook in boiling salted water until tender. Drain well and rinse under cold running water before draining thoroughly. Arrange in the bottom of an ovenware dish. Skin the chicken joints and cut off the flesh in thin slices. Season well with salt and pepper and then cook in the butter until golden. Arrange the chicken on top of the endive, top with white sauce and then with grated cheese. Bake at 350°F/180°C/Gas Mark 4 for 30 minutes and serve very hot.

Braised Endive

1 bunch endive
¾ pint/375ml beef stock
Salt and pepper
1 oz/25 g Parmesan cheese
Wash and drain the endive. Tear it into large pieces and blanch in boiling salted water for 8 minutes. Drain well and arrange in a shallow ovenware dish. Pour on the beef stock and season well. Bake at 350°F/180°C/Gas Mark 4 for 20 minutes and serve sprinkled with finely grated cheese. Serve as an accompaniment to chicken or ham.

For notes on cultivation see page 73

120

LETTUCE

To most people, lettuce means salad, and it is certainly the mainstay of the salad bowl, but also makes a number of good cooked dishes. This is very useful for those who suffer from a glut crop, as the lettuce cannot be frozen or otherwise preserved, but soups freeze very well. In addition, lettuce may be braised to eat as a vegetable, or can be cooked with fresh green peas. Lettuce soups may be served either hot or cold, and are basically made by cooking shredded lettuce with a little bacon fat or butter, then simmering in chicken stock with a herb or spice seasoning and a little onion to flavour (spring onions are good cooked with lettuce). An addition of peas or almonds can be made to lettuce soup, after the cooked vegetable and liquid have been sieved to a purée. Cream or milk may also be added, but if the soup is to be frozen, it is better to prepare it without these additions which can be made during the reheating stage.

Braised Lettuce

4 small well-hearted lettuce
1 small onion
1 rasher bacon
1 tablespoon/15ml olive oil
½ oz/15g butter
4 tomatoes
1 tablespoon/15g chopped parsley
Salt and pepper
1 teaspoon/5g sugar
Pinch of nutmeg
Wash the lettuce and keep them whole. Put into boiling salted water, bring to the boil again, then take out the lettuce and drain well. Heat oil and butter and add chopped onion and bacon. Stir until soft and golden. Peel tomatoes, remove pips, and cut flesh in pieces. Add to onions and stir for 5 minutes. Put in lettuce, parsley and seasonings, cover tightly and simmer for 30 minutes. This is very good with lamb.

For notes on cultivation see page 73

SALAD CROPS

The best green salad is made with lettuce and a mixture of other greenstuff. This can include chicory, endive, watercress, onions, leeks, cucumber, peppers and a variety of herbs. Lettuce can also form the basis of a mixed salad with the addition of radishes, tomatoes, hard-boiled eggs, young carrots and peas. Crisp lettuce leaves often form the garnish for cold meat or fish, patés and other first courses, but the leaves must not be limp and dull, but should be crunchy and delicious enough to eat in their own right. Lettuce leaves should not be cut, but should be torn in pieces after thorough washing and drying. French dressing with a hint of mustard and sugar is the perfect accompaniment to green salad.

Mustard and cress is too often thought of as only a garnish for sandwiches, but it is very good mixed with other greenstuff in a salad, or may be dressed with a French dressing to serve on its own, or with an accompaniment of thinly sliced radishes or spring onions. Radishes are very good on their own, eaten with a smear of unsalted butter (leave a little of the green stem on so that they are easy to handle).

Spring onions may be left whole for salads, with the green tips trimmed neatly, or they can be sliced in thin rings and mixed with other salad vegetables, or served in a separate bowl in French dressing. Onions are also good mixed with a little commercial soured cream seasoned with salt and pepper, a pinch of curry powder or mustard, and a few thin slices of cucumber may be added. Another way of using spring onions is to chop them finely and add to potato salad, or to sprinkle on thin slices of orange, garnished with olives and French dressing, and this is a particularly good accompaniment to rich meats such as duck and pork.

For notes on cultivation see pages 74-75

TOMATOES

Tomatoes are used almost as widely as onions to flavour hundreds of dishes. They go well with meat, fish, eggs and cheese, partner rice and pasta, and are invaluable for soups and sauces. Often it is recommended that tomatoes should be skinned, and this is best done by holding each tomato with a fork over a flame, or by dipping them in hot and then cold water. For perfection, the pips should also be removed before using the tomatoes. Sliced tomatoes make a delicious salad, with French dressing and a garnish of chopped basil or mint. Tomatoes are also good in sandwiches, on their own or mixed with hard-boiled eggs, ham or cheese. Very large tomatoes can be sliced downwards, leaving the slices joined at the base, and the slits filled with slices of hard-boiled egg. Served with mayonnaise, this is a favourite French first course or light luncheon. Another use for very large tomatoes is to cut off their tops, scoop out the pips, and fill the fruit with rice salad, or seafood in mayonnaise. With a filling of chopped meat or fish, breadcrumbs and seasoning they can be baked in a little stock for a good main meal. Tomatoes can be grilled, fried or baked to accompany dishes, and benefit from a good sprinkling of herbs. Green tomatoes which are just beginning to turn colour may also be grilled or fried, and both green and red tomatoes make excellent chutney.

Baked Tomatoes and Eggs

Large tomatoes
Eggs
Cut lids off tomatoes and scoop out seeds. Break an egg into each one, season and bake at 350°F/180°C/Gas Mark 4 for 15 minutes. Add a little cream or grated cheese before baking if liked.

For notes on cultivation see pages 75/76

BLACKBERRIES

Cultivated blackberries are large and juicy, and so are very good served fresh with sugar and cream. When cooked, they are the natural partners of apples, pears and quinces, and their flavour is enhanced by a few drops of rosewater, or a couple of rose geranium leaves (remove the leaves before serving). Blackberries freeze very well, are good mixed with apples for jam, and make the favourite bramble jelly.

Autumn Pudding

1 lb/400g blackberries
8 oz/200g apples
1/2 pint/250ml cider
8 oz/200g castor sugar
5 large slices white bread
Put the blackberries into a saucepan with the cider and sugar. Peel, core and slice the apples, and add to the pan. Simmer until the fruit is soft but unbroken. Take the crust off the bread and line a pudding basin with four slices, trimming so they fit neatly. Pour in the hot fruit and cover with the remaining bread. Put a plate on top and heavy weights and leave in the refrigerator for 24 hours. Turn out and serve with cream.

Bramble Jelly

4 lb/2kg blackberries
2 lemons
1/2 pint/250ml water
Sugar
Put the blackberries into a pan with the juice of the lemons and the water, and simmer for 1 hour. Strain overnight through a jelly bag and measure the juice. Allow 1 lb/400g sugar to 1 pint/500ml juice. Heat the juice gently, stirring in the sugar until dissolved, then boil hard to setting point. Pour into hot jars.

For notes on cultivation see page 76

BLACKCURRANTS

Blackcurrants are excellent for all kinds of pies and puddings, and the flavour is heightened with a few drops of Cassis, the blackcurrant liqueur. Try a pinch of ground cinnamon in any accompanying pastry too. The fruit has good setting qualities and makes a pleasant jam, while blackcurrant syrup is worth making for the freezer.

Blackcurrant Shortcake

1 lb/400g blackcurrants
4 oz/100g sugar
4 oz/100g butter
4 oz/100g castor sugar
2 eggs
4 oz/100g self-raising flour
Pinch of salt
1/2 pint/250ml double cream
Strip the currants from their stems, and cook the currants with the sugar and 4 tablespoons/60ml water until just tender, then cool. Cream the butter and castor sugar until light and fluffy. Beat the eggs lightly and add to the butter mixture alternately with the flour sifted with salt. Put into two 7 in sandwich tins and bake at 375°F/190°C/Gas Mark 5 for 25 minutes. Cool and sandwich together with blackcurrants and whipped cream.

Blackcurrant Syrup

3 lb/1.5kg blackcurrants
1/2 pint/250ml water
Sugar
Put fruit and water into a saucepan and cook gently for an hour, crushing the fruit from time to time. Strain through a jelly bag overnight and measure the juice. Allow 12 oz/300g sugar to each pint/500ml juice, and stir in the sugar until dissolved. Strain into freezer containers (ice cube shapes are useful) and freeze. Use diluted for drinks, or as a sauce for ice cream, or a base for mousses and ices.

GOOSEBERRIES

Large ripe eating gooseberries are splendid eaten raw, or cut in half and served with a sprinkling of sugar. Most of the crop however remains hard and green, but the berries are very popular cooked in pies and puddings, in sauce for savoury dishes, and in jam and chutney. Gooseberries bottle and freeze well. In sweet dishes, their flavour is enhanced by a head of elderflowers which give the fruit a hint of muscat.

Gooseberry Sauce

1 1/2 oz/40g butter
1 oz/25g plain flour
8 oz/200g gooseberries
Salt, pepper and sugar
Melt half the butter and stir in the flour. Cook gently until light brown. Gradually add 3/4 pint/375ml water and cook to make a thin sauce. Top and tail the gooseberries and add to the sauce. Simmer until the berries are soft, and then sieve. Reheat gently, and season to taste with salt, pepper and sugar. Add the remaining butter just before serving. This is the traditional sauce to serve with mackerel, but is good with any oily fish.

Gooseberry Chutney

3 lb/1.5kg gooseberries
3 medium onions
8 oz/200g sultanas
12 oz/300g soft brown sugar
1 1/2 pints/750ml white vinegar
2 teaspoons/10g mustard powder
1 teaspoon/5g turmeric
1 teaspoon/5g ground ginger
Salt, pepper and nutmeg
Wash the gooseberries and top and tail them. Put through a coarse mincer with the onions. Put into a thick pan with the sultanas, sugar, vinegar, mustard, turmeric and ginger, and a good pinch each of salt, pepper and nutmeg. Simmer for 2 hours and put into jars.

For notes on cultivation see page 77

For notes on cultivation see page 77

LOGANBERRIES

These berries are very similar to raspberries, but slightly more acid. This makes them more suitable for cooking than for eating raw, and loganberries may be used for any raspberry, blackberry or mulberry recipe. The fruit goes well with apples, and with other summer berries, so it may well be added to give a rich colour and slightly sharp flavour to a variety of puddings and jams.

Loganberry Sponge

2 oz/50g butter
6 oz/150g castor sugar
2 eggs
4 oz/100g self-raising flour
12 oz/300g loganberries
1 large eating apple
Cream the butter and sugar. Beat the eggs lightly and work into the mixture alternately with the flour. Add the loganberries, and the peeled, cored and sliced apple, and fold in carefully. Put into a greased pudding basin, cover and steam for 1¼ hours. If preferred, the pudding may be put into an ovenware dish and baked at 350°F/180°C/Gas Mark 4 for 1 hour. Serve with custard or cream.

Loganberry and Apple Jelly

4 lb/2kg loganberries
2 lb/1kg cooking apples
2 pints/1l water
Sugar
Put the loganberries into a thick pan. Cut up the apples without peeling and coring them. Add the water and simmer for 1 hour until soft. Strain through a jellybag overnight and measure the juice. To each pint/500ml of juice allow 1 lb/400g sugar. Heat the juice gently, stirring in the sugar until dissolved. Boil hard to setting point and pour into hot jars.

RASPBERRIES

Fresh raspberries are delicious served plainly with castor sugar and cream, and they mix well with other summer fruit such as strawberries, red-currants and peaches. A pinch of cinnamon brings out the flavour of raspberry dishes, and so does a pinch of ground coffee in the accompanying pastry. Raspberries lose their flavour and shape when stewed, and are not good for bottling. They freeze very well and make excellent jam and jelly.

Raspberry Pudding

1 lb/400g raspberries
4 oz/100g castor sugar
1 oz/25g butter
4 oz/100g fresh white breadcrumbs
3 large eggs
Put the raspberries into a thick saucepan with the sugar, and heat gently until the juice runs. Sieve the fruit and juice, and return to the saucepan with the butter. Reheat gently and pour over the breadcrumbs. Leave to stand for 30 minutes. Beat the eggs lightly and mix with the raspberry purée. Put into an ovenware dish and bake at 350°F/180°C/Gas Mark 4 for 1 hour. Serve hot or cold, dusted with icing sugar, and with cream. Frozen raspberries may be used, and should be thawed before use.

Perfect Raspberry Jam

3 lb/1.5kg raspberries
3 lb/1.5kg sugar
1 oz/25g butter
Warm a thick preserving pan gently and rub it with the butter. Put in the raspberries and heat very slowly until the juice runs freely. Meanwhile, put the sugar into an ovenware dish in a low oven to heat. When the raspberry juice is running well, add the warm sugar and beat well. Stir over a low heat for 30 minutes. Pour into warm jars and cover.

For notes on cultivation see page 78

For notes on cultivation see page 78

RHUBARB

Young pink sticks of rhubarb are the best to use for pies and puddings, while the older thicker ones are excellent for making into jams and chutneys. The best way to cook rhubarb is to cut the sticks into short pieces and cook them in a saucepan or in the oven in a little raspberry or plum jam, or marmalade. This colours the rhubarb and supplements the flavour far better than the traditional water and sugar. Only cook the fruit until it is tender, but still keeps a good shape. Rhubarb mixes well with oranges and with dried fruit, and the flavour is delicious with the addition of candied angelica, or ginger.

Rhubarb Batter

1 lb/400g rhubarb
6 oz/150g fresh breadcrumbs
2 oz/50g melted butter
4 oz/100g soft brown sugar
½ lemon
1 teaspoon/5g ground cinnamon
¼ pint/125ml hot water
Cut the rhubarb into 1 in/2.5cm chunks. Mix the crumbs and butter together lightly with a fork. Mix the sugar with the grated rind and juice of the lemon, and with the cinnamon. Grease a pie dish and put in a layer of fruit, then sugar and buttered crumbs. Put on the remaining fruit, sugar and crumbs. Pour in the water. Bake at 350°F/180°C/Gas Mark 4 for 40 minutes. Serve hot or cold with custard or cream.

Rhubarb Fool

1 lb/400g rhubarb
8 oz/200g marmalade
½ pint/250ml single cream
Pinch of ground ginger
Cut the rhubarb in pieces and simmer with the marmalade until tender. Sieve and cool. Stir in the cream and ginger and serve chilled.

For notes on cultivation see page 79

TOP FRUIT

STRAWBERRIES

Always eat strawberries freshly gathered, but do not hull them until immediately before eating. Some people eat them with salt, or a shake of pepper, but the traditional castor sugar and cream are probably the most popular accompaniments to strawberries. Gourmets swear by serving them in orange juice, or with claret, port or Champagne poured over them. The strawberry changes in both texture and flavour when cooked, but strawberry jam is always a favourite. Great care must be taken when freezing strawberries to achieve a good result.

Strawberry Jam

4 lb/2kg strawberries
1 teaspoon/5g citric acid
3½ lb/1.75kg sugar
Put the strawberries into a thick pan with the acid and simmer for 30 minutes. Stir in the sugar until dissolved and then boil hard to setting point. Cool for 15 minutes, stir well and pour into hot jars.

Strawberry Shortcake

8 oz/200g plain flour
2 teaspoons/10g baking powder
¼ teaspoon/1g salt
4 oz/100g butter
4 fl oz/100ml milk
1½ lb/600g strawberries
4 oz/100g sugar
1½ oz/40g butter
¼ pint/125ml double cream
Sift together the flour, baking powder and salt, and work in the butter thoroughly. Lightly mix in the milk to make a soft dough, and divide into two pieces. Put each portion into an 8in/20cm sandwich tin and prick with a fork. Bake at 400°F/200°C/Gas Mark 6 for 15 minutes. Meanwhile, hull the strawberries. Lightly crush half of them and sprinkle with sugar. When shortcakes are cooked, spread butter on top of one. Cover with crushed berries and top with second shortcake. Cool slightly, then top with whipped cream and whole berries.

For notes on cultivation see page 79

APPLES

For cooking purposes, apples fall into two categories - crisp and fluffy. Use crisp apples for pies or any dish in which the shape of slices is important. Use fluffy apples which break up in cooking for purées, mousses, cakes and apple sauce. For a special flavour cook apple slices in butter and sugar instead of water (allow 2 oz/50g butter to 1 lb/400g apples, plus sugar to taste). Flavour apples with the traditional cloves, or with cinnamon or ginger, a little lemon or orange rind and juice, or some rosehip syrup. Team apples with blackberries or raspberries, quinces, plums or apricots for sweet recipes. For savoury dishes, use apples with pork, goose, duck and pheasant, and add a little grated apple to the horseradish sauce served with beef.

Dorset Apple Cake

8 oz/200g self-raising flour
Pinch of salt
4 oz/100g margarine
12 oz/300g eating apples
4 oz/100g sugar
2 oz/50g currants
Milk
3 oz/75g butter
1 oz/25g soft brown sugar
Sift together the flour and salt and rub in the margarine until the mixture is like fine breadcrumbs. Peel and core the apples, and chop them up roughly. Mix them with the flour and stir in the sugar and currants. Add enough milk to make a stiff dough, and stir well together. Put into two greased 7 in/17.5cm sponge tins and bake at 425°F/220°C/Gas Mark 7 for 15 minutes. Reduce heat to 300°F/150°C/Gas Mark 2 and bake for 1 hour. While warm, sandwich together with two-thirds of the butter. Cut the remaining butter in small pieces, mix with brown sugar and spread on top. Eat warm and fresh.

For notes on cultivation see page 80

APRICOTS

Apricots must be really golden and ripe to eat raw, but slightly under-ripe fruit can be poached in a heavy sugar syrup, or cooked in the oven with sugar. A little Kirsch, Curaçao or rum goes well with apricots and may be added to many puddings. The apricot is a good fruit for accompanying ham, pork and poultry. If only a few fruit are available, they can be mixed with apples to give their flavour to pies and puddings. This is a versatile fruit which makes excellent jam and pickles, bottles and freezes well.

Apricot and Apple Pie

1 lb/400g shortcrust pastry
1½ lb/600g cooking apples
4 oz/100g granulated sugar
3 oz/75g soft brown sugar
1½ oz/40g plain flour
Juice of 1 lemon
1 teaspoon/5g ground cinnamon
½ teaspoon/3g ground nutmeg
¼ teaspoon/1g salt
1 lb/400g fresh apricots
½ teaspoon/3g almond essence
1 oz/25g butter
Roll out the pastry and line a pie dish with half of it. Peel the apples and slice thinly. Mix with the granulated and brown sugars, flour, lemon juice, spices and salt, and put into the pie dish. Cut the apricots in half, remove stones, and put the fruit cut side down on the apples. Sprinkle with the essence and put on small pieces of butter. Cover with pastry and bake at 400°F/200°C/Gas Mark 6 for 20 minutes. Reduce heat to 350°F/180°C/Gas Mark 4 and bake for 25 minutes. If liked, sweet shortcrust pastry may be used for this pie, which is good hot or cold, preferably with thick cream.

CHERRIES

For cooking purposes, the Morello cherry is the most suitable, but black or white eating cherries can of course be eaten raw or cooked. Cooking in red wine gives them good flavour and colour, and their flavour is enhanced by cherry brandy or Kirsch. Cherries are a favourite garnish with duck, and can be made into a good salad to serve with poultry.

Cherry and Walnut Salad

8 oz/200g black cherries
2 oz/50g walnut halves
¼ pint/125ml French dressing
2 tablespoons/30ml double cream
Squeeze of lemon juice
Stone the cherries and put into a serving dish. Drop the walnut halves into boiling water, skin them, and chop roughly. Mix with the cherries and pour over the French dressing. Drain off the surplus juice and top the salad with cream to which the lemon juice has been added. Serve with poultry or ham.

Cherry Compote

1 lb/400g cherries
½ pint/250ml red wine
7 oz/175g sugar
½ teaspoon/3g ground cinnamon
½ teaspoon/3g ground nutmeg
Pinch of ground cloves
2 tablespoons/30g redcurrant jelly
Stone the cherries and put them into the wine with the sugar and the spices. Cook until the fruit is just tender but not broken. Drain the cherries and put into a serving bowl. Return the syrup to the saucepan and boil until thick. Stir in the redcurrant jelly and cool, and then pour over the cherries. Serve very cold with whipped cream. If liked the mixture may be served hot over vanilla ice cream. Black cherries are best for this, but Morello cherries can be used with a little more sugar to taste.

For notes on cultivation see page 81

FIGS

Figs must be eaten when they are freshly picked because they are very perishable. They are good just peeled and sliced, but cream may be served with them, plus a little lemon or orange juice, or a spoonful of rum. Figs can be frozen in syrup, but they are a surprisingly good basis for jams and pickles.

Fig Jam

1 lb/400g fresh figs
8 oz/200g apples
3 lemons
Piece of cinnamon stick
Piece of root ginger
2 cloves
1 lb/400g sugar
Peel the figs and blanch them in boiling water for 1 minute. Drain them, rinse in cold water, and cut in thin slices. Put into a thick pan with peeled and sliced apples. Add the juice of 3 lemons and the grated rind of 1 lemon. Put the spices in a piece of muslin and suspend in the pan. Cover and cook gently until the fruit is tender. Add the sugar and stir until dissolved. Boil rapidly for 15 minutes, then pour into small hot jars and cover.

Fig Chutney

2 lb/1kg fresh figs
1 lb/400g onions
4 oz/100g crystallised ginger
1 pint/500ml white vinegar
8 oz/200g soft brown sugar
2 teaspoons/10g salt
½ teaspoon/3g pepper
Peel the figs and cut them into small pieces. Cut the onions and ginger into small pieces. Put the vinegar, sugar, salt and pepper into a thick pan and bring to the boil. Add the remaining ingredients and bring back to the boil. Simmer for about 1½ hours until the mixture is thick. Put into small jars and cover. This chutney has a delicate flavour which is delicious with poultry and ham.

For notes on cultivation see page 81

GRAPES

Perfect grapes make an elegant finish to a meal and are rarely cooked. They do however make a good garnish for fish - sole and haddock in particular - or can be added to rabbit dishes. Plainly roasted pheasant tastes better than ever if simply stuffed with fresh grapes before cooking, which melt away leaving a rich pan juice. If there is a glut of grapes which are not quite perfect for the table, they can be made into a very good jam to use for tarts, or on toast.

Grape Jam

2 lb/1kg grapes
1 lb/400g sugar
Use black or green grapes which are just ripe but juicy. Take out the pips. Put the grapes and sugar into a thick pan, bring slowly to the boil, and then simmer for 1 hour. Put into small jars and cover.

Toffee Grapes

1 lb/400g grapes
2 oz/50g castor sugar
½ pint/250ml double cream
3 oz/75g soft brown sugar
Use large juicy grapes, either black or green. Peel them and remove the pips. Put into an ovenware dish and sprinkle with castor sugar. Whip the cream to soft peaks and spread lightly over the fruit. Chill the dish in the refrigerator for two or three hours. Just before serving, spread the brown sugar on top, and place under a hot grill until the sugar melts and turns to a hard crisp caramel. Serve at once. This recipe may be used for many other types of fruit, or a mixture of them. Raspberries, strawberries, peaches and apricots are particularly good, and a little appropriate liqueur may be added to the fruit base before adding the cream and caramel topping.

For notes on cultivation see page 82

PEACHES

The best peaches to eat raw must be large, soft and juicy. If they are a little smaller and harder, they are excellent cooked in the same ways as apricots. This is another fruit which goes well with savoury food, particularly pork, ham and bacon, and cream cheese. They make excellent jam, bottle and freeze well. It is worth putting a few spoonfuls of brandy into the heavy syrup when bottling peaches to provide a treat for winter parties.

Peach Dumplings

8 oz/200g shortcrust pastry
4 peaches
2 oz/50g butter
2 oz/50g castor sugar
Pinch of ground nutmeg
12 oz/300g soft brown sugar
Roll out the pastry and cut into four squares. Peel the peaches and take out the stones, leaving the fruit as whole as possible. Fill each cavity with butter and sugar, and sprinkle with nutmeg. Put a peach in the centre of each pastry square, form into parcels and seal the edges with a little water. Put the brown sugar in a saucepan with 8 tablespoons/120ml water and heat for 5 minutes to make a thick syrup. Spoon some over the dumplings, and bake at 425°F/220°C/Gas Mark 7 for 10 minutes. Reduce heat to 350°F/180°C/Gas Mark 4 and continue baking for 30 minutes, basting with more syrup every 10 minutes. Serve warm or cold with cream.

Grilled Peaches

4 peaches
Butter and sugar
Peel and halve the peaches. Brush with melted butter and sprinkle with sugar. Grill and serve with ham, pork or chicken.

For notes on cultivation see page 82

PEARS

Juicy dessert pears are suitable for eating raw, or for lightly poaching to serve with chocolate or raspberry sauce. A fresh ripe pear is delicious eaten with a piece of Brie or Camembert cheese. Pears can be rather insipid, and when bottled or frozen they need a little extra flavouring such as vanilla, cloves or rum. Pears may be cooked slowly in red wine and the hard winter cooking pears may be left to cook in wine for many hours in a slow oven until they become deep red and tender.

Honey Pears

4 ripe pears
Juice of 2 lemons
6 oz/150g honey
1 teaspoon/5g ground cinnamon
1 oz/25g butter
Peel and core the pears, and cut in half. Put in a greased ovenware dish, cut side up. Mix the lemon juice and honey and pour over the pears, then sprinkle with cinnamon and dot with butter. Bake at 350°F/180°C/Gas Mark 4 for 20 minutes. Serve hot or cold with cream.

Spiced Pears

2 lb/1kg small pears
Whole cloves
8 oz/200g sugar
1/2 pint/250ml white vinegar
Piece of lemon rind
Piece of root ginger
Piece of cinnamon stick
2 teaspoons/10g whole allspice
Peel and core the pears, and cut in half. Put a clove in each half. Put the sugar and vinegar in a thick pan, and heat gently to dissolve the sugar. Tie the lemon rind and spices in a piece of muslin and suspend in the pan. Add the pears to the vinegar and simmer until they are tender and almost transparent. Pack in hot preserving jars. Boil the syrup for 3 minutes and pour on pears. Seal tightly. Serve with ham or pork.

For notes on cultivation see page 83

PLUMS

Large ripe plums are delicious eaten raw, and they can also be halved and sprinkled with sugar and a little Kirsch or cherry brandy. It is a mistake to stew plums in water - they are better arranged in layers in a casserole with sugar and a sprinkling of cinnamon, or a little lemon or orange rind. Add a little water or red wine to come half-way up the plums, and cook them in a slow oven (300°F/150°C/Gas Mark 2) until the juice runs. Plums bottle and freeze well and make a useful jam.

Spiced Plum Tart

12 oz/300g sweet shortcrust pastry
1 1/2 lb/600g plums
7 oz/175g sugar
1 teaspoon/5g ground cinnamon
1 tablespoon/15ml lemon juice
1 oz/25g butter
Roll out the pastry to line a 9 in/22.5cm pie plate, fluting the edges. Cut the plums in half and take out the stones. Put the fruit cut side down on the pastry. Mix the sugar and cinnamon and sprinkle half on the plums. Pour over the lemon juice and dot with the butter. Bake at 350°F/180°C/Gas Mark 4 for 40 minutes. Sprinkle with the remaining sugar. Serve hot or cold with cream.

Plum Conserve

3 lb/1.5kg plums
Juice of 3 lemons
3 1/2 lb/1.75kg sugar
4 tablespoons/60ml dark rum
Cut the plums into small pieces and put them into a thick pan with the lemon juice and sugar. Stir gently while bringing to the boil, and boil hard for 3 minutes, stirring all the time. Add the rum and leave to stand for 5 minutes, stirring often. Pour into hot jars and cover. This makes a change from the traditional plum jam, and is an excellent tart filling.

For notes on cultivation see page 83

ORDER FORMS

HOME GROWN is an ideal gift because it can help your friends to help themselves and profit more from their gardens than they had ever thought possible.

STANLEY

To: **Stanley Garden Tools Ltd**
Woodhouse Mill
Sheffield S13 9WJ

Please send_____copy/copies of HOME GROWN AT £2.80 per copy post-paid. I enclose PO/cheque for_____ made payable to Stanley Garden Tools Ltd

name (capitals)

address

Allow 21 days for delivery.
This offer applies only to the United Kingdom whilst stocks of this printing last. For overseas rates, write to Stanley Garden Tools Ltd

---

To: **Stanley Garden Tools Ltd**
Woodhouse Mill
Sheffield S13 9WJ

Please send_____copy/copies of HOME GROWN AT £2.80 per copy post-paid. I enclose PO/cheque for_____ made payable to Stanley Garden Tools Ltd

name (capitals)

address

Allow 21 days for delivery.
This offer applies only to the United Kingdom whilst stocks of this printing last. For overseas rates, write to Stanley Garden Tools Ltd

---

To: **Stanley Garden Tools Ltd**
Woodhouse Mill
Sheffield S13 9WJ

Please send_____copy/copies of HOME GROWN AT £2.80 per copy post-paid. I enclose PO/cheque for_____ made payable to Stanley Garden Tools Ltd

name (capitals)

address

Allow 21 days for delivery.
This offer applies only to the United Kingdom whilst stocks of this printing last. For overseas rates, write to Stanley Garden Tools Ltd

---

To: **Stanley Garden Tools Ltd**
Woodhouse Mill
Sheffield S13 9WJ

Please send_____copy/copies of HOME GROWN AT £2.80 per copy post-paid. I enclose PO/cheque for_____ made payable to Stanley Garden Tools Ltd

name (capitals)

address

Allow 21 days for delivery.
This offer applies only to the United Kingdom whilst stocks of this printing last. For overseas rates, write to Stanley Garden Tools Ltd

---

To: **Stanley Garden Tools Ltd**
Woodhouse Mill
Sheffield S13 9WJ

Please send_____copy/copies of HOME GROWN AT £2.80 per copy post-paid. I enclose PO/cheque for_____ made payable to Stanley Garden Tools Ltd

name (capitals)

address

Allow 21 days for delivery.
This offer applies only to the United Kingdom whilst stocks of this printing last. For overseas rates, write to Stanley Garden Tools Ltd

---

To: **Stanley Garden Tools Ltd**
Woodhouse Mill
Sheffield S13 9WJ

Please send_____copy/copies of HOME GROWN AT £2.80 per copy post-paid. I enclose PO/cheque for_____ made payable to Stanley Garden Tools Ltd

name (capitals)

address

Allow 21 days for delivery.
This offer applies only to the United Kingdom whilst stocks of this printing last. For overseas rates, write to Stanley Garden Tools Ltd